Financing the 2020 Election

Financing the 2020 Election

Edited by
Molly E. Reynolds and John C. Green

BROOKINGS INSTITUTION PRESS
Washington, D.C.

Published by Brookings Institution Press
1775 Massachusetts Avenue, NW
Washington, DC 20036
www.brookings.edu/bipress

Co-published by Rowman & Littlefield
An imprint of The Rowman & Littlefield Publishing Group, Inc.
4501 Forbes Boulevard, Suite 200, Lanham, Maryland 20706
www.rowman.com

86-90 Paul Street, London EC2A 4NE

The Brookings Institution is a nonprofit organization devoted to research, education, and publication on important issues of domestic and foreign policy. Its principal purpose is to bring the highest quality independent research and analysis to bear on current and emerging policy problems.

British Library Cataloguing in Publication Information Available

Library of Congress Cataloging-in-Publication Data

Names: Reynolds, Molly, editor. | Green, John Clifford, 1953- editor.
Title: Financing the 2020 election / Edited by Molly Reynolds and John C. Green.
Description: Washington, DC : Brookings Institution Press, [2023] | Includes
    bibliographical references and index.
Identifiers: LCCN 2023011005 | ISBN 9780815740254 (cloth) |
    ISBN 9780815739791 (paperback) | ISBN 9780815739807 (ebook)
Subjects: LCSH: Campaign funds—United States—History. | Presidents—United States—
    Election—2020. | United States. Congress—Elections—2020. | United States—Politics
    and government—21st century.
Classification: LCC JF2112.C28 F56 2023 | DDC 324.7/809730905—dc23/
    eng/20230501
LC record available at https://lccn.loc.gov/2023011005

Dedicated to Colin Ruhter,
Caroline, Nathaniel, Mary Kate Lutz

Contents

List of Tables and Figures   ix

About the Contributors   xiii

Preface and Acknowledgments   xv

1. Financing of the 2020 Election: Change and Continuity   1
   Molly E. Reynolds and John C. Green

2. The Regulatory Environment of the 2020 Election   21
   R. Sam Garrett

3. Financing the 2020 Presidential Elections   51
   John C. Green

4. Financing the 2020 Congressional Elections   99
   Molly E. Reynolds

5. Party Money in the 2020 Election   125
   Robin Kolodny and Diana Dwyre

6. Interest Group Money in the 2020 Election   157
   Jay Goodliffe

7. Political and Policy Implications of the 2020 Election   193
   Robert G. Boatright

Index   223

List of Tables and Figures

TABLES

Table 1.1. Direct and Indirect Federal Campaign Expenditures in
the 2020 Election ... 6

Table 2.1. Selected Entities in the Campaign Finance Regulatory
Environment ... 25

Table 2.2. Selected Federal Contribution Limits, 2020 Election
Cycle ... 32

Table 2.3. Selected Federal Contribution Limits to Political Party
Committees, 2020 Election Cycle ... 38

Table 3.1 2020 Presidential Campaigns, Net Receipts and
Disbursements ... 58

Table 3.2 Contributions to Major Presidential Campaigns in
2020 Election ... 63

Table 3.3 Noncandidate Spending, Major 2020 Presidential
Election Campaigns ... 66

Table 3.4 Top Ten Noncandidate Group Independent
Expenditures, 2020 Presidential Election Campaigns ... 86

Table 4.1 Average Source of House and Senate Candidates'
Receipts, 2020 Congressional Elections (hundreds of
thousands of dollars) ... 103

Table 4.2 Party-Connected Contributions, 2020 Congressional
Elections ... 104

Table 4.3 Noncandidate Spending in 2020 Congressional Races,
Independent Expenditures and Internal Communications ... 107

Table 4.4 Major Party-Aligned Super PACs, 2019–20
Congressional Elections — 108

Table 4.5 Average House and Senate General Election Candidate
Campaign Expenditures, 2020 Congressional Elections — 116

Table 4.6 Average Nonparty Spending on Behalf of Candidates,
2020 Congressional Elections — 117

Table 5.1 Georgia Senate Runoff Joint Fund-Raising Committee
Receipts, 2020–2021 — 135

Table 5.2 National Party Committee Receipts, by Source,
Election Years, 2000–2020 (in 2020 dollars, except as
indicated) — 139

Table 5.3 Top Party-Aligned Super PACs, 2020 (millions of dollars) — 142

Table 6.1 Traditional PACs, Disbursements ($ in millions) and
Number, 2008–2020 Presidential Elections — 158

Table 6.2 Top Twenty Traditional PACs, Total Congressional
Contributions and Recipient Party, 2020 Election — 160

Table 6.3 Top Five Traditional PACs with Internal
Communications Spending, 2020 Election — 164

Table 6.4 Independent Expenditures, Totals and Percentages by
Source, 2010–2020 — 166

Table 6.5 Top Traditional PAC Independent Expenditures,
2008–2020 Presidential Elections — 168

Table 6.6 Top Individual Contributors to Super PACs, 2020
Election — 170

Table 6.7 Characteristics of Donors and Size of Donations to Top
Super PACs, 2020 Election — 171

Table 6.8 Top Twenty-Five Super PACs, Independent
Expenditures, 2020 Election — 173

Table 6.9 Total Spending by Types of Super PACs, 2020 Election — 178

Table 6.10 Top Senate and House Races, Aggregate Independent
Expenditures, 2020 Election — 178

Table 6.11 Georgia Senate Runoff Races: Independent
Expenditures by Parties and Other Groups, 2020–2021 — 180

Table 6.12 Top-Spending Tax-Exempt Groups, 2012–2020 — 184

FIGURES

Figure 1.1 Direct Federal Campaign Expenditures in Presidential
Elections, 1976–2020 — 12

Figure 3.1 Democratic Presidential Nomination 2020: Cumulative Receipts 74

Figure 3.2 Democratic Presidential Nomination 2020: Cash on Hand 74

Figure 3.3 Presidential General Election 2020: Cumulative Receipts, Cash on Hand 81

Figure 3.4 The General Election Campaign 2020: Net Candidate, Voter Outreach, and Independent Expenditures 82

Figure 4.1 Party Contributions, Coordinated Expenditures, and Independent Expenditures, 2020 Congressional Elections 106

Figure 5.1 Hard and Soft Money Receipts of National Party Committees, 1992–2020 131

Figure 5.2 Sources of National Party Committee Money, 2000–2020 132

Figure 5.3 National Party Share of Joint Fund-Raising Receipts, 2008–2020 133

Figure 5.4 National Party Receipts: Transfers from Affiliated Party Committees, 2000–2020 136

Figure 5.5 Contributions to Party Special Accounts, 2016–2020 137

Figure 5.6 National Party Committee Disbursements, 2002–2020 143

Figure 5.7 Party Spending on U.S. House Races, 2000–2020 146

Figure 5.8 Party Spending on U.S. Senate Races, 2000–2020 147

Figure 5.9 Noncandidate Spending: Party and Nonparty Sources, 2010–2020 149

Figure 6.1 Congressional Candidate Expenditures and Traditional PAC Contributions to Congressional Candidates, 1978–2020 159

Figure 6.2 Traditional PAC Contributions to U.S. House General Election Candidates by Candidate Type, 1996–2020 161

Figure 6.3 Traditional PAC Contributions to U.S. Senate General Election Candidates by Candidate Type, 1996–2020 162

Figure 6.4 Traditional PAC Contributions to U.S. House General Election Candidates by Party, 1996–2020 163

Figure 6.5 Traditional PAC Contributions to U.S. Senate General Election Candidates by Party, 1996–2020 163

Figure 6.6 Super PAC Receipts from Individuals, Corporations, and Unions, 2010–2020 169

Figure 6.7 Tax-Exempt Groups, Aggregate Spending, 2004–2020 183

About the Contributors

Robert G. Boatright is professor of political science at Clark University and director of research at the National Institute for Civil Discourse (NICD) at the University of Arizona. He is the author or editor of several books, including *Getting Primaried: The Causes and Consequences of Congressional Primary Challenges* (2013) and *Interest Groups and Campaign Finance Reform in the United States and Canada* (2011). He is currently completing a book on the history of primary election reforms.

Diana Dwyre is professor of political science at California State University, Chico. She has published extensively on U.S. campaign finance, political parties, elections, and the U.S. Congress, and coauthored *Limits and Loopholes: The Quest for Money, Free Speech and Fair Elections* (2008) and *Legislative Labyrinth: Congress and Campaign Finance Reform* (2001) with Victoria Farrar-Myers. She is currently working on a book with Robin Kolodny of Temple University tentatively titled *The Fundamentals of U.S. Campaign Finance: Why Do We Have the System We Have.*

R. Sam Garrett holds a PhD in political science, MPA, and BA (summa cum laude), all from American University's School of Public Affairs. He serves as specialist in American national government at the Congressional Research Service, Library of Congress. Sam was selected as a 2005 Presidential Management Fellow. Sam is an adjunct faculty member in the department of government at American University and at the University of Georgia's Washington Semester Program. He is the author of *Campaign Crises: Detours on the Road to Congress* (2010).

Jay Goodliffe is professor and chair of the department of political science at Brigham Young University and a research fellow at the Center for the Study of Elections and Democracy. He studies campaign finance in the United States and is coauthor of *Who Donates in Campaigns? The Importance of Message, Messenger, Medium, and Structure* (2018).

John C. Green is distinguished professor of political science and emeritus director of the Ray C. Bliss Institute of Applied Politics, University of Akron. He has written extensively on American campaign finance, political parties, and religion and politics. He is editor of *The State of the Parties: The Changing Role of American Politics Parties* (2022), now in its ninth edition, and coauthor of *Secular Surge* (2021).

Robin Kolodny is professor of political science at Temple University. She has published extensively on political parties, campaign finance, and political consultants in the United States and in comparative perspective; and authored *Pursuing Majorities: Congressional Campaign Committees in American Politics* (1998). She is currently working on a book with Diana Dwyre of California State University, Chico, tentatively titled *The Fundamentals of U.S. Campaign Finance: Why Do We Have the System We Have*.

Molly E. Reynolds is senior fellow in governance studies at Brookings Institution. She studies Congress, with an emphasis on congressional rules and procedure, the congressional budget process, and congressional reform. She is the author of the book *Exceptions to the Rule: The Politics of Filibuster Limitations in the U.S. Senate* (2017), which explores creation, use, and consequences of the budget reconciliation process and other procedures that prevent filibusters in the U.S. Senate.

Preface and Acknowledgments

This book is the sixteenth installment in a series on federal campaign finance in presidential election years, originating with Herbert Alexander's *Financing the 1960 Election*, some sixty years ago. We are honored to have helped carry on this remarkable tradition, which we hope will continue in the future.

Each of the presidential elections in the series was unique in some respects, and the 2020 election was no exception, occurring during the COVID-19 global pandemic. The pandemic had a major impact on the federal campaigns as well as the election results, as noted throughout the pages that follow. But it also had an impact on the production of this book. First, the pandemic delayed the filing of federal campaign finance reports and the processing of those reports by the Federal Election Commission. These problems presented challenges to all matter of users of these data, including the present authors. Consequently, the organization of this book did not begin until the spring of 2021, with the goal of completing the work by the end of the calendar year. However, these plans were interrupted by a series of unforeseen events, some personal, some institutional, so that the work was completed a year later. We are very grateful for the perseverance and patience of our authors in overcoming many obstacles. Readers will surely agree that the results were well worth the effort.

We would like to acknowledge the assistance of our colleague David B. Magleby, the editor of five previous installments in this series. Dave's wisdom and experience were crucial to planning this volume, and although he was unable to contribute to the manuscript, his help was invaluable. We would also like to thank an anonymous reviewer whose comments and suggestions were very helpful.

The Ray C. Bliss Institute of Applied Politics at the University of Akron provided material support for the project. We would like to thank Sheila Krumholz, executive director of OpenSecrets, and especially Brendan Glavin, senior data analyst, for assistance in providing our authors with accurate and consistent campaign finance data. We are in debt to the staff of Brookings Institution Press, particularly editors William Finan and Yelba Quinn, and to the staff and editor Jon Sisk of its publishing partner, Rowman & Littlefield.

Molly E. Reynolds
John C. Green

1

Financing of the 2020 Election

Change and Continuity

Molly E. Reynolds and John C. Green

The 2020 election will be remembered for many things, including, as one account put it, "disease, discord, and downturn."[1] But it will also be remembered for a dramatic increase in campaign expenditures, more than doubling the amount from the 2016 election in real terms. It had become commonplace to discuss federal campaign finance in terms of millions of dollars, but in 2020 *billions* of dollars became a common unit of measure. For example, Joe Biden's presidential campaign raised and spent more than $1 billion; and one of his primary rivals, Michael Bloomberg, spent more than $1 billion of his own funds. Meanwhile, Donald Trump's campaign and its alliance with the Republican National Committee combined to raise and spend about $1 billion as well. Further, a surge in Super PAC spending exceeded $2 billion.

These examples highlight the global expansion of federal campaign finance in 2020, fueled by electoral competition, technological developments, organizational innovation, and the continued nationalization of federal campaigns. These factors contributed to the acceleration of three noteworthy trends:

1. the growth of individual contributions to candidates and noncandidate committees, including increases in both small *and* large donations;
2. the growth of independent expenditures by noncandidate organizations, reducing the relative importance of other kinds of expenditures; and

3. the growth in the number and activity of Super and Hybrid PACs, sup-
    planting in relative terms the activities of other sources of independent
    expenditures.

However, the independent impact of these record-breaking election expenditures is far from clear.

This book documents and assesses the extraordinary financial activity in
2020, adding the newest installment to a series of books that began with
Herbert B. Alexander's *Financing the 1960 Election.*[2] Each substantive
chapter in this volume was written by scholars with special expertise in key
aspects of federal campaign finance. Before previewing their work, it is useful
to review the political context of the election as well as a general overview of
federal campaign finance in 2020.

CONTEXT OF THE 2020 ELECTION

Presidential elections are defined in large part by the occupant of the White
House, especially if reelection is sought. By one measure, the 2020 campaign
began nearly four years before Election Day, when President Trump filed
reelection paperwork on the same day he was inaugurated, January 20, 2017.
This decision was unprecedented among contemporary presidents and fit
Trump's penchant for violating political norms. From the perspective of an
observer marking that day as the start of the 2020 campaign, some of the
events that followed were predictable continuations of past trends in presidential politics; others were unusual but consistent with the broader context
of the election; still others were novel and unexpected by even the most
attentive observers.

Throughout his presidency, Trump was frequently beset by low poll
numbers, reflecting his contentious style and controversial policies. In fact,
when he left office in January 2021, his Gallup average approval rating over
the course of his presidency was 41 percent—four percentage points lower
than any previous president.[3] Indeed, Trump began 2020 with the lowest
approval rating at the start of an election year for a president running for
reelection since Gerald Ford in 1976,[4] in part due to his impeachment by
the House of Representatives and acquittal by the Senate, both along party
lines. As the presidential campaign began in earnest, the expectation was that
Trump would face political headwinds.

Such low approval ratings masked the partisan polarization in public support for Trump, a hallmark of the times. Over the course of his presidency,

only 7 percent of Democrats, on average, approved of his performance—but, among Republicans, the figure was 88 percent.[5] These strong preferences for and against Trump surely contributed to the high levels of engagement on the part of both Democrats and Republicans with the presidential race. According to the Pew Research Center in July 2020, 83 percent of registered voters indicated that it "really matters" who won the presidency—the highest proportion of respondents giving this response in the two decades.[6]

However, Trump's low approval ratings and a polarized public might have been counteracted by the strength of the economy in January 2020. During his term, Trump benefited from the lowest unemployment rate in half a century.[7] Many politicians would have balked at challenging a sitting president during a strong economy. Although Democrats were energized and perceived that Trump was nonetheless vulnerable, they were not unified behind a single vision of what sort of candidate was best to take on Trump. Thus, it was hardly surprising that a record twenty-nine Democratic candidates sought their party's 2020 presidential nomination. This diverse field included a wide array of officeholders and celebrities, most with impressive credentials. But attention quickly fixed upon former vice president Joe Biden (favored by the party establishment and quickly dubbed the front-runner) and U.S. Senator Bernie Sanders (a favorite of the progressive wing of the party and the runner-up for the 2016 nomination).

This large field of candidates winnowed steadily, with Biden facing strong challenges from Sanders and other candidates, so much so that former New York City mayor Michael Bloomberg launched a lavishly self-funded campaign as a moderate substitute for Biden. Meanwhile, Trump campaigned aggressively for renomination, despite facing no real opposition, and received a record number of Republican primary votes.

Almost on cue, Sanders emerged from the early nomination contests with strong momentum. Then, with the help of the party establishment, Biden won the South Carolina primary and rode that momentum into key victories on Super Tuesday, largely clearing out the candidate field. Consequently, the race was settling into a Biden-Sanders contest—until the COVID-19 pandemic suddenly struck the United States. The pandemic brought the nomination contest to a quick end, leaving Biden the presumptive nominee.

The sudden advent of the COVID-19 pandemic and its cascading effects on the American economy scrambled the relationship between a strong economy and Trump's reelection prospects. On the one hand, the pandemic response generated the most severe economic slowdown since the Great Depression.[8] But on the other hand, the economic stimulus payments distributed in the spring of 2020 may have helped blunt the negative effect of the economic crisis on Trump's electoral chances.[9]

Biden adopted a "basement strategy," ceding the limelight to Trump, who struggled with managing the public response to the pandemic. Adding to the president's challenges was the wave of protest and civil unrest that followed the killing of an unarmed black man, George Floyd, by a white police officer in May 2020. During the spring and summer, the Democratic Party rallied around Biden, so that by the time of the national conventions, he was well prepared to face Trump in the fall. Public opinion polls showed Biden comfortably ahead nationally and leading in key battleground states, and some analysts began predicting a "blue wave" that would give Biden large coattails in congressional races. Other analysts were more cautious, recalling that Trump had won the Electoral College in 2016 with less than a majority of the popular vote.

The pandemic's consequences for the economy were not, of course, the only mechanism by which COVID-19 affected the 2020 election. By Election Day, more than 200,000 Americans had died of the virus, leaving countless family members and friends to confront their loss, trauma that may have affected their political behavior.[10] The pandemic affected all aspects of the campaign. President Trump's affinity for rallies was limited by restrictions on large indoor gatherings, leading the campaign to schedule large outdoor events. Meanwhile, the Biden campaign held fewer, smaller events. With in-person events and face-to-face contact limited, and more Americans staying home, social and mass media were even more important for carrying campaign messages.

Election administrators nationwide were left to determine how to conduct the election safely, leading to substantial expansion of voting by mail and other convenience forms of casting a ballot. According to the Census Bureau, 69 percent of voters across the country voted either by mail or in person prior to Election Day.[11] As a result, millions of Americans had voted before several major events occurred that could have affected their choices, including the death of Supreme Court Justice Ruth Bader Ginsburg in September and Trump's own COVID diagnosis in October.

The campaign produced a sharp increase in voter turnout, reaching a contemporary record of 66 percent of eligible voters.[12] Biden received 51.9 percent of the national popular vote but won 306 Electoral College votes by a narrow margin, carrying the three closest states—Georgia, Arizona, and Wisconsin—by a scant 43,000 ballots. And the president-elect had "negative" coattails in the House of Representatives (with the Republicans picking up fourteen seats) and essentially no coattails in the Senate (where the Democrats only gained one seat). However, the close results in Georgia produced a rare double runoff on January 6, 2021, where the Democrats gained two more Senate seats. These victories created a 50-50 tie in the Senate, broken by newly elected Vice President Kamala Harris. Thus, the Democrats obtained unified control of the federal government by the slimmest of margins.

President Trump continued to break long-established norms by refusing to concede the election until ten weeks after Election Day. Trump insisted that he had won, and he disputed the election results in court, in public declamations, and with pressure on state election officials—but to no avail. Indeed, these activities likely undermined the Republican Senate candidates in the Georgia runoff elections. More seriously, Trump's rhetoric contributed to an unprecedented occupation of the Capitol in Washington, D.C., on January 6 by hundreds of his supporters, resulting in millions of dollars of damage, numerous injuries, and at least five deaths. This disorder temporarily interrupted the certification of the 2020 Electoral College results, and once order was restored, the election was certified in the early morning of January 7, 2021. The House of Representatives then impeached Trump for a second time—and he was again acquitted by the Senate after he left office, with some Republican votes against Trump in both instances. In a fitting coda to his first term, Trump continued to strengthen his campaign organization, preparing for another presidential bid in 2024.

OVERVIEW: FEDERAL CAMPAIGN EXPENDITURES IN 2020 ELECTION

To set the stage for the substantive chapters that follow, table 1.1 provides a high-level overview of the record-breaking 2020 campaign expenditures. It is based on summary data for all 13,530 federal committees active in the 2020 election cycle, aggregated by committee type (see the table footnotes for details). For purposes of comparison, the same analysis was also conducted of all 11,150 committee reports from 2016 election cycle, the results of which are reported in the text.[13] It is worth noting that an additional 2,380 committees filed reports in 2020, a 21 percent increase over 2016.[14]

Table 1.1 reports the source and type of 2020 federal campaign expenditures. The source of campaign expenditures (first column) includes the federal political committees and other groups covered in the substantive chapters that follow (see chapter 2 for definitions of these entities). The type of campaign expenditures is divided into *direct campaign expenditures*

Table 1.1   Direct and Indirect Federal Campaign Expenditures in the 2020 Election

SOURCE OF EXPENDITURES	DIRECT EXPENDITURES	INDIRECT EXPENDITURES
Presidential Candidate Committees (PCCs)[a]	$4,073,903,380	
Congressional Candidate Committees (PCCs)[b]	$3,978,413,718	
Presidential Joint Fundraising Committees (JFCs)[c]		$680,220,391
Non-Presidential Joint Fundraising Committees (JFCs)[d]		$84,270,185
National Party Committees[e]		$1,669,331,579
Coordinated Expenditures	$80,459,422	
Independent Expenditures	$390,517,356	
Other Party Committees[f]		$404,947,328
Coordinated Expenditures	$6,546,397	
Independent Expenditures	$2,195,373	
Connected Political Action Committees (PACs)[g]		$312,493,044
Internal Communication Expenditures	$22,755,968	
Independent Expenditures	$45,601,926	
Non-connected Political Action Committees (PACs)[h]		$448,727,800
Independent Expenditures	$38,002,609	
Leadership Political Action Committees (PACs)[i]		$112,691,000
Independent Expenditures	$6,344,782	
Hybrid Political Action Committees (PACs)[j]		$847,484,898
Independent Expenditures	$550,305,551	
Super Political Action Committees (PACs)[k]		$761,139,910
Independent Expenditures	$2,120,248,234	
Other Independent Expenditures[l]	$101,819,026	
Tax-Exempt Groups *Independent Expenditures*[m]	$126,725,316	
ALL (SUBTOTALS)	$11,543,839,058	$5,321,306,135
GRAND TOTAL		**$16,865,145,193**

(continued)

Table 1.1   (Continued)

Source: Analysis by authors of 2020 FEC Committee Summary file https://www.fec.gov/data/browse-data/ ?tab=committees and other FEC reports

Notes:
a. *Total disbursements by all major and minor party presidential candidate PCCs and other committees authorized by candidates*
b. *Total disbursements by all major and minor party congressional candidate PCCs and other committees authorized by candidates*
c. *Total disbursements by the principal JFCs of the Biden and Trump PCCs, and other participating committees, excluding transfers to authorized committees*
d. *Total disbursements by JFCs with participants other than presidential PCCS and other participating committees, excluding transfers to authorized committees*
e. *Total disbursements by the Democratic and Republican National Committees (DNC, RNC) and four major party congressional campaign committees (CCCs), excluding coordinated and independent expenditures (listed separately in the table) as well as all contributions and transfers to other committees*
f. *Total disbursements by all other party committees for federal election activity, excluding coordinated and independent expenditures (listed separately in the table) as well as all contributions and transfers to other committees*
g. *Total disbursements by Connected PACs, excluding communication and independent expenditures (listed separately in the table) as well as all contributions and transfers to other committees*
h. *Total disbursements by Non-connected PACs, excluding independent expenditures (listed separately in the table) as well as all contributions and transfers to other committees*
i. *Total disbursements by leadership PACs, excluding independent expenditures (listed separately in the table) as well as all contributions and transfers to other committees*
j. *Total disbursements by hybrid PACs, excluding independent expenditures (listed separately in the table) as well as all contributions and transfers to other committees*
k. *Total disbursements by super PACs, excluding independent expenditures (listed separately in the table) as well as all contributions and transfers to other committees*
l. *Total of all independent expenditures not listed elsewhere in the table (mostly by individuals)*
m. *Includes electioneering communication and independent expenditures by 501(c) tax-exempt organizations as reported at www.opensecrets.org/527s/527cmtes.php?level=C&cycle=2004*

(second column) and *indirect campaign expenditures* (third column). Direct campaign expenditures are focused on persuading voters, including the familiar campaign activities by candidates, parties, and interest groups. Indirect campaign expenditures are focused on the less-familiar provision of campaign infrastructure, such as fund-raising, expertise, and administration. Subtotals for the direct and indirect campaign expenditure columns are found at the bottom of the table along with a grand total of all expenditures.

Although the expenditure data in table 1.1 are incomplete due to disclosure limitations (discussed where relevant below),[15] the results are nonetheless impressive: at least $16.8 billion was spent during the 2020 election, $11.5 billion in direct expenditures (68 percent) and another $5.3 billion in indirect expenditures (32 percent).[16] These figures more than doubled the comparable figures of $8.1 billion for the 2016 election, $5.6 billion in direct expenditures and $2.5 billion in indirect expenditures (all in 2020 constant dollars).[17]

Not listed in table 1.1 are financial transactions among committees to avoid double counting, such as contributions to candidates by PACs and transfers among party committees. For the sake of completeness, these figures are discussed briefly in the text where relevant.

Candidate Committees

As in the recent elections, candidate committees were the largest source of direct campaign expenditures in 2020. Table 1.1 shows that all the presidential candidates' principal campaign committees (PCCs) spent a combined total of $4 billion in the nomination and general election campaigns. Meanwhile, all the congressional candidates' PCCs spent a combined total of almost $4 billion in primary and general election campaigns. These expenditures were more than twice the size of comparable expenditures in 2016, where $1.6 billion was spent by presidential candidate PCCs and $1.8 billion by congressional candidate PCCs.

In 2020, federal PCCs provided 69 percent of all direct expenditures and 47 percent of (grand) total expenditures. One reason for this increase was the expansion of candidate committees in 2020 (4,119) from 2016 (3,022). From this perspective, it is quite appropriate to describe the 2020 election as "candidate centered."

For practical reasons, it makes sense to list all expenditures by PCCs in the direct expenditure column, although conceptually some such expenses may be for campaign infrastructure rather than persuading voters.[18] For example, a rough categorization of campaign expenditures for Biden's PCC found that 13 percent of disbursements were for fund-raising and administration; the parallel figure for Trump's PCC was 14 percent. Still, 79 percent of Biden's expenditures and 68 percent of Trump's expenditures were for media of various kinds.[19] This pattern has been noted for congressional campaign spending as well.[20]

Although not listed in table 1.1, the largest source of funds for candidate committees was contributions from individuals. In 2020, such individual contributions totaled $7 billion, accounting for 71 percent of all contributions to candidate committees,[21] up from $2.4 billion in 2016. One kind of individual contribution drew particular attention: an increase in small donations—that is, unitemized contributions of $200 or less.[22] In 2020, such funds accounted for 25 percent of all contributions to presidential PCCs ($801 million) and 32 percent of all contributions to congressional PCCs ($1.2 billion). These figures represent a dramatic increase over 2016, when the comparable figures were $485 million and $214 million, respectively. (Overall, unitemized contributions to all kinds of committees totaled $4.7 billion in 2020, up from $2.2 billion in 2016.)

Joint Fund-Raising Committees

Although not listed in table 1.1, a substantial portion of the individual contributions to presidential and congressional PCCs, large and small, came through joint fund-raising committees (JFCs). JFCs associated with the major party presidential nominees[23] transferred $1.2 billion to presidential PCCs and other party committees in 2020, while non-presidential JFCs transferred $472 million to congressional PCCs and other participating committees; the comparable figures for 2016 were $722 million and $218 million, respectively. In 2020, unitemized contributions accounted for 35 percent ($701 million) of the contributions to the presidential JFCs but just 5 percent ($30 million) of the contributions to non-presidential JFCs; in 2016, the comparable contributions figures were 31 and 3 percent, respectively. Although the number of presidential JFCs increased only slightly in 2020 (from four to five), the number of non-presidential JFCs increased substantially (1,045) from 2016 (611).

As table 1.1 shows, JFCs also made indirect campaign expenditures in 2020, including for fund-raising and voter outreach.[24] Presidential JFCs spent $680 million on indirect expenditures in 2020, up from $287 million in 2016. Meanwhile, non-presidential JFCs spent $84 million in 2020, up from $55 million in 2016. Overall, the indirect campaign spending by both kinds of JFCs accounted for 14 percent of all indirect expenditures in 2020 and about 5 percent of total expenditures. JFCs were clearly a major element of financing the 2020 election.

Party Committees

Apart from participating in JFCs, party committees also engaged in direct campaign expenditures in 2020. As table 1.1 shows, the national party committees[25] made $80.4 million in coordinated expenditures with their candidates as well as $391 million in independent expenditures in support of their candidates; the comparable figures were $78 million and $273 million in 2016, respectively. Meanwhile, other party committees (mostly major-party state and local committees) made $6.5 million in coordinated expenditures and $2.1 million in independent expenditures in 2020; the comparable figures were $5.5 million and $650,000 in 2016, respectively. The number of national party committees was the same in 2020 and 2016 (6), whereas the number of state and local party committees engaged in federal activity increased slightly in 2020 (469) from 2016 (455).

Although not listed in table 1.1, the national party committees also contributed $3.3 million to the PCCs, while other party committees contributed

$4.8 million; comparable figures were $2.5 million and $1.9 million in 2016, respectively.

Interestingly, the indirect campaign expenditures of party committees were four times larger than their direct campaign spending. As table 1.1 shows, the national party committees spent almost $1.7 billion in 2020, while other party committees spent another $404.9 million in federal election activity;[26] the comparable figures were larger than in 2016, $882 million and $163 million, respectively.

All told, the combined party committees' expenditures accounted for 4 percent of all direct expenditures, 40 percent of all indirect expenditures, and 15 percent of total expenditures. The major political parties were certainly an important factor in the 2020 election, especially regarding campaign infrastructure and services to candidates.

Traditional PACs

Like party committees, political action committees (PACs) engaged in direct and indirect campaign expenditures in 2020. As table 1.1 shows, a subset of Traditional PACs, those with a separate segregated fund (SSF) and "connected" with a sponsoring organization (such as corporations, labor unions, and associations), made $22.7 million in internal communications expenditures to their members.[27] These figures may have been lower in 2020 than in 2016, where the comparable figures were $31 million.[28] These Connected PACs also spent $45.6 million in independent expenditures, down from $56 million in 2016. Connected PACs spent another $312.4 million in indirect expenditures;[29] the comparable 2016 figure was $260 million.

As table 1.1 shows, Non-connected PACs (without a sponsoring organization) made $38 million in independent expenditures in 2020 and, in addition, spent $449 million on indirect expenditures; the comparable 2016 figures were $26 million and $194 million, respectively. Meanwhile, Leadership PACs (organized by officeholders and candidates) made $6.3 million in independent expenditures and $112.6 million in indirect expenditures in 2020, largely to advance the aspirations of the relevant candidate.[30]

Although not listed in table 1.1, all Traditional PACs combined also contributed $878 million to candidates PCCs and other committees; the comparable figure for 2016 was $801 million.

In 2020, the combined direct expenditures of Traditional PACs (Connected, Non-connected, and Leadership) accounted for 1 percent of all direct expenditures, 16 percent of all indirect expenditures, and 6 percent of total expenditures. Overall, the number of Traditional PACs combined rose in 2020 (5,405) compared to 2016 (5,256). Although there appear to have been some shifts among the different types of Traditional PACs, these entities remained a factor in 2020, especially in congressional elections.

Hybrid and Super PACs

Two relatively new kinds of PACs were very active in 2020, Hybrid and Super PACs. Technically known as "independent expenditure only" committees (IEOC), these PACs may raise and spend unlimited funds for independent expenditures in campaigns. Super PACs maintain only an IEOC account, whereas Hybrid PACs combine the features of Traditional and Super PACs, maintaining both SSF and IEOC accounts.

As table 1.1 shows, Hybrid PACs made independent expenditures of $550 million in 2020, eleven times more than in 2016, when the comparable figure was $50 million. Hybrid PACs also spent $847 million on indirect campaign expenditures, also a dramatic increase over 2016, when the comparable figure was $110 million. One factor in this increase was the expansion in the number of Hybrid PACs in 2020 (394) compared to 2016 (141).

Meanwhile, Super PACs made $2.1 billion in independent expenditures, double the comparable 2016 figure of $1.1 billion. Super PACs also spent $761 million in indirect campaign expenditures, a large increase over the 2016 figure of $614 million. Here, too, one factor for this increase was the expanded number of Super PACs in 2020 (1,774) compared to 2016 (1,339).

In 2020, combined Hybrid and Super PAC expenditures accounted for 23 percent of all direct campaign expenditures, 30 percent of all indirect campaign expenditures, and 25 percent of total campaign expenditures.

Although not listed in table 1.1, Hybrid PACs also contributed $6.2 billion to candidates' PCCs and other committees; the comparable figure for 2016 was $709 million. These very large numbers were due in large measure to expanded activity by ActBlue and WinRed PACs, fund-raising platforms that earmarked individual donations to other federal committees.[31] These groups played a major role in the growth of unitemized donations in 2020. At the same time, many Hybrid and Super PACs also raised substantial sums in very large donations from very wealthy people. Hybrid and Super PACs clearly came of age in the 2020 election.

Additional Independent Spenders

Table 1.1 reports that "other" independent expenditures, mostly made by individuals, totaled $101.8 million in 2020.[32] The table also reports the independent expenditures (and electioneering communications) by tax-exempt groups, which was estimated at $126.7 million in 2020. These figures may underestimate the actual campaign spending by such groups due to limitations in disclosure; their indirect expenditures are unknown.[33] The activities of tax-exempt groups drew attention in 2020 in part because such groups made donations to Super PACs, raising concern about increased influence of "dark money."[34]

Interestingly, both additional sources of independent expenditure figures were about one-half of the size of comparable 2016 figures, $212 million and $256 million, respectively, suggesting that when combined, these two sources of independent expenditures accounted for about 2 percent of all direct campaign expenditures in 2020 and about 1 percent of total expenditures. The rise of Super PACs may have displaced these sources of independent expenditures to a significant degree.

To put the 2020 direct campaign expenditures in historical context, figure 1.1 plots all the direct campaign expenditures of presidential PCCs, congressional PCCs, and all noncandidate organizations in presidential election years from 1976 to 2020 (see the footnotes to the figures for data sources).

All three sources of direct expenditure slowly trended upward from 1976 to 1996, after which each took a different path. First, congressional candidate expenditures continued the slow upward trend until 2012, dipped in 2016, and then grew dramatically in 2020. Second, presidential candidate expenditures began to move upward as fewer candidates participated in the public financing system until 2008, dipped in 2012 and 2016, and then grew

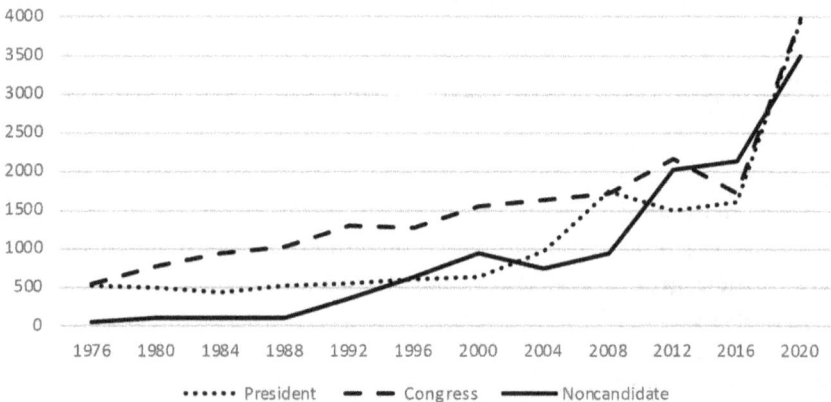

Figure 1.1 Direct Federal Campaign Expenditures in Presidential Elections, 1976–2020 (2020 constant dollars). *Source*: OpenSecrets, analysis of FEC Summary Files: 1992–2020, www.fec.gov/campaign-finance-data/; 1976–1988, www.fec.gov/fec-reports-financial-activity-1976-1994/; for campaign expenditures by tax-exempt groups, www.opensecrets.org/527s/527cmtes.php?level=C&cycle=2004

dramatically in 2020. Third, noncandidate expenditures showed an uneven pattern, due to the advent and decay of different sources of noncandidate campaign expenditures:

- a slow increase of noncandidate expenditures through 2000, reflecting the rise of party soft money;
- a decline in noncandidate expenditures in 2004, when soft money was banned, followed by slow growth from 2008 to 2012, reflecting electioneering communications by tax-exempt groups plus the advent of Super PACs; and
- a modest increase in noncandidate spending in 2016, followed by a sharp expansion in 2020, reflecting the maturing of Super and Hybrid PACs.

All told, figure 1.1 shows more than a tenfold increase in direct campaign expenditures from 1976 to 2020 in real terms. At this writing, there are good reasons to expect that these trends will persist in the 2024 election cycle.

PREVIEWING THE SUBSTANTIVE CHAPTERS

The substantive chapters that follow provide a more detailed examination of key aspects of the broader patterns presented in table 1.1 and figure 1.1.

In chapter 2, R. Sam Garrett describes the regulatory environment in which candidates, parties, PACs, and other actors raised and spent funds in the 2020 election. These entities are governed by specific, complex, and sometimes arcane rules. Although few major changes were made in these regulations between 2016 and 2020, the existing rules help explain the behavior of the various entities participating in the campaign finance system during a time of rapid change.

In chapter 3, John C. Green reports on the finances of the nomination and general election components of the 2020 presidential contest. The patterns include a record level of direct campaign expenditures in pursuit of the White House, including lavish self-financed primary campaigns. In addition, direct spending by noncandidate sources expanded, especially during the general election. He also finds significant innovations in the Trump and Biden campaigns that may persist for 2024.

In chapter 4, Molly E. Reynolds provides a parallel analysis of the congressional contests, which set records for spending: the ten most expensive House and Senate races in history took place in 2020. Fund-raising by candidates for their own campaigns showed substantial increases, thanks to a sizable increase in donations from individuals, especially in small amounts. Direct expenditures from noncandidate sources in congressional races also increased, especially in the form of independent expenditures.

In chapter 5, Robin Kolodny and Diana Dwyre explore the role of party money in 2020, which saw historically high levels of spending by national party committees. The use of JFCs expanded over previous election cycles, helping party committees efficiently secure maximum contributions from wealthy donors, including new types of party accounts for the conventions, headquarters buildings, recounts, and legal fees. Party committees were also quite active in independent expenditures, especially in congressional campaigns.

In chapter 6, Jay Goodliffe describes the financial activity by interest groups by means of Traditional PACs, Hybrid and Super PACs, and tax-exempt groups. In the 2020 election cycle, these groups combined to spend record amounts directly in campaigns, especially Hybrid and Super PACs, which involved an increased role of very large contributions from very wealthy donors stretching across the political spectrum. He finds examples of both continuity and dramatic change in the ways interest groups sought to influence elections via political finance.

In chapter 7, Robert G. Boatright puts the factors and trends described in the previous chapters in political context, with a special focus on the prospects for campaign finance reform. Although records were set across a wide range of types of raising and spending, the eye-popping aggregate sums were perhaps not the most important story of the 2020 campaign. Rather, the legacy may be a heightened symbolic value of political money rather than its role in fueling campaigns operations.

A SIXTY-YEAR ANNIVERSARY

The 2020 election marks the sixty-year anniversary of *Financing the 1960 Election*, the first of a series of fifteen books (with this one being the sixteenth) describing federal campaign finance in presidential election years, written by Herbert E. Alexander, his contemporary and future colleagues.

Financing the 1960 Election was an early product of Citizens' Research Foundation, a nonprofit organization devoted to studying campaign finance, founded in 1958 with Alexander as its director. The 1960 book originated as a chapter in *The Presidential Election and Transition, 1960–1961*,[35] following the publication of Alexander Heard's *The Costs of Democracy* in 1960,[36] and leading to Alexander's service as director of the President's Commission on

Campaign Costs 1961–62.[37] Building on these foundations, Alexander and the Citizens' Research Foundation labored for the next forty years, constructing an impressive edifice of campaign finance research and analysis, including more than two hundred publications.[38]

The series of *Financing* books are the best-known product of Alexander's scholarship, and they have influenced generations of scholars, activists, and public officials. The series can be divided into three parts:

- The first part includes books on the 1960, 1964, and 1968 elections,[39] covering the decade leading up to the passage of the Federal Election Act of 1971 (FECA), the legislation that ushered in the modern era of campaign finance reporting and regulation (see chapter 2). The crucial information provided by these books and Alexander's other research contributed to passage of FECA and the subsequent amendments to FECA in 1974, 1976, and 1978.
- The second part includes six books on the post-FECA elections of 1972, 1976, 1980, 1984, 1988, and 1992, the last three with coauthors.[40] These books took advantage of the expanded disclosure of campaign finance activity required by FECA to document its implementation and operation in the new era.
- The third part includes six books on the 1996, 2000, 2004, 2008, 2012, and 2016 elections.[41] In recognition of the growing complexity of the campaign finance system, these books were edited collections. As Alexander neared retirement, the initial volume was edited by John C. Green with Alexander's assistance, and then David B. Magleby became the main editor (one volume had multiple editors). These collections are a fitting tribute to the ongoing research community Alexander helped form and nurture.

Of course, the federal campaign finance system in 2020 was vastly larger than in 1960, with a broader range of finance activity, greater diversity of financial actors, and wider scope of regulation. But it is worth noting that the present system has addressed many of the major concerns raised in 1960, whereas others were still prominently debated in 2020 (see chapter 7). Indeed, the campaign financing trends of the past sixty years have, in some respects, returned to the basic patterns identified in *Financing the 1960 Election*. In 2020, the three major portions of election campaigns (by candidate, party, and interest group committees) were prominent, characterized by largely unlimited spending, a prominent role for large contributions, and enlarged resistance to regulation. At the same time, the increase in small donations, the diversity of entities involved, and the near balance of partisan and ideo-logical resources in 2020 was a contrast to 1960.

The reporting and disclosure of campaign finances is a fitting example of this contrast. Alexander was a relentless champion of complete, accurate, and timely information about political finance. Indeed, furthering this goal has been a principal purpose of the *Financing* books. Although not without its limitations, the present disclosure process has many virtues: the reporting features of the Federal Election Commission and state agencies are robust, and they are bolstered by nonprofit organizations dedicated to the dissemi-nation of such information and the independent analyses of the data, fitting successors to the Citizens' Research Foundation.

In 2021, two innovative watchdog groups, the Center for Responsive Politics and the National Institute on Money in Politics, merged to become OpenSecrets, launching a state-of-the-art effort to track the flow of money in politics at the national, state, and local levels.[42] The new organization describes its mission thus:

> Nonpartisan, independent and nonprofit, OpenSecrets is the nation's premier research group tracking money in U.S. politics and its effect on elections and public policy. Our mission is to track the flow of money in American politics and provide the data and analysis to strengthen democracy. Our vision is for Americans to use this knowledge to create a more vibrant, representative, and accountable democracy.[43]

A key asset of the organization is its award-winning website, which provides easy access to campaign finance data, enhanced by contextual information, sophisticated analyses, and unique reporting on money and politics. In its new configuration, OpenSecrets will be an even greater boon to journalists, scholars, activists, and public officials alike.

OpenSecrets was a partner in this volume, serving as the primary source of information on campaign finance in each of the chapters. Brendan Glavin, senior data analyst and formerly with the Campaign Finance Institute (now part of OpenSecrets), worked closely with the authors to help ensure accu-rate and consistent data.[44] Glavin's invaluable assistance and the partnership with OpenSecrets is very much in the spirit of Herbert Alexander and the *Financing* volumes.

NOTES

1. Andrew E. Busch and John J. Pitney, *Divided We Stand* (Lanham, MD: Row-man & Littlefield, 2021), 69–108.

2. Herbert E. Alexander, *Financing the 1960 Election* (Princeton, NJ: Citizens' Research Foundation, 1962).

3. Jeffrey M. Jones, "Last Trump Job Approval 34%; Average Is Record-Low 41%," *Gallup*, January 18, 2021, https://news.gallup.com/poll/328637/last-trump -job-approval-average-record-low.aspx.

4. Nathaniel Rakich, "Trump Is the Most Unpopular President since Ford to Run for Re-Election," *FiveThirtyEight*, January 7, 2020, https://fivethirtyeight.com/ features/trump-is-the-most-unpopular-president-since-ford-to-run-for-reelection/.

5. Jones, "Last Trump Job Approval 34%; Average Is Record-Low 41%."

6. Pew Research Center, "Election 2020: Voters Are Highly Engaged, But Nearly Half Expect to Have Difficulties Voting," August 2020, https://www.pewre search.org/politics/202/08/13/election-2020-voters-are-highly-engaged-but-nearly-hald-expect-to-have-difficulties-voting.

7. Peter K. Enns and Julius Lagodny, "We Predicted the States Biden Would Win 100 Days before the Election," *Washington Post*, November 12, 2020, https://www .washingtonpost.com/politics/2020/11/12/we-predicted-states-biden-would-win-100 -days-before-election/.

8. David C. Wheelock, "Comparing the COVID-19 Recession with the Great Depression," *Economic Synopses* 39 (2020), 10.20955/es.2020.39.

9. Seth Masket, "How Much Did COVID-19 Affect the 2020 Election?" *FiveThirtyEight*, January 27, 2021, https://fivethirtyeight.com/features/how-much -did-covid-19-affect-the-2020-election/.

10. National Center for Health Statistics, "Provisional Death Counts for Coronavirus Disease 2019 (COVID-19)," https://www.cdc.gov/nchs/nvss/vsrr/COVID19/ index.htm.

11. Zachary Scherer, "Majority of Voters Used Nontraditional Methods to Cast Ballots in 2020," April 29, 2021, https://www.census.gov/library/stories/2021/04/ what-methods-did-people-use-to-vote-in-2020-election.html.

12. Drew Desilver, "Turnout Soared in 2020 as Nearly Two-Thirds of Eligible U.S. Voters Cast Ballots for President," Pew Research Center, January 28, 2021, https://www.pewresearch.org/fact-tank/2021/01/28/turnout-soared-in-2020-as -nearly-two-thirds-of-eligible-u-s-voters-cast-ballots-for-president/.

13. Table 1.1 is based on the FEC Committee summary files for 2020 and 2016 and other FEC reports.

14. Some of the aggregate figures presented here may appear to differ slightly from other figures reported elsewhere in the book because of different ways of combining and analyzing the same financial reports. For an example of how these data were used in a somewhat different but valid fashion than in table 1.1, see Karl Evers-Hillstrom, "Most Expensive Ever: 2020 Election Cost $14.4 Billion," *OpenSecrets*, February 11, 2021, https://www.opensecrets.org/news/2021/02/2020-cycle-cost-14p4-billion-doubling-16.

15. The pandemic created some special limitations on disclosure of campaign finance information due to difficulties in the filing of reports by committees as well as in the processing of these reports by the FEC. For example, the FEC noted, "The data presented in these statistical summaries do not include all reports filed on paper.

To minimize COVID-19 exposure, the Commission closed its office headquarters in mid-March 2020 and the processing of reports submitted on paper will be delayed until the agency resumes normal operations. Financial activity of paper filers will be accounted for in the first statistical release after the reopening of the agency's office."

16. For ease of presentation in the text, table 1.1 entries are rounded.

17. In this chapter, all figures from previous years are expressed in 2020 constant dollars.

18. Although candidate committees are required to report expenditures in detail, there are no standardized categories for purposes for which funds are expended.

19. For these data, see https://www.opensecrets.org/2020-presidential-race/joe-biden/candidate?id=N00001669 and https://www.opensecrets.org/2020-presidential-race/donald-trump/candidate?id=N00023864.

20. Steve Ansolabehere and A. Gerber, "The Mismeasure of Campaign Spending: Evidence from the 1990 U.S. House Elections," *Journal of Politics* 56, no. 4 (1994): 1106–18.

21. The 2020 figure is low compared to past elections because of the nearly $1.5 billion spent by self-financed candidates. But looked at from another perspective, such self-financing is individual donations.

22. See Ollie Gratzinger, "Small Donors Give Big Money in 2020," *OpenSecrets*, October 30, 2020, https://www.opensecrets.org/news/2020/10/small-donors-give-big-2020-thanks-to-technology/.

23. Biden's JFCs were the Biden Victory Fund, Biden Action Fund, and Biden Fight Fund; the Trump JFCs were Trump Make American Great Again Committee and Trump Victory Fund.

24. See Jessica Piper, "Mar-a-Lago, $20K Worth of Flowers and Lots of Consulting: When Joint Fundraising Money Goes beyond Campaigns," *OpenSecrets*, September 3, 2019, https://www.opensecrets.org/news/2019/09/joint-fundraising-committees-go-beyond-campaigns-mar-a-lago.

25. The national party committees included the Democratic National Committee (DNC) and Republican National Committee (RNC); and the Congressional Campaign Committees, the Democratic Senatorial Campaign Committees (DSCC) and the National Republican Senatorial Committee (RNSC), the Democratic Congressional Committee (DCCC) and the National Republican Congressional Committee (NRCC).

26. In 2020, many and complex transfers were made among the various party committees, a practice allowed by law.

27. Internal communication expenditures must be reported only if they exceed $2,000 per election. So, these figures do not include all communication expenditures undertaken in 2020.

28. Due to filing and reporting challenges, this figure understates the level of internal communications in 2020 (see chapter 6 for more details).

29. Because the organization sponsoring a SSF PAC can pay the costs of administering an SSF PAC with organizational funds, the indirect campaign expenditures likely do not include administrative expenses. Thus, the indirect campaign expenditures for these PACs are understated.

30. See Yue Stella Yu, "Luxury Hotel Stays, Private Flights, New Nonprofits: Leadership PACs Can Pay for Them," *OpenSecrets*, December 12, 2019, https://www.opensecrets.org/news/2019/12/leadership-pacs-cash-flows-to-closely-linked-businesses.

31. See https://www.opensecrets.org/political-action-committees-pacs/actblue/C00401224/summary/2020 and https://www.opensecrets.org/political-action-committees-pacs/winred/C00694323/summary/2020.

32. Individuals making more than $250 in independent expenditures must file a report with the FEC.

33. The tax-exempt organizations report under Internal Revenue Service rules. The information disclosed on campaign-related expenditures is general and lacks the details required in FEC reports. An exception is electioneering communications, which occur in broadcast media made thirty days before a primary or sixty days before a general election that identify a specific federal candidate and are receivable by fifty thousand or more people in the candidate's district or state; these reports are filed with the Federal Communications Commission. Thus, many of the election expenditures of such groups are not disclosed. The names of the donors to such groups are not disclosed because the information is part of the donors' confidential federal income tax returns.

34. For example, Anna Massoglia, "'Dark Money' Groups Steering Millions to Super PACs in 2020 Elections," *OpenSecrets*, February 7, 2020, https://www.opensecrets.org/news/2020/02/dark-money-steers-millions-to-super-pacs-2020.

35. Paul T. David, ed., *Presidential Election and Transition, 1960–1961* (Washington, DC: Brookings Institution, 1961).

36. Herbert E. Alexander, *The Costs of Democracy* (Chapel Hill: University of North Carolina Press, 1960).

37. See Herbert E. Alexander, ed., *Studies in Money in Politics*, vol. 1 (Princeton, NJ: Citizens' Research Foundation, 1965).

38. For more information about Alexander and his publications, see http://www.cfinst.org/HerbertEAlexander/Bio.aspx.

39. Herbert E. Alexander, *Financing the 1964 Election* (Princeton, NJ: Citizens' Research Foundation, 1966); Herbert E. Alexander, *Financing the 1968 Election* (Lexington, MA: Heath, 1971).

40. Herbert E. Alexander, *Financing the 1972 Election* (Lexington, MA: Heath, 1976); Herbert E. Alexander, *Financing the 1980 Election* (Lexington, MA: Heath, 1983); Herbert R. Alexander and Brian A. Haggerty, *Financing the 1984 Election* (Lexington, MA: Heath, 1987); Herbert E. Alexander and Monica Bauer, *Financing the 1988 Election* (Boulder, CO: Westview, 1991); Herbert E. Alexander and Anthony Corrado, *Financing the 1992 Election* (Armonk, NY: Sharpe, 1995).

41. John C. Green, ed., *Financing the 1996 Election* (Armonk, NY: Sharpe, 1999); David B. Magleby, ed., *Financing the 2000 Election* (Washington, DC: Brookings Institution Press, 2002); David B. Magleby, Anthony Corrado, and Kelly D. Patterson, eds., *Financing the 2004 Election* (Washington, DC: Brookings Institution Press, 2006); David B. Magleby, ed., *Financing the 2008 Election*

(Washington, DC: Brookings Institution Press, 2011); David B. Magleby, ed., *Financing the 2012 Election* (Washington, DC: Brookings Institution Press, 2014); David B. Magleby, ed., *Financing the 2016 Election* (Washington, DC: Brookings Institution Press, 2019).

42. OpenSecrets, "Leading Money-in-Politics Data Nonprofits Merge to Form OpenSecrets, a State-of-the-Art Democratic Accountability Organization," https://www.opensecrets.org/news/category/press-releases/.

43. https://www.opensecrets.org/about/.

44. Of course, the use and interpretation of these data are the responsibility of the authors and editors.

2

The Regulatory Environment of the 2020 Election

R. Sam Garrett[1]

When Herbert E. Alexander wrote *Financing the 1960 Election*, two main kinds of organizations—candidates and political parties—were central to his analysis. Alexander also described interest groups as they existed at the time, such as unions, but the political environment was generally simpler than it is today, as were a collection of federal statutes that were widely regarded as ineffective at regulating political activity.[2] On all these fronts, much has changed since 1960, and the 2020 campaign environment was vastly different than the one Alexander chronicled. However, campaigns are still ultimately about candidates, and most voters, with busy lives and not focused on politics, identify their Election Day preferences through party affiliation.

This chapter discusses the 2020 regulatory environment with an emphasis on explaining the rules that apply to different entities and why those rules matter. Seemingly arcane regulatory definitions, such as for "contributions" and "expenditures," or "candidate committees," "party committees," or "political action committees," all have major implications for campaign practices. If one wants to adhere to the Watergate adage of "following the money," the regulatory environment provides the map.[3]

Limits on amounts of contributions and sources of contributions (or, in some cases, outright prohibitions) and disclosure about financial transactions are fundamental principles in federal campaign finance policy. Importantly, however, there have been major changes in the regulatory environment and in the kinds of entities that influence political campaigns since Congress established, and courts adjudicated, much of the existing campaign finance policy framework throughout the twentieth century. The regulatory environment for the 2020 election cycle is the product of more than a century of campaign practices, organizations, and legal developing around each other and responding to each other.

Key points of that environment include the following.

- Campaign finance law (the Federal Election Campaign Act, FECA) generally regulates entities known as "political committees," which include candidate, party, and political action committees (PACs).
- Political committees (except Super PACs and specific accounts in Hybrid PACs) are subject to individual contribution limits, but no aggregate limits cap total individual giving.
- Independent expenditures to elect or defeat federal candidates are unlimited, assuming that the spending is not coordinated with a campaign, and may be undertaken by party and political committees but also by individuals.[4]
- Entities subject to Federal Election Commission (FEC) regulation must "disclose" (report) their financial activity to the commission and, by extension, to the public. They also must include certain "disclaimers" (identifying information) on their advertising and other communications.
- Campaign finance law regulates conduct to influence federal elections, not broader political or policy advocacy. In some cases, entities regulated primarily under tax law (the Internal Revenue Code, IRC) may also influence elections and operate under different disclosure rules.
- A regulated entity's status as a political committee or a politically active entity affects whether it may make contributions, independent expenditures, or both, and the kind of disclosure required.
- As campaign finance regulation has grown more complex in recent decades, so has the policy environment surrounding it, from the kinds of issues subject to policy debate to the variety of congressional committees or agencies potentially involved in regulation.

WHY CAMPAIGN FINANCE POLICY MATTERS

Few aspects of campaign management are subject to regulation in the United States, but campaign fund-raising and spending are heavily regulated. Here the terms "policy" and "regulation" generally are used to mean federal requirements affecting the campaign finance environment. These requirements include constitutional provisions; statutory law enacted by Congress and signed by the president; agency regulations (sometimes called "rules") or other guidance that provides advice but is not a formal requirement; and court opinions that interpret whether Congress, agencies, or regulated entities have exceeded their authority.

The campaign finance regulations that Congress establishes, federal agencies implement and enforce, and courts interpret determine what people and organizations in the campaign environment may do and how they may do it. In turn, what is sometimes called the "regulated community" of candidates, donors, parties, and anyone else subject to campaign finance law must be keenly aware of these rules. Civil and criminal penalties, campaign crises, and public scandals can accompany noncompliance. At the same time, campaigns and related entities are in the business of winning elections. Political practitioners—candidates, political consultants, and lawyers who specialize in protecting campaign organizations from noncompliance—also are keenly aware of what law and regulation prohibit and what they do not. Even if some fund-raising or organizational practices are controversial, campaigns and other groups are likely to pursue them if they help win elections. The regulations, therefore, set the boundaries for what ultimately become strategic decisions about how campaigns are waged.[5]

ACTIVITIES AND ENTITIES REGULATED UNDER CAMPAIGN FINANCE POLICY

Like other areas of public policy, campaign finance has its own vocabulary rooted in law enacted by Congress, rules issued by federal agencies, and interpretations by the courts. This chapter, and the rest of the book, generally uses the terms that have specific meanings and where following precise language is important for accuracy. At the same time, the book employs some of its own acronyms, noted below, for consistency throughout the chapters that follow.[6]

In the broadest sense, the campaign finance regulatory environment affects certain *activities* and certain *entities*. In terms of activities, campaign finance law generally regulates money raised or spent to elect or defeat federal candidates. This activity is known as "express advocacy" because it explicitly calls for (or facilitates) election or defeat of specific candidates. Examples of such activities include political advertising calling for election or defeat of candidates, fund-raisers to solicit funds, and even some messages that refer to clearly identified candidates without calling for their election or defeat (such as "electioneering communications," discussed later in this chapter).

On the other hand, the campaign finance regulatory environment generally does not address activity that avoids specific calls to elect or defeat candidates. Even much activity that might be considered broadly political, such as general interest group advocacy, or political advertising that solely addresses policy issues rather than candidates, does not fall under the campaign finance regulatory regime. These general public policy messages are called "issue advocacy," and they are not subject to campaign finance regulation as discussed here unless otherwise noted.

Although the activities regulated under campaign finance law are relatively straightforward, the *entities* regulated are more complicated, due largely to decades of lawmaking, agency regulations, and court opinions, much of which this chapter summarizes. Most significantly, the FECA primarily addresses entities defined as "political committees,"[7] including candidate campaign, party, and political action committees (PACs). In general, all political committees are subject to contribution limits, disclosure requirements, and disclaimer requirements. Beyond those general similarities, different kinds of political committees play unique roles in campaigns and are subject to different kinds of regulation.

Table 2.1 provides an overview of the kinds of entities and practices that were subject to campaign finance regulation in 2020 and by whom. The policy history discussed later in this chapter provides additional detail about how different activities and entities developed and have been regulated.

- Candidate committees are what readers likely think of as a "campaign." Also known as "authorized committees" or "principal campaign committees" (PCCs), these are the organizations that candidates have established to raise and spend funds to develop and deploy strategy, theme, and message. Contributions to and from PCCs are limited, as discussed later in this chapter. If they choose to do so, candidates may make unlimited contributions to their own campaigns.[8] As with all political committees, PCCs are also subject to disclosure and disclaimer requirements (see chapters 3 and 4 on candidate PCCs in 2020).
- Party committees raise and spend funds to support or oppose candidate committees. The most prominent examples at the federal level are the Democratic National Committee (DNC) and the Republican National Committee (RNC), the governing bodies of the nation's two major political parties (sometimes called "headquarters committees"). In addition to the DNC and RNC, parties also form separate political committees for different purposes. Most prominently, these include one political committee per chamber of Congress dedicated to electing party candidates.

Table 2.1   Selected Entities in the Campaign Finance Regulatory Environment

Entity Type	Brief Description	Examples	Contributions permitted to candidates?	Primary Regulatory Statute
Candidate's principal campaign committee (PCCs)	House, Senate, or presidential campaigns	Biden for President; Donald J. Trump for President, Inc.	Yes	FECA
Party committees (RNC, DNC, CCCs)	Party entities dedicated to recruiting candidates and electing nominees	National Republican Campaign Committee; Democratic Congressional Campaign Committee	Yes	FECA
SSF political action committees (Connected, Non-connected, Leadership PACs)	Entities organized to support electoral goals of corporations/union, independent group, or politician	United Mine Workers of America—Coal Miners PAC; Walmart Inc. PAC; CHERPAC	Yes	FECA
Joint fund-raising committees (JFC)	Entities organized to raise funds for multiple candidate or party committees	Biden Victory Fund; Trump Victory Fund	Routes contributions to multiple committees	FECA
Super PACs	Independent-expenditure only committees; post-*Citizens United* only	Senate Leadership Fund; Women Vote!	No	FECA
Hybrid PACs	SSF PACs that operate separate accounts for limited contributions and for unlimited independent expenditures	ActBlue; WinRed	Yes, from accounts accepting limited contributions	FECA
Tax-exempt 501(c)(4)	Social welfare organizations	People for the American Way	No	IRC
Tax-exempt 501(c)(5)	Labor unions	AFL-CIO	No	IRC
Tax-exempt 501(c)(6)	Business associations	U.S. Chamber of Commerce	No	IRC

Source: Author analysis of FECA, FEC disclosure reports, and OpenSecrets organizational summaries.

Notes: Abbreviations in the "entity type" column are used for consistency throughout this book, although they do not necessarily appear in policy or practitioner parlance. The author abbreviated some names in the "example" column for space. The table excludes discussion of Section 527 of the Internal Revenue Code. All political committees (candidate committees, parties, PACs) are regulated under IRC §527 for tax purposes. However, these entities typically do not have taxable income. In the early 2000s, some organizations regulated by §527 claimed not to be political committees but nonetheless engaged in efforts to elect or defeat candidates. The table also does not reflect individual entities' incorporation status or corporate or legal relationships between different organizations.

These entities are known as "congressional campaign committees" (CCCs, sometimes called "Hill committees," a reference to their roles in electing congressional majorities on Capitol Hill). For the two major parties, these are the Democratic Congressional Campaign Committee (DCCC) and Democratic Senatorial Campaign Committee (DSCC); and the National Republican Congressional Committee (NRCC) and National Republican Senatorial Committee (NRSC). A variety of state and local party committees also may participate in federal elections subject to FECA. In addition to making contributions and independent expenditures supporting their candidates (or electioneering communications referring to them), parties may also make limited "coordinated party expenditures" to support their candidates.[9] As with all political committees, all these entities are subject to contribution limits, disclosure, and disclaimer requirements (see chapter 5 on party committees in 2020).

- Whereas candidate committees and party committees are relatively self-explanatory, "political action committees" (PACs) are more complicated, largely because they developed at different times due to unique regulatory circumstances, and thus different entities use variations on the "PAC" terminology (see chapters 3, 4, 5, and 6 on different kinds of PACs in 2020).

- Traditionally, the term "PAC" referred to one kind of entity, a "separate segregated fund" (SSF). SSFs first emerged in the 1970s as corporations and unions sought options for influencing elections despite FECA's ban on corporate and union contributions and expenditures as it existed at the time.[10] Through SSF PACs, corporations, unions, other similar economic organizations,[11] or independent organizations may raise voluntary contributions in permissible amounts and to make contributions, independent expenditures, or electioneering communications supporting or opposing (or referencing for electioneering communications) federal candidates.

- SSFs formed by corporations, unions, and related organizations are known as "Connected" PACs, whereas those formed by independent organizations are known as "Non-connected." Connected and Non-connected PAC contributions are subject to limits under FECA. A Connected PAC, such as a corporate or union entity, may not use the PAC to make contributions or expenditures that are otherwise prohibited. A corporation could not, for example, permissibly get around the ban on corporate contributions simply by routing prohibited funds through its PAC.[12] As with other committees, disclosure and disclaimer requirements apply to SSFs.

- Leadership PACs are another form of SSF. The names come from the origins of such PACs as fund-raising tools for members of the congressional leadership, who use the committees to raise funds to build legislative majorities and support their colleagues.[13] Leadership PACs emerged in the 1970s as members of Congress sought ways to raise funds for their colleagues in addition to making contributions from their own campaigns. Through Leadership PACs, members of Congress can make limited contributions to other campaigns. Although Leadership PACs are popularly identified with the member or candidate who creates these committees, for regulatory purposes they are unaffiliated with the candidate's principal campaign committee (PCC). In some cases, candidates use Leadership PACs to defray costs indirectly related to their campaigns, such as travel for party fund-raising or other events. Leadership PACs are subject to contribution limits as well as disclaimer and disclosure requirements. (For purposes of this book, the combination of Connected, Non-connected, and Leadership PACs are referred to as "Traditional PACs," both because of their history and to distinguish them from newer kinds of PACs.)

- Super PACs are subject to disclosure and disclaimer requirements, but because they may only make independent expenditures, they are not subject to contribution limits. These committees, which the FEC classifies as "independent-expenditure only committees" (IEOCs), are a product of the post-*Citizens United* environment, discussed later in this chapter. Some SSF Non-connected PACs also operate separate accounts that resemble Super PACs in that they may accept unlimited contributions for use in independent expenditures. These entities are known as Hybrid PACs.

- Although campaign finance law primarily regulates political committees, any person or entity that engages in independent expenditures or electioneering communication (see below for definitions) in a campaign must disclose that activity to the FEC.[14] Three kinds of tax-exempt groups regulated primarily under the Section 501(c) of the Internal Revenue Code are particularly noteworthy, even though these groups are not political committees. The most active such groups are "social welfare" groups organized and regulated under Section 501(c)(4). These entities typically are membership organizations devoted to specific policy issues. Section 501(c)(5) regulates labor unions and Section 501(c)(6) regulates business leagues known as "trade associations." To maintain their tax-exempt status, these organizations may not *primarily* engage in political campaigning, but their spending on independent expenditures and electioneering communications became more noteworthy after the 2010 *Citizens United* decision (discussed below; see chapter 6 on tax-exempt groups in 2020).

Entities That Regulate: Congress

In the legislative branch, two congressional committees have shaped campaign finance policy since the 1970s. In the House of Representatives, the Committee on House Administration exercises primary jurisdiction over federal elections, including campaign finance. The Senate Rules and Administration Committee is the counterpart committee on that side of the Capitol. Both committees play leading roles in shaping campaign finance legislation and conducting oversight of related policy issues and of the FEC.

Other committees exercise jurisdiction over related issues and can affect campaign finance policy, but they do not specialize in the topic in the same way as the Committee on House Administration and the Senate Rules and Administration Committee. Most prominently, the House and Senate Judiciary Committees have jurisdiction over constitutional amendments, including those that would authorize Congress and the states to further regulate campaign finance. Members of Congress regularly introduce such amendments, but they have never been adopted. Other committees, such as the House Energy and Commerce Committee and Senate Commerce Committee, oversee telecommunications issues and thus could consider legislation or oversight related to topics such as political advertising.

Finally, committees specializing in government investigations can and have conducted wide-ranging reviews of campaign finance practices on issues such as foreign money in U.S. elections and connections with national security. Examples include the 1990s work of the House Government Reform and Oversight Committee concerning prohibited foreign funds in U.S. elections and the post-2016 Senate Intelligence Committee investigation on foreign interference and online political advertising.[15]

How campaign finance legislation moves through Congress can vary. Traditionally, the committees discussed above, especially the House Administration and Senate Rules Committees, hold hearings on unique bills. That process continues today. In addition, sometimes this traditional, committee-based legislation has been superseded by large "omnibus" bills, often negotiated by chamber leadership.[16] This process is especially true in the annual appropriations cycle. Appropriations bills thus can become the legislative "vehicles" of last resort when traditional "stand-alone" legislation devoted to specific policy issues is not advancing. In campaign finance, these bills can contain not only operating funds for the Federal Election Commission, but also funding restrictions or other policy provisions that can have campaign finance implications.[17] One of the most significant such changes in the past decade occurred in 2014 (FY2015), when Congress substantially increased contribution limits to political parties after the Supreme Court's 2014 *McCutcheon* decision invalidated previous aggregate contribution limits for party contributions (see below).

Entities That Regulate: Federal Agencies

In 1974, Congress established the Federal Election Commission (FEC) to administer and enforce civil aspects of campaign finance law. As currently structured, the FEC is a six-member independent regulatory agency. Commissioners are nominated by the president and subject to Senate confirmation. Under FECA, no more than three of the six commissioners may be affiliated with the same political party.[18] In practice, the agency usually is evenly divided between Democratic and Republican nominees.

The FEC has always been controversial. Congress created the agency in the aftermath of Watergate amid pressure to police private fund-raising. Some members did not want to cede oversight to an independent body. The independent, bipartisan structure eventually won legislative approval. Congress required at least four votes—therefore, at least some measure of bipartisanship—to conduct the agency's most significant business, such as approving enforcement actions and issuing regulations. For some observers, the four-vote requirement is an important safeguard against partisan enforcement, whereas others counter that the requirement plus the even number of commissioners limits the chances that the agency will reach controversial but necessary decisions.[19]

Other agencies have some responsibility for campaign finance issues as well. The Department of Justice (DOJ) is responsible for criminal enforcement. The Federal Communications Commission (FCC) administers aspects of telecommunications law that can affect political committees. The Internal Revenue Service (IRS) is responsible for administering and enforcing tax laws that can be relevant for political committees, particularly publicly financed presidential candidates.

THE CONSTITUTION AND MAJOR STATUTES
AFFECTING CAMPAIGN FINANCE

As the paramount body of federal law, the U.S. Constitution sets general parameters affecting elections and campaign finance, although the document does not explicitly mention political money. The First Amendment is at the heart of most campaign finance litigation and judicial precedent; it both limits what government can do and protects what nongovernmental actors can do. The relevant provision of the First Amendment specifies that "Congress shall make no law . . . abridging the freedom of speech."[20] The Supreme Court has issued a series of opinions interpreting campaign finance law within the context of the First Amendment that have major implications for political practice and policy options.

The Elections Clause in Article 1 assigns the states with most authority for regulating the federal elections and specifies that "The Times, Places and Manner of holding Elections for Senators and Representatives, shall be prescribed in each State by the Legislature thereof; but the Congress may at any time by Law make or alter such Regulations, except as to the Places of [choosing] Senators."[21] (In practice, states have essentially no role in regulating campaign finance in federal elections. States do, however, sometimes provide policy models for additional federal regulation or deregulation.) Some members of Congress and policy advocates see the Elections Clause as a potentially untapped congressional authority to regulate campaign finance to a greater degree than exists today. However, as discussed below, recent trends point toward deregulation.

EARLY FOUNDATIONS OF FEDERAL CAMPAIGN FINANCE POLICY

Although some elements of federal campaign finance law date to the Civil War period,[22] modern campaign finance policy at the federal level began to take shape in the early 1900s, when Congress enacted legislation regulating some contributions and establishing a rudimentary, and easily avoided, system of publicizing information about financial transactions.

Most notably during this early period, in the 1907 Tillman Act, Congress prohibited corporations and national banks from making campaign contributions.[23] As is often the case with changes in public policy, the Tillman Act resulted from scandal, in this case surrounding corporate fund-raising accompanying President Theodore Roosevelt's 1904 reelection campaign. Roosevelt had crafted an image of a corporate reformer and "trustbuster." The Tillman Act thus was both consistent with the president's policy legacy and provided political cover against heavy and sometimes-controversial corporate funding in what was a largely unregulated campaign finance policy environment at the time.[24]

Congress applied the contribution ban to labor unions in 1940s.[25] Other early statutes, including the Publicity Act and the Federal Corrupt Practices Act, enacted and amended between 1910 and 1925, established basic disclosure requirements and spending limits.[26] These and other early federal regulatory efforts established a principle that remains consistent today: pro-regulatory campaign finance policies are typically framed as remedies to political corruption arising from private campaign financing (see chapter 7 on these issues in 2020).

The Federal Election Campaign Act (FECA) and *Buckley v. Valeo*

Modern campaign finance policy emerged in the 1970s in response to ineffective and antiquated disclosure requirements and contribution limits in what were, by then, decades-old and poorly enforced federal statutes. Congress enacted the 1971 Federal Election Campaign Act (FECA) and substantially amended it in 1974, 1976, and 1979.[27] Some of these FECA amendments responded to the Watergate scandal, which, in addition to various other abuses, involved illegal funding for the 1972 Richard Nixon reelection campaign.[28] FECA remains the nation's primary campaign finance statute and thus the home of most such provisions in federal law, codified in what is known as the United States Code, the body of permanent law that Congress enacts.[29]

Among other points, FECA and its major amendments required disclosure about campaign receipts and expenditures by political committees. The act also limited contributions to and from such committees. Thus, all political committees are principally governed by FECA and related FEC regulations. Political advertising and other activities classified as independent expenditures or electioneering communications must also report those activities to the FEC under FECA.

The 1976 *Buckley v. Valeo* case considered several challenges to the 1974 FECA amendments. Most important for the long-term regulatory environment, *Buckley* established a distinction between contributions and expenditures based on what the Supreme Court determined were different risks of corruption with each practice.[30] The version of FECA challenged in *Buckley* capped both contributions and expenditures. The *Buckley* ruling, however, invalidated the expenditure limits (except for publicly financed presidential campaigns) as an unconstitutional restriction on protected First Amendment political speech.[31] Although contribution limits constrained the donor's political speech, the court held, doing so was a reasonable effort to limit potential corruption.[32] Federal campaign contribution limits for the 2020 cycle appear in table 2.2.

Table 2.2 Selected Federal Contribution Limits, 2020 Election Cycle

	To Candidate Committees PCC	To National Party Committees DNC, RNC, CCCs, special accounts	To Traditional PACs SSF accounts, Connected, Non-connected, and Leadership	To Super, Hybrid PACs independent expenditure accounts
From Individuals	$2,800 per candidate, per election[a]	$35,500 per year, plus $106,500 for each special party account	$5,000 per year	Unlimited
From National Party Committees	$5,000 per candidate, per election[b]	Unlimited transfers among national party committees	$5,000 per year	Unlimited
From Traditional PACs[c]	$5,000 per election	$15,000 per year, plus $45,000 for each special party account	$5,000 per year	Unlimited
From Super, Hybrid PACs[d] independent expenditure accounts (not considered contributions under FECA)	Prohibited (permitted to make independent expenditures only)	Prohibited (permitted to make independent expenditures only)	Prohibited (permitted to make independent expenditures only)	N/A[e]

Source: Adapted by the author from Federal Election Commission, "Archive of Contribution Limits, 2019–2020," available at https://www.fec.gov/help-candidates-and-com-mittees/candidate-taking-receipts/archived-contribution-limits/.

Notes:
a. Individuals may give $2,800 to any one candidate committee during the primary and during the general (and, runoff, if applicable) election campaigns.
b. This amount refers to direct contributions, not coordinated party expenditures. Parties may make purchases on behalf of, and in concert with, candidate campaigns. Limits vary by type of race and the state in question. For 2020 limits, see Federal Election Commission, "Price Index Adjustments for Expenditure Limitations and Lobbyist Bundling Disclosure Threshold," *Federal Register* 85, no. 34, 9772. The table also excludes a special $49,600 limit for contributions by party committees to Senate campaigns (shared between the national party and its Senate campaign committee).
c. The term "Traditional PAC" refers to those PACs permitted to make contributions to federal candidates with separate segregated funds (SSFs). This entry also refers to "multicandidate" PACs, which are the most common type of PAC. Multi-candidate PAC status is triggered when these committees make certain aggregate contributions to multiple candidates. Hybrid PACs using their accounts subject to contribution limits could contribute in the same amounts listed in the "From Traditional PACs" row.
d. As noted above, Hybrid PACs using their accounts subject to contribution limits could contribute the same amounts listed in the "From Traditional PACs" row.
e. Discussion of transfers/contributions among Super PACs and among Hybrid PACs using independent expenditure accounts is beyond the scope of this chapter.

Buckley established which contribution, spending, and disclosure mechanisms were constitutionally valid.[33] *Buckley*, therefore, continues to mean that, in practice, contributions can be limited, and reasonable disclosure can be required, but spending generally cannot be limited. Specifically, spending by campaigns (except publicly financed presidential ones), candidates, individuals, or any other entity spending independently cannot be limited per the *Buckley* precedent. Most such spending funds political advertising. *Buckley* established that "express advocacy," which explicitly calls for election or defeat of a candidate, is subject to campaign finance regulation. On the other hand, "issue advocacy," which at least arguably concerns policy issues rather than electoral outcomes, generally is not. All these topics would become major issues of debate for the subsequent forty years, ultimately building to the 2010 *Citizens United* decision discussed below—and, as of this writing, the latest major Supreme Court decision affecting the regulatory environment.

Finally, *Buckley* endorsed the concept of disclosure in campaign finance as a means of limiting potential quid pro quo corruption. Most notably, FECA requires public reporting of the sources and amounts of contributions. For contributions from individuals, for example, political committees must report the name, address, occupation, and employer for those who give an aggregate of more than $200 (per calendar year or election cycle, depending on the recipient type).[34] Required disclosure has been a consistent theme in federal campaign finance policy. However, after the Supreme Court's 2010 *Citizens United* ruling, as new kinds of organizations have emerged, disclosure has received renewed attention in the regulatory environment (see below).

The Bipartisan Campaign Reform Act (BCRA) and *McConnell v. FEC*

By the mid-1990s, momentum was building in Congress to address perceived loopholes that had developed in FECA. Pro-regulatory lawmakers argued that the unlimited independent spending *Buckley* permitted had led to a proliferation of "outside money" (i.e., money "outside" the regulatory framework), such as by PACs affiliated with corporations and unions. They also argued that corporate and labor money fueled broadcast communications that were derided as "sham ads," posing as issue advocacy but functionally engaging in express advocacy by naming candidates and urging the public to support or oppose their policy positions but not explicitly calling for their election or defeat (thus avoiding regulation under FECA per the *Buckley* decision).

Congress responded by enacting the Bipartisan Campaign Reform Act (BCRA) in 2002, the first major amendments to FECA since 1979.[35] Like FECA, which BCRA amended, the statute is complex and made several changes throughout federal campaign finance law, but a few key points are important for understanding the regulatory environment in 2020.

First, BCRA banned "soft money" in federal elections. Before BCRA, large, unlimited contributions for generic "party-building" activities, as opposed to directly supporting electioneering, were a significant source of cash for the major political parties. The "soft money" popular term contrasts with "hard money," which generally signifies the other funds discussed in this chapter, most of which are subject to contribution limits. Soft-money funds were controversial because pro-regulatory legislators saw soft money as violating the spirit of FECA's contribution limits. The act also updated individual contribution limits (particularly the non-PAC limits), indexing them to inflation.

Second, to respond to the "sham" issue ads discussed above, BCRA established a new political advertising concept known as "electioneering communications." Electioneering communications include only broadcast, cable, or satellite ads; refer to a clearly identified federal candidate; and must be targeted to the relevant electorate. The ads also are aired within sixty days of a general election or within thirty days of a primary. Practically speaking, the provision meant that although corporations, unions, or other groups could still use their treasuries to fund ads supporting or opposing candidates, they could not do so during preelection periods (assuming that the ads met the electioneering communication standard).

These communications appear to be less important in recent elections than in the immediate aftermath of BCRA, largely due to subsequent deregulatory developments. Nonetheless, at the time, they represented a significant congressional effort to further regulate political advertising as well as corporate and union political money. This component of BCRA, therefore, represented one of the most robust periods of campaign finance regulation in the modern era. Such stringent regulation would be short lived.

BCRA largely survived an initial legal challenge, brought by, among others, Senator Mitch McConnell (R-KY). In its 2003 *McConnell v. FEC* decision, the Supreme Court upheld almost the entire statutory text.[36] Soon, however, other legal challenges, based on how the act applied in practice, had more success in federal courts. For example, in 2007, the court limited the scope of the electioneering communication provision.[37] More generally, the mid-2000s featured a series of judicial opinions (including those that the Supreme Court issued) that weakened BCRA and, more important, foreshadowed a major challenge to some of the foundational regulatory principles in place at least since Congress enacted FECA.[38]

Citizens United and Implications for the Regulatory Environment

The Supreme Court's January 2010 decision in *Citizens United v. Federal Election Commission* is one of the most consequential campaign finance cases of the past fifty years, and certainly since *Buckley*.[39] Like *Buckley*, *Citizens United* is a complex and detailed ruling.[40] Most consequentially, *Citizens United* struck down a previous prohibition in FECA on corporate independent expenditures in federal elections. The decision also has been widely understood to apply to unions, although it did not expressly address those groups. In practice, the decision meant that corporations and unions could now use their treasury funds to independently call for the election or defeat of federal candidates. *Citizens United* did not affect the FECA prohibition on direct corporate and union contributions to candidates, parties, and SSF PACs, nor did it affect disclosure and disclaimer requirements. The decision also did not affect an individual's ability to spend unlimited amounts on independent expenditures, a precedent that dates to *Buckley*.

Citizens United continues to shape the policy debate in Congress and beyond. Supporters of additional campaign finance regulation argue that the decision runs afoul of congressional intent in FECA and Supreme Court precedent in *Buckley*. Proponents of the decision argue that the case appropriately restored protections for independent political speech that FECA and *Buckley* had limited.

One of the most important implications of *Citizens United* concerns the development of a new kind of political committee known as "super political action committees" or "Super PACs" (discussed above). Super PACs arose only indirectly from *Citizens United*, as a second case that was already making its way through the federal courts when the Supreme Court issued its *Citizens United* ruling permitted the new entities. The decision in that second case, *SpeechNow v. FEC*, relied on the *Citizens United* precedent.[41] In *SpeechNow*, the U.S. Court of Appeals for the District of Columbia Circuit held that unlimited contributions to PACs that made only independent expenditures were constitutionally protected. The ruling thus reinforced *Citizens United*'s emphasis on new avenues for corporations and unions to spend money to affect federal elections. It also affected how certain tax-exempt groups regulated primarily by tax law rather than campaign finance law may engage in campaigns.

To summarize, with *Citizens United*, corporations and unions could spend directly on elections if they chose to do so. With *SpeechNow*, they could choose to give funds to other entities, which became known as Super PACs, to spend independently on their behalf. *Citizens United* and *SpeechNow* also fostered development of the Hybrid PACs (discussed above), in which an SSF PAC operates a separate account that can receive unlimited contributions for use in independent expenditures.

These Hybrid PACs, sometimes called "Carey committees" after related litigation, are not Super PACs per se, but, essentially, the separate account that accepts unlimited contributions for the purpose of independent expenditures that functions like a Super PAC. The Hybrid PAC concept developed in 2011 after a Non-connected SSF PAC sued the FEC for permission to accept unlimited contributions for use in independent expenditures. Considering the *Citizens United* and *SpeechNow* precedents, and related policy guidance at the FEC, the agency agreed not to enforce a previous prohibition on a SSF PAC (and other committees in similar circumstances) accepting unlimited contributions for independent expenditures.[42]

RECENT POLICY ACTIVITY AND THE 2020 REGULATORY ENVIRONMENT

Unlike some of the historical periods discussed above, particularly the immediate aftermath of the 2010 *Citizens United* decision, little in federal campaign finance policy or law changed between 2016 and 2020. Much of the legislative activity that did occur between 2016 and 2020 in Congress focused on concerns about foreign interference in U.S. elections during 2016 and fears of additional attacks in 2018 or 2020. Even if Congress had enacted new legislation, the FEC would have been unable to implement the legislation because the agency lost a policy-making quorum twice between 2019 and 2020 after resignations left the commission with fewer than four members.[43] Campaigns and other political committees also continued to adapt their fund-raising strategies to regulatory developments that occurred post-*Citizens United*, such as additional options for party fund-raising.

Ongoing Implications from Changes in Party Financing and Presidential Public Funds

The 2020 cycle featured fund-raising strategies that emphasized various ways to consolidate solicitations and aggregate large contributions, particularly by the parties and presidential campaigns. These developments were not unique to 2020, but in some cases, they did reflect relatively recent changes in the regulatory environment.

As noted previously, the 2014 Supreme Court decision in *McCutcheon v. FEC* invalidated previous aggregate contribution limits. Practically speaking, this meant that individuals and PACs could contribute to as many candidates or parties as they desired as long as they did so in permissible amounts (sometimes called the "base" limits as opposed to the invalidated "aggregate" limits). Before *McCutcheon*, federal law had capped the total amount an individual or PAC could give.[44] In the FY2015 omnibus appropriations law, Congress permitted national parties to raise significantly larger amounts than they had been permitted to raise since BCRA prohibited unlimited party soft-money fund-raising beginning in the 2004 election cycle. The 2014 changes permitted the party committees to create new, separate accounts, with separate fund-raising limits indexed to inflation, for three activities:

- For the 2020 cycle, the national party headquarters committees—most notably the DNC and the RNC—could raise up to $106,500 per individual contributor for presidential nominating conventions.[45]
- The DNC and RNC, and party hill committee in the House and Senate—the DCCC, DSCC, NRCC, and NRSC—could each annually raise $106,500 from an individual contributor in 2020 for two other accounts: one for recounts and other legal compliance issues, another for party buildings.

As table 2.3 shows, an individual donor could give a maximum of more than $850,000 in each year of the 2020 cycle for a total of more than $1.7 million; the analogous contributions from Traditional PACs could total $360,000—if the individual or PAC donor gave to one party in all the ways listed in table 2.3. The new accounts arguably permitted the parties to respond to financial competition from the unlimited contributions that Super PACs could collect post-*Citizens United* and to the fact that Congress was eliminating public financing for nominating conventions (see below). The accounts have, however, been controversial, as they also arguably represent fund-raising akin to the unlimited party soft money that BCRA prohibited.[46]

Another party fund-raising strategy designed to amass large contributions concerns entities is known as "joint fund-raising committees" (JFCs). As Anthony Corrado has explained, the new party accounts and the lack of aggregate contribution limits post-*McCutcheon* "greatly enhanced the value of joint fundraising strategies" and encouraged increasingly complex financial arrangements among participating political committees.[47]

Table 2.3 Selected Federal Contribution Limits to Political Party Committees, 2020 Election Cycle

	Direct Contribution to Party Committee General Accounts	Special Account for Nominating Conventions	Special Account for Legal Compliance and Recounts	Special Account for Party Buildings	Total under Assumptions in Table
From an Individual	$35,500 each to the headquarters committee (e.g., DNC or RNC) and both CCCs (e.g., House and Senate) ($106,500 total) annually	$106,500 to headquarters committee only annually	$106,500 each to the headquarters committee and both CCCs ($319,500 total) annually	$106,500 each to the headquarters committee and both CCCs ($319,500 total) annually	$852,000 annually
From a Traditional PAC	$15,000 annually to the headquarters committee and both CCCs (e.g., House and Senate) ($45,000 total)	$45,000 to headquarters committee only annually	$45,000 each to the headquarters committee and both CCCs ($135,000 total) annually	$45,000 each to the headquarters committee and both CCCs ($135,000 total) annually	$360,000 annually

Source: Adapted by the author from Federal Election Commission, "Archive of Contribution Limits, 2019–2020," available at https://www.fec.gov/help-candidates-and-committees/candidate-taking-receipts/archived-contribution-limits/.

Note: The table does not address state-level contributions. The totals listed in the tables assume that a donor contributed only to one party. In addition, the sums listed in the "Total" column assume that a donor gives the maximum permissible amount to one party as reflected in the scenarios in the table. However, the sums in the "Total" column do not appear in FECA, and as discussed in the chapter text, the McCutcheon decision invalidated previous aggregate contribution limits.

JFCs provide a way for parties and candidates to aggregate fund-raising and disburse funds in permissible amounts to participating political committees. For example, a national party and the Senate and House candidates in a single state might form a JFC to facilitate soliciting donors for a single contribution that, on the surface, would be larger than permissible but that is permissible once the contribution is disbursed in lawful amounts. These arrangements can be attractive to participating political committees because they make fund-raising more efficient. They also permit splitting fund-raising proceeds and costs. Amounts vary by the number and type of participating political committees and on the allocation formula they agree to when forming the JFC. FEC regulations require that one of the participating committees (often a party) acts as the fund-raising agent for all the participants or that the committees form a separate committee to be the fund-raising agent.[48] The participants may continue their own separate fund-raising provided that no single contributor exceeds the relevant contribution limits to the committee, whether through the JFC or directly to a participant. In other words, the JFC provides an additional way to raise money, but it does not create "extra" fund-raising limits for the participants (see chapters 3 and 4 on JFCs).

Directly and indirectly, regulatory changes in recent election cycles spurred some of these fund-raising strategies, especially in presidential campaigns, where the public financing system established by FECA has become inactive (see chapter 3). Since the 1976 election cycle, taxpayers have had the option to designate or "check off" $3 (or $6 for married couples filing jointly) on their individual income tax returns to support matching funds for primary candidates and general-election grants for party nominees. Congress eliminated a third element of the program, grants for party nominating conventions[49] in 2014. Although public funding for candidates remains available, benefits are generally believed to be too low for competitive campaigns. The 2020 general-election grant for major-party nominees would have been $103.7 million—a far cry from what the Biden and Trump campaign raised privately.[50] Even if candidates had applied for funding in 2020, the FEC quorum loss would have prevented allocating public funds for much of the cycle.

Unique Factors Shaping the 2020 Regulatory Environment: COVID and Foreign Interference

Although every election cycle is unique, two highly unusual factors dominated much of the 2020 policy environment and, perhaps, help explain why Congress and regulators did not adopt campaign finance proposals on other issues. These unique factors are the COVID-19 pandemic and concerns about foreign interference in U.S. elections. Although the pandemic had major implications for campaign fund-raising, it generally did not raise campaign finance regulatory issues. The connection to foreign interference has more direct campaign finance implications. Beyond these two issues, policy disagreements between the two parties, and in some cases between the House and Senate, precluded action in most other campaign finance policy areas.

The COVID-19 pandemic caused substantial changes in election administration and voting practices nationwide, as state and local election jurisdictions rushed to find new ways to staff polling places and expand absentee and mail voting options. Many of those efforts required state legislatures, election officials, or both to make statutory or regulatory changes.[51] Political campaigns and other political committees also had to adapt to the pandemic. But unlike in election administration and voting, those challenges did not involve major campaign finance regulatory questions. Political campaigns did, however, face unique fund-raising challenges during the spring of 2020, when fund-raisers traditionally focus on building financial momentum from primary victories and on raising as much as possible for the fall general election. As the Center for Responsive Politics reported, during this key period, campaigns faced dual challenges of canceled in-person fund-raisers and unemployment or financial uncertainty for many potential donors.[52] Online fund-raisers and motivated donors ultimately still led to robust fund-raising, as discussed elsewhere in the book (see chapter 4 for examples).

Turning to the foreign interference issue, FECA completely bans foreign funds from U.S. campaigns. Specifically, the act prohibits direct or indirect contributions, expenditures or independent expenditures, or solicitations involving anyone other than U.S. citizens or permanent resident aliens. Although Congress confined the rest of FECA to federal elections, foreign nationals may not make these contributions, expenditures, or solicitations (or be solicited) "in connection with a Federal, State, or local election."[53] Historically, policy concerns about foreign interference in U.S. elections focused on limited instances of alleged violations of these provisions.[54] Although such episodes are rare, appear to have limited consequences, or both, they are prosecuted and involve stiff criminal penalties.[55]

New foreign-interference concerns emerged in the second half of 2016, before the November election. These reports would lead to multiple congressional, federal agency, and state-level investigations concerning election security—all of which was a major focus of the regulatory environment leading up to the 2020 election cycle. Most of that discussion is beyond the scope of this chapter. In general, federal investigations determined that interference efforts were aimed at undermining public confidence in the American political process; attempting to sway voters and undermine some candidates; and explore potential technical vulnerabilities in U.S. elections systems. Although the investigations determined that the 2016 foreign interference did not alter election results, it did employ what Director of National Intelligence Dan Coats later characterized as "aggressive attempts" using social media to "spread propaganda focused on" social and political division in the United States.[56]

An investigation led by former FBI director Robert F. Mueller, appointed as a Justice Department special counsel to investigate election interference, found that "[t]he Russian government interfered in the 2016 presidential election in sweeping and systematic fashion," including by releasing information hacked from the DNC.[57] Mueller and other investigators also examined whether any campaign finance practices had violated the FECA foreign-national prohibition noted above.[58] The campaign finance and elections legislation pursued, mostly by Democrats, throughout the 116th Congress drew partially on foreign-money concerns. In some cases, legislation, such as the campaign finance overhaul bill H.R. 1 (the For the People Act), passed the House but did not become law amid deep partisan divisions over the scope of the bills. Congress did, however, require additional intelligence reporting surrounding foreign interference in U.S. campaigns and elections.[59]

As private entities, political committees determined individually how to respond to foreign interference threats, if they had the financial and organizational resources to do so at all. The FBI, Department of Homeland Security, and intelligence agencies provided advice on cybersecurity to political committees and other entities involved in the electoral process.[60] The FEC also issued advisory opinions permitting political committees to accept reduced-cost cybersecurity and information technology services in specific circumstances.[61]

Publicly available government information suggests that some foreign interference occurred during the 2020 cycle but less consequentially than in 2016. In March 2021, the National Intelligence Council, which reports to the director of national intelligence, released an unclassified version of an intelligence community assessment (ICA) based on information obtained through December 2020.[62] The assessment found "no indication that any foreign actor attempted to alter any technical aspect of the voting process in the 2020 elections, including voter registration, casting ballots, vote tabulation, or reporting results."[63]

The intelligence community also assessed that the Russian and Iranian governments conducted "influence operations" or "influence campaigns" designed to undermine public confidence in the electoral process, undermine or support presidential candidates; and that actors in other countries made limited attempts to lower public confidence or otherwise interfere with the 2020 U.S. elections.[64] The assessment did not analyze the effects of foreign interference on U.S. political processes or election outcomes.

Ongoing Debate over Transparency in Disclosures and Disclaimers

Disclosure is a key component of FECA's anticorruption provisions. Even as contribution or expenditure limits might change, provisions that require public information about financial transactions provide at least some measure of accountability. Policy debates often concern equity, specifically whether similar requirements apply to similar groups and conduct.

As new sources of campaign spending surfaced after *Citizens United*, disclosure became even more important than it had been previously. Historically, Democrats and Republicans in Congress generally agreed on the importance of disclosure even if they disagreed on other campaign finance matters. That consensus began to erode after *Citizens United*. Several legislative attempts to mandate additional disclosure since 2010 have stalled. Much of the tension over expanding disclosure requirements concerns whether or how entities that are not political committees should publicly report their donors. As noted previously, any entity that makes electioneering communications or independent expenditures already must report to the FEC, but this does not necessarily mean that the original sources of funds will be disclosed. This is the crux of what some observers call "dark money," an unofficial term that generally implies funds for which an original donor's identity is concealed or unclear.

Although donor disclosure in campaign finance remains the norm, regulatory developments over the past decade generally indicate a trend toward deregulation. The saga of whether nonpolitical committees, such as tax-exempt groups, must report their donors to the FEC spans at least the past decade and involves multiple rulemakings and protracted litigation.[65] In short, during much of that period, nonpolitical organizations could avoid listing donors if contributions were not earmarked "for the purpose of furthering" electioneering communications or independent expenditures.

In August 2020, the U.S. Circuit Court of Appeals for the District of Columbia upheld a district court decision invalidating an FEC regulation that permitted omitting some independent expenditure donors from FEC reports. The ruling affects disclosure requirements but does not appear to open a new avenue for political money. It could provide additional transparency surrounding contributions that flow through tax-exempt groups and eventually fund independent expenditures calling for election or defeat of candidates, but its ultimate consequence depends on FEC implementation. As of this writing, the commission has not issued regulations implementing the opinion.[66]

Separately, in May 2020, the IRS issued regulations specifying that 501(c) organizations no longer had to disclose their donors to the agency unless requested.[67] Although not specifically related to campaign finance, opponents criticized the change as potentially making campaign finance investigations involving the groups more difficult, while proponents countered that the previous reports were burdensome.

DISCUSSION

The complexity of the 2020 regulatory environment is a product of more than a century of public policy. Some congressional efforts to make things relatively simple, such as capping both contributions and expenditures, did not survive Supreme Court scrutiny. Every time a statute or regulation was invalidated, Congress or the FEC then had to consider alternative ways that would achieve a similar goal, and at the same time, win judicial approval if it were litigated. This dynamic explains, for example, why there are now different categories of political advertising or legally separate political entities that pursue similar aims. The campaign industry itself, particularly campaign finance lawyers and strategists, is also responsible for the changes in the regulatory environment. They have both requested clarity through new legislation, regulation, or litigation and have tried to stay one step ahead of the latest regulatory developments (or, some would argue, have exploited loopholes).

Just as campaigns have become more sophisticated, so, too, have the roles of federal statutes and agencies regulating that environment. The FEC and DOJ remain the main regulatory players in campaign finance policy, just as FECA remains the nation's core statute on the subject. If history is a guide, new challenges, such as changes in campaign technology and emerging threats from foreign actors, could facilitate roles for congressional committees, statutes, or agencies that have previously played limited roles in campaign regulation. The roles of the IRS and tax-exempt groups provide a contemporary example of such an evolution.

Deregulatory litigators' successes in federal courts seem likely to continue. Indeed, some observers have argued that a July 2021 Supreme Court ruling on donor disclosure in tax law that is, on the surface, unrelated to campaign finance could be the basis for a future challenge to FECA donor disclosure.[68] In addition, in 2022 the Supreme Court, in *Ted Cruz for Senate v. FEC*, invalidated a previous limit on campaign repayment of candidate loans. Although the ruling was relatively narrow, some observers have suggested that the case could establish a future challenge to the contribution limits themselves.

Readers might be wondering why the chapter did not further address high-profile legislative efforts to enact campaign finance legislation ahead of the 2020 cycle to document foreign interference in 2016 (some of which also occurred in the 2020 cycle), or to explore possible campaign finance connections to the first Trump impeachment investigation.[69] These issues certainly were historically noteworthy, but they did not substantially alter the regulatory environment. For the most part, legislation was debated but not enacted into law. Foreign interference and impeachment proceedings raised important questions about campaign practices or individual people and candidates but did not alter the regulatory environment overall, which is this chapter's focus.

Similarly, the FEC enforced the law where it could reach agreement but did not adopt new regulations altering the status quo. The loss of the commission's policy-making quorum also precluded action on rulemaking and major enforcement actions. Also importantly, it is possible that the FEC, DOJ, or both will pursue enforcement matters concerning the 2020 cycle in the future. FECA requires the commission to maintain confidentiality until enforcement matters are closed, a process that can take years.[70] The DOJ also is typically tight-lipped about its enforcement activities while they are in progress.

Threats from foreign interference in U.S. elections have shown some bipartisan agreement on issues such as reporting requirements and helping political committees defend themselves. Commitment to the long-standing FECA foreign-national prohibition also appears to be secure. Nonetheless, consensus on more domestic and contentious campaign finance policy questions in Congress and at the FEC remains largely elusive.

NOTES

1. This chapter represents the views of the author and not necessarily those of the Congressional Research Service, Library of Congress, or any other institution with which he is affiliated.

2. See Herbert E. Alexander, *Financing the 1960 Election* (Princeton, NJ: Citizens' Research Foundation, 1962).

3. The "follow the money" phrase often is attributed to journalists Carl Bernstein and Bob Woodward's *All the President's Men* (New York: Simon & Schuster, 1974) and the film of the same name. According to one account, the origins of the phrase are disputed. See Kee Malesky, "Follow the Money: On the Trail of Watergate Lore," NPR, June 16, 2012, https://www.npr.org/2012/06/16/154997482/follow -the-money-on-the-trail-of-watergate-lore.

4. Independent expenditures are those "not made in concert or cooperation with or at the request or suggestion of [a] candidate, the candidate's authorized political committee, or their agents, or a political party committee or its agents." See 52 U.S.C. §30101(17).

5. Readers should be aware of what the chapter does not address. This chapter highlights selected federal statutes, regulation, and litigation but omits some important details for clarity and length. It also does not address compliance or enforcement issues for individual political committees.

6. Some of these abbreviations and other terminology are unique to the book and would not necessarily appear in policy or practitioner parlance.

7. On the FECA "political committee" definition, see 52 U.S.C. §30101(4) and 52 U.S.C. §301010(5).

8. Publicly financed presidential candidates are subject to contribution limits as well.

9. Limits vary by type of race and the state in question. For 2020 limits, see Federal Election Commission, "Price Index Adjustments for Expenditure Limitations and Lobbyist Bundling Disclosure Threshold," *Federal Register* 85, no. 34 (2020): 9772. Additional discussion of 2020 activity appears later in this volume.

10. For historical discussion, see Robert E. Mutch, *Campaigns, Congress, and the Courts: The Making of Federal Campaign Finance Law* (New York: Praeger, 1988).

11. Besides corporations and unions, the other kinds of economic organizations that may have a Connected PAC are membership organizations, trade associations, cooperatives, and corporations without stock.

12. For Connected PACs, the sponsoring organization may pay the administrative costs of the PAC but may only solicit contributions from the sponsoring organization's members (and is allowed to pay for "internal communications" with such members). Non-connected PACs must cover the administrative costs of the PAC themselves but may solicit contributions from anyone.

13. FECA only briefly addresses Leadership PACs. See, for example, 52 U.S.C. §30114(c). As with all political committees, Leadership PAC compliance with particular regulatory requirements depends heavily on circumstances. Additional discussion is beyond the scope of this chapter.

14. This scenario assumes that the spender exceeds relevant financial thresholds in the act.

15. See, for example, U.S. House of Representatives, Committee on Government Reform and Oversight, "Investigation of Political Fundraising Improprieties and

Possible Violations of Law, Interim Report," 4 vols., House report 105-829 (Washington, DC: Government Printing Office, 1998); and U.S. Senate, Select Committee on Intelligence, "Open Hearing: Social Media Influence in the 2016 Election," S. Hrg. 115-242 (Washington, DC: Government Printing Office, 2017).

16. This trend is particularly true in budgetary policy but also applies in other policy areas, including campaign finance. For general overviews, see, for example, Walter J. Oleszek, "The 'Regular Order': A Perspective," Congressional Research Service report R46597, November 6, 2020, crsreports.congress.gov/product/pdf/R/R46597; James M. Curry and Frances E. Lee, *The Limits of Party: Congress and Lawmaking in a Polarized Era* (Chicago: University of Chicago Press, 2020); and Molly E. Reynolds, *Exceptions to the Rule: The Politics of Filibuster Limitations in the U.S. Senate* (Washington, DC: Brookings Institution Press, 2017).

17. Discussion of legislative budget procedure affecting the kinds of policy provisions that can be included in appropriations bills is beyond the scope of this chapter.

18. On FEC establishment generally, see 52 U.S.C. §30106.

19. On FEC history and implications of the agency's structure, see, for example, Michael M. Franz, "The Devil We Know? Evaluating the Federal Election Commission as Enforcer," *Election Law Journal* 8 (2009): 167–87; R. Sam Garrett, "Administering Politics: Rediscovering Campaign Finance and Public Administration," *Administrative Theory & Praxis* 38 (2016): 188–205; Mutch, *Campaigns, Congress, and the Courts*; and Karen Sebold, "The Toothless Tiger: An Overview of the Structural and Partisan Issues that Affect the Federal Election Commission," paper presented at the State of the Political Parties quadrennial meeting, University of Akron, November 2021.

20. U.S. Constitution, Amdt. 1.

21. U.S. Constitution, Art. 1. Other constitutional provisions, particularly those concerning presidential elections and voting rights, are beyond the scope of this chapter. This chapter does not attempt a detailed constitutional or legal discussion. For overviews, see, for example, Samuel Issacharoff, Pamela S. Karlan, Richard H. Pildes, and Nathaniel Persily, *The Law of Democracy: Legal Structure of the Political Process* (St. Paul, MN: Foundation Press, 2016); Daniel Hays Lowenstein, Richard L. Hasen, Daniel P. Tokaji, and Nicholas Stephanopoulos, *Election Law: Cases and Materials* (Durham: Carolina Academic Press, 2017); and L. Paige Whitaker, "Campaign Finance Law: An Analysis of Key Issues, Recent Developments, and Constitutional Considerations for Legislation," Congressional Research Service report R45320, updated September 24, 2018, crsreports.congress.gov/product/pdf/R/R45320.

22. See, for example, Mutch, *Campaigns, Congress, and the Courts*.

23. 34 Stat. 864.

24. For additional discussion, see, for example, Edmund Morris, *Theodore Rex* (New York: Modern Library, 2001), 354–60; and Robert E. Mutch, *Buying the Vote: A History of Campaign Finance Reform* (New York: Oxford University Press), 27–61.

25. See 57 Stat. 167 (1943) and 61 Stat. 136 (1947).

26. For overviews of campaign finance policy foundations during the Progressive Era and subsequent deregulatory challenges, see, for example, Mutch, *Buying the Vote*; John Samples, *The Fallacy of Campaign Finance Reform* (Chicago: University of Chicago Press, 2006); and Anthony Corrado, "Money and Politics: A History of Federal Campaign Finance Law," in *The New Campaign Finance Sourcebook*, ed. Anthony Corrado, Thomas E. Mann, Daniel R. Ortiz, and Trevor Potter (Washington, DC: Brookings Institution Press, 2005), 7–47.

27. FECA was originally codified at 2 U.S.C. §431 *et seq.* It is now codified at 52 U.S.C. §30101 *et seq.*

28. On Watergate history generally, see Bernstein and Woodward, *All the President's Men*. On campaign finance policy implications, see, for example, Mutch, *Campaigns, Congress, and the Courts*.

29. On FECA and the 1970s amendments as enacted, see P.L. 92-225 (1971), P.L. 93-443 (1974), P.L. 94-283 (1976), and P.L. 96-187 (1979).

30. One issue in *Buckley* was the public financing of presidential campaigns, and that is discussed in chapter 3.

31. *Buckley* is 424 U.S. 1.

32. On the court's rationale concerning different corruption risks, see, for example, Daniel R. Ortiz, "The First Amendment and the Limits of Campaign Finance Reform," in *The New Campaign Finance Sourcebook*, ed. Anthony Corrado, Thomas E. Mann, Daniel R. Ortiz, and Trevor Potter (Washington, DC: Brookings Institution Press, 2005), 92–93.

33. The court upheld spending limits for publicly financed presidential campaigns on the grounds that participating candidates chose to voluntarily accept public funds and could be required to meet reasonable conditions on receiving those funds.

34. On reporting requirements generally, see 52 U.S.C. §30104.

35. For BCRA as enacted, see P.L. 107-155. The statute amended FECA. For additional discussion of the statute, legislative history, and judicial challenges, see R. Sam Garrett, "Outside Money and Inside Policy: Campaign Finance Before and After *Citizens United*," in *Campaigns and Elections American Style: The Changing Landscape of Political Campaigns*, ed. James A. Thurber and Candice J. Nelson (New York: Routledge, 2019), 304–28.

36. *McConnell v. Federal Election Commission* (2003), 540 U.S. 93.

37. *Wisconsin Right to Life v. FEC* (*WRTL II*), 2007, 551 U.S. 449.

38. For additional discussion of litigation, see, for example, Issacharoff et al., *The Law of Democracy*; Lowenstein et al., *Election Law*; and Whitaker, "Campaign Finance Law."

39. On *Citizens United*, see 558 U.S. 310.

40. For additional discussion of the evolution of the case and campaign implications, see, for example, Garrett, "Outside Money and Inside Policy."

41. *SpeechNow.org v. FEC*, 599 F.3d 686 (D.C. Cir. 2010).

42. For additional background, see Federal Election Commission, "FEC Statement on *Carey v. FEC*: Reporting Guidance for Political Committees that Maintain

a Non-Contribution Account," press release, October 5, 2011, https://www.fec.gov /updates/fec-statement-on-carey-fec/.

43. See, for example, Kenneth P. Doyle, "Commissioner's Resignation Freezes FEC Enforcement, Rulemaking," *Bloomberg Government*, August 28, 2019.

44. On *McCutcheon*, which invalidated aggregate contribution limits, see 572 U.S. 185.

45. As enacted, see P.L. 113-235. As codified, see 52 U.S.C. 30116(9).

46. For historical discussion of the accounts' origins and practical contribution scenarios, see Anthony Corrado, "The Regulatory Environment of the 2016 Election," in *Financing the 2016 Election*, ed. David B. Magleby (Washington, DC: Brookings Institution Press, 2019), 64–70.

47. Corrado, "The Regulatory Environment of the 2016 Election," 69.

48. See 11 C.F.R. §102.17. See also, for example, Federal Election Commission, "Joint fund-raising with other candidates and political committees," https:// www.fec.gov/help-candidates-and-committees/joint-fundraising-candidates-political-committees/.

49. For additional discussion, see Corrado, "The Regulatory Environment of the 2016 Election."

50. On 2020 public financing amounts, see Federal Election Commission, "Understanding Public Funding of Presidential Elections," https://www.fec.gov/help -candidates-and-committees/understanding-public-funding-presidential-elections/.

51. See, for example, Amanda Zoch, "2020 Legislative Action on Elections," National Conference of State Legislatures, June 21, 2021, ncsl.org/research/electio ns-and-campaigns/2020-legislative-action-on-elections-magazine2021.aspx.

52. Karl Evers-Hillstrom, "Political Donations Dropped Off as Coronavirus Pandemic Peaked," Center for Responsive Politics, June 9, 2020, opensecrets.org/news /2020/06/political-donations-dropped-off-as-coronavirus-pandemic-peaked/.

53. 52 U.S.C. §30121.

54. See, for example, U.S. House of Representatives, Committee on Government Reform and Oversight, "Investigation of Political Fundraising Improprieties"; and Garrett, "Administering Politics."

55. See, for example, Richard C. Pilger, ed., *Federal Prosecution of Election Offenses* (Washington, DC: U.S. Department of Justice, 2017), 138–40.

56. On the Coats statement, see Hudson Institute, "Dialogues on American Foreign Policy and World Affairs, Dan Coats and Walter Russell Mead," interview transcript, July 17, 2018, https://www.hudson.org/research/14456-full-transcript -dialogues-on-american-foreign-policy-and-world-affairs-director-of-national-intel-ligence-dan-coats-and-walter-russell-mead.

57. U.S. Department of Justice, Special Counsel Robert S. Mueller III, "Report on the Investigation into Russian Interference in the 2016 Presidential Election," vol. 1, March 2019, https://www.justice.gov/archives/sco/file/1373816/download, 1.

58. On interpretation of how the foreign-national prohibition applied to 2016 presidential fund-raising, see, for example, Bob Bauer, "Campaign Finance

Law: When 'Collusion' Becomes a Crime," Just Security, June 2, 2017, https://www
.justsecurity.org/41593/hiding-plain-sight-federal-campaign-finance-law-trump
-campaign-collusion-russia-trump/.

59. See, for example, provisions in the FY2020 National Defense Authorization
Act, P.L. 116-92; 133 Stat. 2119 and 133 Stat. 186.

60. See, for example, Federal Bureau of Investigation, "Protected Voices," https://
www.fbi.gov/investigate/counterintelligence/foreign-influence/protected-voices.

61. See Federal Election Commission, advisory opinions 2018-11, 2018-12, and
2019-12, https://www.fec.gov/data/legal/advisory-opinions/.

62. The intelligence community is a collection of several federal agencies, such as
the Central Intelligence Agency, Federal Bureau of Investigation, and military intelligence services that gather and analyze foreign intelligence.

63. U.S. National Intelligence Council, *Foreign Threats to the 2020 US Federal
Elections*, Intelligence Community Assessment 2020-00078D (unclassified version),
March 10, 2021, https://www.dni.gov/files/ODNI/documents/assessments/ICA
-declass-16MAR21.pdf, i.

64. U.S. National Intelligence Council, *Foreign Threats to the 2020 US Federal
Elections*, i.

65. For additional discussion, see, for example, Garrett, "Outside Money and
Inside Policy."

66. For an overview, see, for example, Zainab Smith, "Appeals Court Affirms
Invalidation of Disclosure Rule in Crossroads GPS v. CREW (18-5261)," *FEC
Record*, August 26, 2020, https://www.fec.gov/updates/appeals-court-affirms-invali-
dation-disclosure-rule-crossroads-gps-v-crew-18-5261/.

67. See U.S. Department of the Treasury, Internal Revenue Service, "Guidance
under Section 6033 Regarding the Reporting Requirements of Exempt Organizations," *Federal Register*, May 28, 2020, 31959.

68. See *Americans for Prosperity v. Bonta* (594 U.S. ___ (2021)).

69. For historical background, see, for example, Aaron Blake, "The Impeachment
Case Against Donald J. Trump, as It Stands," *Washington Post*, November 22, 2019,
https://www.washingtonpost.com/politics/2019/11/22/impeachment-case-against
-donald-trump-right-now/; U.S. House of Representatives, "Impeachment of Donald J. Trump, President of the United States," Report of the Judiciary Committee,
together with dissenting views, H. Rept. 116-346 (Washington, DC: Government
Printing Office, 2019); and U.S. National Intelligence Council, *Foreign Threats to
the 2020 US Federal Elections*.

70. 52 U.S.C. §30109(a)(12).

3

Financing the 2020 Presidential Elections

John C. Green

The 1960 presidential election was the major topic of Herbert E. Alexander's *Financing the 1960 Election*,[1] and some of its features resemble the 2020 election: a wealthy presidential candidate (John F. Kennedy); a well-known vice president as rival (Richard M. Nixon); the impact of new technology (television); new financing of primary and the general election campaigns (candidate-centered politics); close and controversial results. Of course, the scale and scope of the two elections was very different. Indeed, the complexity of the fifth presidential election of the twentieth-first century would likely amaze observers of the fifteenth presidential election of the twentieth century.

In 2020, at least $6 billion was spent directly to persuade voters in the presidential elections (primaries and general election)—an all-time record in nominal as well as constant dollars.[2] Two-thirds of these expenditures, $4 billion, were made by the candidates' principal campaign committees (PCCs), while noncandidate committee spending in the presidential contests accounted for the remaining one-third, $2 billion, including expenditures by party committees, Traditional PACs, Super and Hybrid PACs,[3] and tax-exempt groups. Both the Trump and Biden finance operations showed significant innovation. For the Trump campaign, it was an extraordinary integration of fund-raising with the Republican National Committee; and for the Biden campaign, it was innovative coordination of funding from PACs, Super PACs, and tax-exempt groups. Some aspects of these innovations continued after the presidential campaign.

RULES, RIVALS, AND RESOURCES

As in previous elections, presidential campaign finance in 2020 was influenced by federal laws, the nature of competition, and the activities of the participants. On the first count, the rules for raising and spending money undergirded the financial patterns. On the second count, a very large and diverse set of Democratic rivals opposed Donald Trump, an unusually controversial president. On the third count, Trump and his opponents used varied strategies to obtain and use financial resources. And all these features were affected by the sudden appearance of the COVID-19 pandemic midway through the 2020 election cycle.

Rules

Federal campaign finance law imposes mandatory rules for candidates and other actors in presidential campaigns (see chapter 2). Although the law saw few changes in 2020 compared to recent elections, developments continued within the basic outlines of the law. One continuity was the lack of candidate participation in presidential public financing.[4] Another continuity was the way mandatory regulations helped define a two-year election calendar, divided into a nomination campaign and a general election campaign, with the nomination campaign further subdivided into a primary season and a bridge period.

The presidential nomination campaign begins with the election cycle (January 1 of the year before the presidential election). The primary season begins with the scheduled primary contests (early in the election year) and ends when active campaigning ceases and the nominee is no longer in doubt (the exact date of which varies from election to election). The nomination campaign prior to the scheduled contests has traditionally been called the "invisible primary," when rival candidates and their supporters compete for resources with which to contest the primaries.[5] Here the 2020 primary season is defined as beginning on January 1, 2019, and ending on March 31, 2020 (with the "invisible primary" occurring between January 1, 2019, and February 3, 2020).

The nomination campaign concludes with a bridge period, stretching from the end of the contested primaries through the national party conventions (thus varying in length from election to election). During this period, the primary fund-raising limits still apply to candidate committees, even though the general election campaign is functionally under way. Here the 2020 bridge period is defined as beginning on April 1, 2020, and ending on August 31, 2020.

Once the major-party presidential nominees are officially chosen by the national conventions (in the summer of the election year), the general election campaign begins, reaching a crescendo on Election Day in November and concluding with the calendar year. Here the 2020 general election campaign is defined as beginning on September 1, 2020, and ending on December 31, 2020.

Both the nomination and general election campaigns can be thought of as team efforts, reflecting the organizational networks associated with the candidates.[6] Rival candidates seeking the presidential nominations deploy their own teams; and in the general election, the party nominees deploy a broader team representing party constituencies. Candidates' principal campaign committees (PCCs) are at the center of these teams alongside various kinds of allied, aligned, and assisting organizations, operating with varying degrees of separation from the candidate's PCCs (see chapter 2). In this regard, the 2016 nomination campaign saw a great deal of innovation in such entities by the Republican presidential candidates, but such creativity was attenuated among Democratic presidential candidates in 2020, largely because of the controversy surrounding Super PACs (see chapter 7 and below).

In 2020, all kinds of noncandidate committees were active in the nomination campaign, especially in the bridge period and the general election campaign. As in the past, spending by noncandidate entities increased during the bridge period as major party constituencies rallied around the presumptive nominees. Likewise, these efforts accelerated during the general elections campaign (these combinations will be referenced as "Team Biden" and "Team Trump" when relevant).

Rivals

Beyond federal law, presidential campaign finance is influenced by the structure of competition among rival candidates, including the details of the primary contests and the number of candidates involved.

Presidential nomination campaigns involve a *sequence* of more than fifty primaries and caucuses, the results of which allocate national party convention delegates to the candidates. The dates and details of these contests are determined by a combination of party rules and state laws, producing a variegated topography of competition. As in 2016, the 2020 primary contests began with the four traditional events in February 2020 (Iowa caucuses, New Hampshire primary, Nevada caucuses, and South Carolina primary), followed by fifteen contests on Super Tuesday, the first week of March. The remaining scheduled contests were scattered over the next four months, with the national conventions occurring in late summer. This topography was complicated by responses to the pandemic, including the cancellation and rescheduling of some of the contests.

In 2020, potentially important schedule changes among the Democrats included moving the California primary to Super Tuesday and replacing caucuses with primaries in nine states.[7] In addition, the Democratic National Committee once again sponsored a series of candidate debates. But in 2019 and 2020, the criteria for candidates qualifying for the debates involved poll standings plus a measure of broad-based fund-raising success: for the first two debates, a minimum of 65,000 unique donors (with at least 200 unique donors per state in 20 states and/or territories); for the third debate, a minimum of 130,000 unique donors (with at least 400 unique donors per state in 20 states and/or territories); and for subsequent debates, a minimum of 225,000 unique donors (with at least 1,000 unique donors per state in 20 states and/or territories; see chapter 7). These criteria put an emphasis on small donations.

In contrast to the primaries, the general election campaign is a set of fifty-one *simultaneous* contests ending on Election Day, the results of which allocate electoral votes to the candidates. Here, too, the states and District of Columbia have some variation, including rules for allocating electors, modes of voting (absentee, early in-person, election day in-person), and dates when ballots can be cast and accepted. In 2020, this topography was affected by responses to the pandemic.

In the sequential primaries, candidates can adjust their financial strategies in response to individual contests, and success in one contest can generate "momentum" fostering success in subsequent contests. Most candidates participate to some degree in every contest if they have the necessary resources and reasonable prospects for success. In the simultaneous general elections, the nominees have no contest results with which to respond, and most candidates focus their efforts on a handful of competitive "battleground" states, which may shift as the campaign progresses. Thus, candidates are less likely to adjust their financial strategies, focusing instead on adjusting tactics to implement their strategies.

All of these tendencies intersect with the number of candidates in the race. Nomination campaigns frequently involve multiple candidates. All else being equal, a large candidate field makes the strategies of individual candidates less stable and predictable. On the one hand, this means that individual candidates can prevail in the early contests with only a small portion of the vote, but on the other hand, the numerous competing rivals can fragment the vote and available resources.

Indeed, most multi-candidate primary fields are eventually winnowed into two-candidate races. Some primary campaigns begin with a de facto two-candidate field, as in 2016 for the Democrats, and a single-candidate field occurs when an incumbent president faces only token opposition for renomination, as for the Republicans in 2020. Because of the dominance of the two-party system, general election campaigns tend to be two-candidate races, although the presence of minor party and independent candidates can produce more complexity and affect the outcome.

In 2020, the Democratic nomination field reached an all-time high (twenty-nine candidates),[8] exceeding the record set by the Republican primary campaign in 2016 (seventeen candidates). The large multi-candidate Democratic field winnowed steadily prior to the primary contests, then very quickly once the contests began, leaving Biden the presumptive Democratic nominee. Meanwhile Trump was the only significant Republican candidate. Both major-party nominees engaged in intense campaign activities during the bridge period and the general election.

Resources

Campaign finance laws and the structure of competition set the basic parameters for candidates' finances, with each candidate calculating how best to raise and spend the funds necessary to be successful—first in obtaining their party's nomination, then in winning the general election.

In this regard, three fund-raising approaches are commonly recognized in presidential campaigns: a high-dollar "insider" strategy, a small-dollar "outsider" strategy, and a mixed strategy employing elements of the high-dollar and small-dollar approaches. Although candidates may prefer one strategy over another, many are forced by political circumstances to adopt a particular strategy, especially during the nomination campaign.

A high-dollar fund-raising strategy relies on national prominence and strong connections with established fund-raising networks to raise funds in large amounts. One common tactic is to form a Leadership PAC, an exploratory committee, or another kind entity to lay the groundwork for the campaign before the candidacy is formally announced. Another tactic is to recruit a cadre of high-dollar fund-raisers, known as "bundlers," and to hold extensive in-person fund-raising events.

If successful, a high-dollar fund-raising strategy reinforces candidate prominence, dissuades potentially strong rivals from entering the race, secures a resource advantage in the initial contests, and provides financial resilience if the candidate encounters setbacks in the nomination campaign.

The goal is a decisive victory early in the primary campaign, at which point the strategy can be applied to preparing for the general election campaign during the bridge period. Republican George W. Bush used this approach in 2000 as did Democrat Hillary Clinton in 2008 and 2016. In 2020, Pete Buttigieg, Kamala Harris, and Amy Klobuchar attempted variations on this strategy.[9]

A small-dollar strategy depends on candidate novelty and clear issue positions to raise money from beyond established financial networks. A common tactic is to solicit multiple small donations via social media, email, telephone calls, and direct mail. If successful, such a strategy establishes credibility, undermines better-financed opponents, and produces sufficient funds to compete in the initial contests. The goal is to secure early victories to generate momentum that will translate to success by the end of the primary season. Then the strategy can be applied to preparing for the general election campaign during the bridge period. Democrat Howard Dean in 2004, Republican Ron Paul in 2008, and Bernie Sanders in 2016 pursued small-dollar strategies. In 2020, Sanders attempted this strategy again, as did Elizabeth Warren.[10]

However, in 2020 the distinction between high-dollar and small-dollar strategies was blurred by the strong incentives for all Democratic candidates to qualify for nomination campaign debates by raising small donations. This incentive, plus general developments in digital fund-raising technology and earmarking conduit organizations (such as ActBlue and WinRed), helped dramatically expand small donations to most candidates.

Some candidates deploy mixed strategies from the outset of their campaign, using elements of high-dollar and small-dollar fund-raising, such as Democrat Barack Obama and Republican John McCain in 2008. In 2020, Biden and Trump used mixed strategies, analogous to the 2012 and 2016 presidential campaigns, respectively. Another variation is the self-financing of nomination campaigns, in whole or in part, a strategy used by Republicans Steve Forbes in 1996 and Mitt Romney in 2008. In 2016, Donald Trump substantially self-financed his nomination campaign, but his novel appeal also attracted small donations, especially during the bridge period. In 2020, Democrats Michael Bloomberg and Tom Steyer largely self-funded their own lavish campaigns.

The development of organizational networks linked in various ways to candidates' principal campaign committees (PCCs) are often part of the financial strategy, including allied organizations (such as Leadership PACs or exploratory committees), aligned organizations (such as Super PACs and tax-exempt groups), and assisting organizations (Traditional PACs, party committees, and Hybrid PACs).[11]

Super PACs and tax-exempt groups can fit well with a high-dollar fund-raising strategy, especially when funded by a few very large donations from well-connected donors. In 2012, both Barack Obama and Mitt Romney benefited from Super PACs in this fashion; and in 2016, most candidates in both parties were also assisted by Super PACs. But Super PACs and tax-exempt groups can also assist insurgent candidates by providing a high level of spending for otherwise poorly financed campaigns. Such wealthy patrons have long been a staple of presidential nomination campaigns, but typically by means of personal independent expenditures or the activities of tax-exempt groups. In 2000, before Super PACs existed, some wealthy individuals funded independent "issue ads" against John McCain in the Republican primaries.[12] In 2012, Republicans Newt Gingrich and Rick Santorum ben-efited from such patrons via their candidate-aligned Super PACs. In 2020, Biden, Buttigieg, Harris, Klobuchar, Warren—and even Sanders—benefited from this kind of spending at crucial movements in their campaigns. How-ever, the controversy surrounding Super PACs in the Democratic primaries substantially reduced the number and scope of candidate-aligned Super PACs in 2020 (see chapter 7).

As with Super PACs, joint fund-raising committees (JFCs) involving can-didate, party, and other kinds of committees fit well with high-dollar fund-raising, allowing well-connected donors to give large donations that are then divided between the participating entities. However, JFCs can also be part of a small-dollar strategy by soliciting small donations via direct appeals to citizens. Both patterns occurred for the major-party nominees in 2020.

PRESIDENTIAL PCC NET RECEIPTS AND NET DISBURSEMENTS IN 2020

Table 3.1 lists the total net receipts and disbursements for all presidential candidates' principal campaign committees (PCCs) during the 2020 election cycle. For the major-party nominees, Biden and Trump, the figures are sub-divided into the primary season (January 1, 2019, to March 31, 2020), the bridge period (April 1 to August 31, 2020), and the general election (Sep-tember 1 to December 31, 2020). For the other candidates, the total figures are for the primary season only.

In the 2020 election cycle, all candidate PCCs combined raised and spent some $4 billion, more than double the total funds raised and spent in the 2016 election cycle ($1.7 billion and $1.6 billion, respectively) as well as in the 2012 election cycles ($1.8 billion and $1.6 billion, respectively) in constant 2020 dollars.[13] As in previous election cycles, most PCCs expended

Table 3.1 2020 Presidential Campaigns, Net Receipts and Disbursements

Candidate	*(millions of dollars)* Net Receipts	Net Disbursements
Democratic Party		
Biden	1,067	1,067
Primary Season[a]	139	107
Bridge Period[b]	405	245
General Election[c]	523	715
Bloomberg	1,096	1,121
Steyer	345	353
Sanders	215	215
Warren	128	131
Buttigieg	101	95
Klobuchar	53	53
Harris	43	43
Yang	42	42
Booker	26	26
Delaney	23	23
O'Rourke	18	18
Gillibrand	15	15
Gabbard	15	15
Castro	10	10
Williamson	8	8
Bennet	7	7
Other Candidates	34	21
Republican Party		
Trump	750[d]	740
Primary Season[a]	225	222
Bridge Period[b]	218	215
General Election[c]	307	303
Other Candidates	4	4

Source: OpenSecrets, analysis of FEC data, https://www.fec.gov/campaign-finance-data/presidential-candi-date-data-summary-tables/?year=2020&segment=6. See this source for candidates in the rows labeled "Other Candidates."
Notes: Net Receipts and Disbursements remove offsets and contribution refunds.
a. January 1, 2019, to March 31, 2020
b. April 1 to August 31, 2020
c. September 1 to December 31, 2020
d. Includes net cash on hand at end of 2017–2018 election cycle

nearly all the funds raised during the period of active campaigning. As will be discussed below, Trump was an exception in this regard.

Democratic Candidates

In the 2020 primary season, Democratic PCCs raised and spent $3.2 billion, about six times more than the $520 million raised and $469 million spent by Democratic candidate PCCs in the 2016 primary season.

The major reason for this increase was very large amounts raised and expended by self-financed candidates. Michael Bloomberg supplied his campaign with more than $1 billion of his own funds (a bit more than Biden's combined receipts for the *entire* 2020 election cycle), while Tom Steyer provided his campaign with $345 million (about two and one-half times Biden's primary season receipts).[14] These extraordinary levels of self-funding dwarfed previous self-financed presidential campaigns of all sorts. For example, Ross Perot spent some $112 million of his own money on his 1992 independent presidential campaign.[15]

Excluding self-financed candidates, the Democratic field raised and spent nearly $1.8 billion in the primary season, three times the funds raised and spent in the 2016 primary season (see above). One reason for this increase was the sevenfold expansion of the field of candidates in 2020 (from four in 2016 to twenty-nine candidates in 2020). In 2020, the average primary funds raised by the PPCs of the non-self-funded candidates was $68 million, less than one-half of the 2016 figure of $130 million.

During the primary season, Joe Biden's 2020 successful nomination campaign raised $139 million and spent $107 million, about two and one-half times less than the $342 million raised and $289 million spent by Hillary Clinton in her successful 2016 nomination campaign. One reason for this pattern was the pandemic-shortened primary season (ending about March 31, 2020, versus May 31, 2016). Biden ended the primary season with a surplus of $24 million, less than Clinton's $64 million in 2016.

During the bridge period, Biden raised $405 million and spent $245 million, about twice Clinton's 2016 bridge-period receipts of $256 million and comparable to her disbursements of $211 million. One reason for this pattern was the longer bridge period in 2020 (five months in 2020 versus two months in 2016). Then, during the 2020 general election, Biden raised $523 million and spent $713 million, about one and one-half times more than Clinton's 2016 receipts of $325 million and more than twice her disbursements of $342 million. In fact, Biden raised almost 20 percent more than the 2012 Obama campaign's general election receipts of $441 million and more than one and one-half times more than Obama's disbursements of $431 million (when Biden was also on the ticket).

Bernie Sanders was Biden's best-financed competitor in the early 2020 nomination contests, raising and spending $215 million during the primary season. These figures were, respectively, 54 and 100 percent larger than Biden's primary season net receipts and disbursements. Before the pandemic cut short the competitive contests, Sanders was on track to rival his 2016 financial totals.

Other Democratic candidates raised and spent less than Sanders in the primary season: Elizabeth Warren raised $128 million (almost as much as Biden), followed by Pete Buttigieg ($101 million) and Amy Klobuchar ($53 million). Emblematic of the financial patterns of many promising but unsuccessful candidates in the crowded Democratic field, the eventual Democratic vice-presidential nominee, Kamala Harris, raised $43 million. These four candidates raised a combined total of $325 million, about 50 percent more than Sanders's total. All of the remaining Democratic candidates combined for $175 million in receipts, about one-fifth less than Sanders's total.

A substantial portion of Biden's funds were raised through three joint fund-raising committees (JFC): the Biden Victory Fund (with the Democratic National Committee and forty-seven state Democratic committees), the Biden Action Fund, and the Biden Fight Fund (both with the Democratic National Committee). These committees raised a total of $713 million and transferred $246 million to Biden's candidate committee in the 2020 election cycle. Respectively, these figures were 15 percent higher than the $622 million raised by Clinton's two joint fund-raising committees in 2016 and 42 percent higher than the $173 million transferred to Clinton's 2016 campaign committee.

In 2020, the Democratic JFC funds were largely raised in the general election, whereas more of the 2016 fund-raising occurred in the primary season. In 2020, Democrats' JFCs transferred $255 million to Democratic Party committees, 2 percent less than the $261 million transferred in 2016.[16] The 2016 campaign featured a controversial practice by the Clinton campaign requiring that the state Democratic parties participating in the JFCs transfer their share of the proceeds back to the DNC (see chapter 5).[17]

It is worth noting that the Biden JFCs spent $154 million, in addition to transfers, for fund-raising and other political activities; 97 percent of these expenditures occurred during the general election ($149 million) and 3 percent during the bridge period ($5 million).

Republican Candidate

In 2020, Donald Trump, like previous incumbent presidents facing only token opposition for their party's nomination, engaged in a broad-based effort to fund the general election, with funds raised and disbursed throughout the 2020 election cycle. Overall, Trump raised $750 million[18] and spent $740 million, about one and three-quarters more than he raised ($429 million) and spent ($405 million) in his 2016 campaign. Unlike most presidential candidates, Trump ended the general election campaign with a $10 million surplus—and continued fund-raising after Election Day and into the next election cycles (see below).

In the 2020 primary season, Trump raised $225 million and spent $222 million, more than three times his 2016 receipts ($70 million) and expenditures ($68 million). During the bridge period, Trump raised $218 million, more than three times his 2016 receipts ($68 million), and spent $215 million, more than seven times his 2016 disbursements ($28 million). During the 2020 general election, Trump raised $307 million, 5 percent more than in 2016 ($291 million), and spent $303 million, 29 percent more than in 2016 ($274 million).[19]

By way of comparison, Trump raised and spent $525 million in the 2020 bridge period and general election combined, about 10 percent less than Clinton raised in 2016 during the comparable period ($581 million) and about 5 percent less than Clinton spent ($553 million). In this regard, Trump's 2020 receipts were about the same as the 2012 Obama campaign during the comparable period ($518 million), but Trump's spending was about 20 percent less than the Obama spending ($664 million).

A substantial portion of Trump's 2020 funds were also raised through two JFCs: the Trump Make American Great Again Committee (with the Republican National Committee and forty-six state Republican party committees) and the Trump Victory Fund (with the Republican National Committee). The two main JFCs raised a total of $1.3 billion and transferred $275 million to Trump's 2020 PCC, figures that were 79 percent higher than the $698 million raised by these same Trump JFCs from 2016 and 88 percent higher than the $146 million transferred to Trump's 2016 PCC. In 2020, the two main JFCs transferred $652 million to Republican Party committees, more than five times the $120 million transferred in 2016. In addition, Trump participated in four JFCs with Republican candidates, resulting in transfers of $500,000 to his PCC (see chapter 5). Like the Clinton campaign in 2016, the Trump campaign engaged in the controversial practice requiring that the state Republican parties participating in the JFC's transfer their share of the proceeds back to the RNC (see chapter 5).[20]

It is worth noting that in addition to funds transferred, the main Trump JFCs spent $548 million on fund-raising and voter outreach operations (see below); 59 percent of these expenditures occurred during the general election ($321 million), 12 percent during the bridge period (65 million), and 29 percent during the primary season ($162 million).[21]

In 2020, Trump's JFC finances were larger than Biden's, including funds raised (175 percent), funds transferred to candidate campaign committees (111 percent), and funds transferred to party committees (265 percent). This pattern reflects not only Trump's incumbent status, but also the strategic decision to integrate fund-raising with the Republican Party from the beginning of Trump's term in office (see below).

For the sake of completeness, minor-party and independent presidential candidates had combined receipts of $26 million and disbursements of $25 million in the 2020 election cycle, roughly the same totals as in the 2016 election cycle, $25 and $27 million, respectively (data not shown in table 3.1).

SOURCES OF PRESIDENTIAL PCC RECEIPTS IN 2020

Table 3.2 reports the estimates of the sources of campaign funds raised by the main major-party candidates in 2020.[22] The first four columns of the table report contributions from individuals by size of donation; the last two columns show funds from the candidates themselves (a form of individual donation) and from all other sources (such as previous campaigns, party committees, and PACs). Each of the six columns reports two figures: the actual dollar amounts raised (underlined) and the percentage of all the funds raised by each candidate during the relevant time periods (*italicized*). As in past presidential elections, the overwhelming proportion of funds raised by presidential candidate committees came from individual donors in one form or another, including from the candidates themselves.

Democratic Candidates

As table 3.2 shows, the eight major Democratic presidential candidates raised a total of $672 million in "small donations" (unitemized contributions of $200 or less) during the 2020 election cycle. Such donations accounted for 22 percent of all these candidates' PCC receipts. But if the self-financed campaigns of Bloomberg and Steyer are excluded, along with Biden's postprimary fund-raising, such donations are 38 percent of the funds raised by the major candidates during the primary season.[23] The $258 million raised during the 2020 primary season by the main candidates was only slightly larger than $253 million raised by the most significant candidates (Clinton and Sanders) during the 2016 primary season, but the difference was stark between the relative importance of small donations to Clinton (22 percent) versus Sanders (44 percent).

The relative importance of small donations varied by candidate in 2020 as well, with Warren leading in table 3.2 with 42 percent, followed by Sanders

Table 3.2 Contributions to Major Presidential Campaigns in 2020 Election

(millions of dollars)

Candidate	Individual Contributions[d]								CANDIDATE**	%	OTHER***	%
	$200 or less	%	$201–$999	%	$1,000–$2,799	%	$2,800	%				
Democratic Party												
Biden	$460	43%	$245	23%	$192	18%	$170	16%	$0	0%	$*	0%
Primary Season[a]	$46	32%	$34	26%	$22	16%	$35	26%	$0	0%	$*	0%
Bridge Period[b]	$183	45%	$77	19%	$69	17%	$77	19%	$0	0%	$*	0%
General Election[c]	$231	44%	$134	26%	$101	19%	$58	11%	$0	0%	$*	0%
Bloomberg	$0	0%	$0	0%	$0	0%	$0	0%	$1,089	99%	$7	1%
Steyer	$3	1%	$0	0%	$0	0%	$0	0%	$342	99%	$0	0%
Sanders	$86	40%	$80	37%	$30	14%	$6	3%	$0	0%	$13	6%
Warren	$54	42%	$42	33%	$13	10%	$5	4%	$*	0%	$14	11%
Buttigieg	$34	34%	$28	28%	$18	18%	$20	20%	$0	0%	$*	0%
Klobuchar	$19	37%	$14	26%	$9	17%	$6	12%	$0	0%	$4	8%
Harris	$16	37%	$10	22%	$8	19%	$7	18%	$0	0%	$2	4%
Republican Party												
Trump	$405	54%	$158	21%	$87	11%	$75	10%	$*	0%	$29	4%
Primary Season[a]	$117	52%	$43	19%	$20	9%	$27	12%	$0	0%	$19	8%
Bridge Period[b]	$133	61%	$41	19%	$24	11%	$23	9%	$0	0%	$0	0%
General Election[c]	$155	50%	$74	24%	$43	14%	$25	9%	$0	0%	$11	3%

Source: OpenSecrets, analysis of FEC individual contribution data, January 1, 2019, through December 31, 2020

*Less than $1 million

** Self-financing or self-loans not repaid

*** Transfers from previous campaigns, PACs, other committees, parties, noncontribution income

Notes:

a. Primary Season, January 1, 2019, through March 31, 2020

b. Bridge Period, April 1 through August 31, 2020

c. General Election, September 1 through December 31, 2020

d. All individual contributions to candidates' principal campaign committee and all contributions transferred from joint fund-raising committees to the candidate campaign committees. All itemized contributions from each individual donor were combined into a single figure, taking into account multiple contributions in different reporting periods.

with 40 percent. However, Sanders raised significantly more dollars than Warren in this regard ($84 million versus $53 million). Biden scored the lowest at 32 percent; the other candidates fell between Biden and Sanders.[24]

These figures may be misleading because of repeated donations, which could move regular givers of small donations above the $200 reporting threshold. For this reason, looking at all donations of less than $999 is also a useful measure of small donations to the campaign. By this measure, Sanders raised 77 percent of his funds from donations of less than $999, and Warren raised 75 percent. In contrast, Biden raised 58 percent of this primary receipts from these two categories combined during the primary season, with the remaining candidates falling between Biden and Warren.

Interestingly, Sanders's small-dollar fund-raising appears to have been less productive in 2020 than in 2016. In 2016, he raised more dollars than in 2020 ($108 million versus $86 million under $200, and $93 million versus $80 million between $201 and $999), and these smaller donations made up a larger percentage of his receipts (44 percent versus 40 percent in 2016; 38 percent versus 37 percent in 2020). Of course, the early end of the primary season due to the pandemic also affected these figures.

Funds in donations in 2020 contrasts with the simultaneous increase in importance of very large donations—the epitome of which were the self-financed campaigns of Bloomberg and Steyer.[25] Indeed, Bloomberg's self-contribution of $1 billion was more than three times larger than all the unitemized donations to his main Democratic rivals during the primary season, and Steyer's self-contribution was roughly 33 percent larger.[26]

Biden's mixed fund-raising strategy relied more heavily on maximum donations of $2,800 (16 percent) and donations between $1,000 and $2,799 (18 percent) than his rivals. In this regard, Biden performed less well than Hillary Clinton's high-dollar primary campaign in 2016 (21 percent and 16 percent, respectively); in addition, Biden generated fewer dollars in 2020 than Clinton in 2016 ($35 million versus $40 million, and $22 versus $35 million, respectively). Not surprisingly, Sanders (3 percent and 14 percent) and Warren (4 percent and 10 percent) raised relatively little in maximum donations, or between $201 and $999, respectively.[27]

Biden's finances improved dramatically in the bridge period and general election, a pattern common among presumptive and actual nominees, given the ability of the candidate to draw on the full range of potential party donors (including those who had supported primary rivals). Biden's donations of $200 or less increased over the primary season fourfold during the bridge period, then another fivefold during the general election, increasing by about 13 percentage points over the primary season. Large gains also occurred for each of the other donation categories: a sixfold increase for donations between $201 and $999 combined bridge period and general election, a sevenfold increase for donations between $1,000 and $2,799, and fourfold for the maximum donation of $2,800. At the same time, the relative percentage of Biden's postprimary funds in these categories was roughly comparable to the primary season.

The breadth of Biden's postprimary fund-raising can be illustrated by a comparison to Hillary Clinton's postprimary fund-raising in 2016. In terms of donations of $200 or less, Biden raised $414 million versus $100 million for Clinton—$211 million versus $115 million in donations between $201 and $999, and $170 million versus $78 million in $1,000 to the maximum. Only in the maximum category did Biden fall behind Clinton, $133 million versus $208 million—which was precisely Clinton's area of strength in her high-dollar fund-raising strategy.

Republican Candidate

In 2020, Donald Trump raised the highest proportion of his funds in small donations of any of the major candidates—54 percent overall, with 52 percent during the primary season, 61 percent in the bridge period, and 50 percent in the general election. Trump's totals in the primary season ($117 million) far exceeded any of his Democratic rivals. Partly due to repeat donations, he also did well with donations between $201 and $999 ($43 million) and among donations between $1,000 and $2,799 ($20 million) compared to the main Democratic candidates. And Trump nearly matched Biden in maximum donations of $2,800 ($27 million).

These figures are dramatically different than Trump's 2016 primary campaign, where he only raised $17 million in individual donations and eventually provided his campaign with $71 million of his own funds. In 2020, Trump contributed $8,021 to his own campaign. The contrast with his previous postprimary receipts is illustrative: in 2020 Trump raised $405 million in donations of $200 or less versus $246 million in 2016; among donations between $201 and $999, the figures were $154 million versus $44 million; among donations between $1,000 and the maximum donation, $87 million versus $30 million; and among the maximum donations, $75 million versus $34 million.

NONCANDIDATE AND PARTY COMMITTEE SPENDING IN 2020

Table 3.3 reports aggregated direct campaign spending by noncandidate committees for and against the major presidential candidates in 2020. The

Table 3.3 Noncandidate Spending, Major 2020 Presidential Election Campaigns

Millions of dollars	Independent Expenditures				Communication Expenditures			
	Super PAC		Other Groups		Internal		Electioneering	
Candidate	For	Against	For	Against	For	Against	For	Against
Democratic Party								
Biden	349.0	297.9	39.7	2.2	0.5	0.0	1.3	0.0
Primary Season[a]	11.8	1.0	0.2	*	0.0	0.0	0.0	0.0
Bridge Period[b]	39.3	92.0	3.1	0.4	*	0.0	0.0	0.0
General Election[c]	297.9	204.5	36.4	1.8	0.5	0.0	1.3	0.0
Bloomberg	*	*	0.0	0.0	0.0	0.0	0.0	0.0
Steyer	0.0	0.0	0.0	0.0	0.0	0.0	0.0	0.0
Sanders	1.2	1.5	0.2	4.9	0.0	0.0	0.0	0.0
Warren	14.8	18.6	0.1	*	0.0	0.0	0.0	0.0
Buttigieg	0.7	0.1	0.0	0.0	0.0	0.0	0.0	0.0
Klobuchar	2.7	0.0	0.0	0.0	0.0	0.0	0.0	0.0
Harris	0.0	*	*	0.0	0.0	0.0	0.0	0.0
Republican Party								
Trump	42.7	278.8	14.1	26.8	0.4	*	0.2	9.9
Primary Season[a]	13.8	19.7	1.9	0.3	0.0	0.0	*	0.0
Bridge Period[b]	9.3	91.9	4.1	9.2	*	*	0.1	2.4
General Election[c]	19.4	167.2	8.1	17.3	0.4	*	0.1	7.5

Source: OpenSecrets, analysis of 2020 FEC data, https://www.fec.gov/campaign-finance-data/communication-filings-data-summary-tables/?year=2020&segment=24
*Less than $100,000

Notes:
a. *January 1, 2019, to March 31, 2020*
b. *April 1 to August 31, 2020*
c. *September 1 to December 31, 2020*

spending includes independent expenditures by Super PACs and other groups, plus partisan and electioneering communication costs by other organizations (including spending by the candidate assisting committees discussed above).

Spending by noncandidate and party committees was at least $2 billion dollars in the 2020 presidential campaigns (see chapter 6), an estimate based on aggregating the figures in table 3.3. This amount is at least two and one-half times larger than the analogous $778 million spent in the 2016 presidential campaign.[28] The largest parts of this dramatic increase came from independent expenditures by noncandidate committees, which more than doubled ($1.1 billion in 2020 versus $478 million in 2016), and more than a thirteenfold increase in electioneering communication by tax-exempt groups ($11 million versus $800,000).

Of course, this aggregate measure of spending can obscure as much as it reveals. For example, the volume of independent expenditures includes both expenditures for and against candidates. Thus, it is important to look at each of these kinds of expenditures separately.

In 2020, independent expenditures by Super PACs equaled about $1 billion or some 90 percent of all the noncandidate expenditures reported in table 3.3; 58 percent of these expenditures were against a candidate and 42 percent were in favor of a candidate. The $11 million in electioneering communication expenditures from tax-exempt groups were even more skewed, with 90 percent against a candidate. Interestingly, the $88 million in independent expenditures from other committees (mostly Traditional PACs) skewed the other way, with 61 percent for a candidate and 39 percent against. A similar pattern held for the $900,000 for internal communication expenditures by Traditional PACs,[29] which were 97 percent for a candidate and only 3 percent against.

Noncandidate independent expenditures from Super PACs and other groups played a modest role in the Democratic primary season, equaling just 4 percent of the disbursements of the candidates listed in table 3.3. Only two candidacies involved double-digit figures: Biden enjoyed $12 million in support of his candidacy (and just $1 million against), whereas Elizabeth Warren enjoyed $14.8 million in support of her candidacy (but $18.6 million against). Sanders also had an independent expenditures deficit, with $1.4 million for his candidacy (and $6.4 million against); Buttigieg ($3.7 million in support) and Klobuchar ($2.7 million in support) both had a favorable balance.

Noncandidate independent expenditures from Super PACs and other groups played a much large role in the bridge period and general election, equaling 68 percent of the combined Biden and Trump disbursements. Both presumptive nominees had negative balances during the bridge period, with less disadvantage for Biden ($39.2 million in support versus $92 million against) compared to Trump ($9.3 million in support versus $91.9 million against). Indeed, the primary season was a version of this pattern for Trump ($13.8 million in support versus $19.7 million against).

However, the pattern shifted sharply in Biden's favor in the general election; Biden had a positive balance ($297.9 million for $204.9 million against), and Trump had a larger negative balance ($19.4 million for and $167.2 million against). A similar pattern but with much smaller amounts occurred for electioneering communication expenditures; Biden had a positive balance ($1.2 million for and $0 against), and Trump had a negative balance ($200,000 for and $9.9 million against). Both presumptive nominees had positive balances with internal communication expenditures—Biden, $500,000; and Trump, $400,000. Overall, Biden (with a net of $90 million *for* his candidacy) had a large advantage over Trump (with a net $257 million *against* his candidacy) in all noncandidate committee expenditures combined.

As in the past, the major party organizations spent much less on independent expenditures in support of their presidential candidates than in other races (see chapters 4 and 6). In the general election, the DNC made $1.3 million in independent expenditures in support of Biden in the general election, and the RNC made $300,000 in support of Trump. Also in the general election, the DNC spent $18.8 million in party-coordinated expenditures for Biden, and the RNC spent $25.3 million in party-coordinated expenditures for Trump. These figures were about the same as in 2016 (see chapter 5). In addition, Team Biden and Team Trump spent more than $400 million on voter outreach field operations, with a large edge for Trump (see below).[30]

CANDIDATES' ORGANIZATIONAL
NETWORKS IN 2020

As in past presidential campaigns, many candidates benefited from allied, aligned, and assisting committees alongside their PCCs in 2020.

The twenty-nine Democrats who sought their party's presidential nomination in 2020 had different kinds of organizational networks. Eight candidates (28 percent of the total) formed allied exploratory committees;[31] nineteen candidates (66 percent) had or formed allied Leadership PACs, which raised a total of $14.7 million in the 2020 election cycle.[32] Thirteen (45 percent) benefited from Super PACs aligned with their campaign, which raised a total of $81.6 million.[33] Eleven candidates (38 percent) had significant assistance from other political committees.[34] In sum, sixteen candidates (55 percent) benefited from two or more of these kinds of organizations.[35] However, unlike the Republican primary candidates in 2016, just one of the 2020 Democratic candidates benefited from a tax-exempt organization (Sanders).

Biden's organizational network included his vice-presidential Leadership PAC, American Possibilities, which spent $500,000 during the 2020 election cycle and ceased operations in October 2019. Although Biden initially opposed Super PACs, he changed his mind as the primary campaign developed. In the fall of 2019, Biden associates organized a Super PAC, Unite the Country,[36] which made $37.5 million in independent expenditures for Biden and $1.4 million against Trump during the 2020 election cycle. The sum of these expenditures equaled 4 percent of all of Biden's PCC disbursements.

After the primary season concluded, Biden benefited from support of some four dozen Super PACs not closely aligned with his candidacy, although Biden indicated in April 2020 that Priorities USA was his preferred Super PAC (see below). The four largest of these organizations were associated with prominent Democratic leaders and associates:

- Priorities USA Action was organized by associates of Barack Obama in 2011;[37] it made independent expenditures of $53 million for Biden and $58 million against Trump. The sum of these expenditures equaled 11 percent of Biden's PCC disbursements.
- American Bridge 21st Century was organized by Hillary Clinton associates in 2010;[38] it made independent expenditures of $40,000 for Biden and $51 million against Trump. The sum of these expenditures equaled 5 percent of Biden's PCC disbursements.
- Independence USA PAC was organized by Michael Bloomberg and associates in 2012 to support moderate Democratic candidates;[39] it made independent expenditures of $53 million for Biden and $2 million against Trump. The sum of these expenditures equaled 5 percent of Biden's PCC disbursements.
- Future Forward USA was organized by liberal political activists in 2018 to support progressive candidates;[40] it made independent expenditures of $74 million for Biden and $54 million against Trump. The sum of these expenditures equaled 12 percent of Biden's PCC disbursements.

During the primary season, Biden deployed 816 bundlers to raise funds.[41] His assisting committees included organized labor, including the AFL-CIO's endorsement. During the general election, Biden's bundlers increased dramatically, as did the number of assisting committees (see below).

Bernie Sanders's organizational network included his Leadership PAC, Progressive Voters of America, which spent $63,000 during the 2020 election cycle. Sanders opposed Super PACs in 2016 and 2020, and actively discouraged supporters from organizing them. However, he benefited from support of three Super PACs not closely aligned with his campaign.[42] He also benefited from a 501 (c)(4) tax-exempt organization, Our Revolution. Founded in August 2016, it was led by Sanders associates and endorsed by Sanders himself. In 2020, it mobilized progressive activists on behalf of Sanders in key early primary states. Although the exact dollar value of this assistance was unclear, it was substantial enough for Common Cause to file a complaint with the FEC.[43] All told, support from all these organizations likely equaled less than 2 percent of Sanders's PCC disbursements. Sanders did not deploy bundlers as part of his small-dollar fund-raising strategy, but he was assisted by more than a dozen grassroots progressive groups, including the Democratic Socialists of America (and nineteen local affiliates) and some labor unions, especially the Vote Nurses Values PAC.

Elizabeth Warren's organizational network included her Leadership PAC, PAC for a Level Playing Field, which was active in the 2018 election cycle as she was preparing for her presidential campaign, but it ceased operations during the 2020 election cycle. Although Warren also opposed Super PACs initially, she eventually accepted the support of an aligned Super PAC organized by associates, Persist PAC, which made independent expenditures of $14.7 million for her.[44] This support equaled 12 percent of Warren's PCC disbursements. Although Warren did not deploy bundlers during the primary season, it was not for lack of support among elite fund-raisers.[45] Her assisting committees included feminist organizations, including an endorsement by NOW.

Pete Buttigieg's organizational network included his Leadership PAC, Hitting Home PAC, which was active in 2018 when Buttigieg was organizing his presidential campaign, but it was largely inactive in the 2020 election cycle. Buttigieg did not benefit from an aligned Super PAC organized by associates but did receive support for VoteVets.org. Founded in 2006 to support the candidacies of progressive veterans, it made independent expenditures of $3.6 million for Buttigieg.[46] This support equaled 4 percent of Buttigieg's PCC committee disbursements. In addition, Buttigieg deployed

150 bundlers during the primary season,[47] and his assisting committees included LGTBQ groups.

Amy Klobuchar's organizational candidacy included her Leadership PAC, Follow the North Star Fund, which spent $500,000 in the 2020 election cycle. She benefited from an aligned Super PAC, Kitchen Table Conversations,[48] which made independent expenditures of $2.7 million for Klobuchar. This support equaled 5 percent of Klobuchar's PCC disbursements. She deployed 150 bundlers in the primary season,[49] and her assisting organizations included feminist and labor committees.

Kamala Harris's organizational network included her Leadership PAC, Fearless for the People, which spent $800,000 in the 2020 election cycle. An aligned Super PAC, People Standing Strong, was organized by her associates, but her campaign ended before it made any independent expenditures. Harris deployed 137 bundlers during the primary season,[50] and her assisting committees included feminist and civil rights groups.

Donald Trump's organizational network eventually included a presidential Leadership PAC Saving America, which he established after Election Day toward the end of the 2020 election cycle.[51] Vice President Mike Pence also had a Leadership PAC, Great America Committee, which spent $1.8 million in the 2020 election cycle. Trump was originally opposed to Super PACs, but he accepted aligned Super PAC support in July 2016.[52]

Like Biden, Trump also benefited from support of about three dozen Super PACs not closely aligned with his campaign in the general election, although Trump indicated in 2019 that America First Action was his preferred Super PAC. The four largest of these organizations were organized by prominent Republican activists:

- America First Action (affiliated with America First Policies, a 501(c)(4) tax-exempt group) was organized by conservative activists in 2017 to further Trump's plans and policies;[53] it made independent expenditures of $45,000 for Trump and $134 million against Biden. The sum of these expenditures equaled 17 percent of Trump's PCC disbursements.
- Great America PAC (associated with Great American Alliance, a 501(c) (4) tax-exempt group) was organized in 2016 by conservative activists;[54] it made $8.5 million in independent expenditures for Trump and $0.5 million against Biden. This support equaled about 1 percent of Trump's PCC disbursements.
- Committee to Defend the President was organized in 2013 by conservative activists as the Stop Hillary PAC and then backed Trump in 2016;[55] it made independent expenditures of $9.4 million for Trump and $4.1

million against Biden. The sum of these expenditures equaled 2 percent of Trump's PCC disbursements.

- Preserve America PAC was organized by Republican activists in the fall of 2020 to support Trump and other GOP candidates;[56] it made independent expenditures of $103 million against Biden. The sum of these expenditures equaled 13 percent of Trump's PCC disbursements.

In addition, Trump deployed hundreds of bundlers during the primary season,[57] which expanded dramatically during the general election. His assisting committees included Tea Party groups and an array of conservative organizations, which also increased substantially during the general election (see below).

THE DYNAMICS OF THE PRESIDENTIAL CAMPAIGN IN 2020

Among the many political norms that President Donald Trump broke was his decision to file for reelection on the *very day* of his inauguration as president—January 20, 2017. Trump thus became the first modern president to formally campaign for reelection while governing throughout his term.[58] This decision gave unusual substance to the long-standing meme of the "permanent campaign" in contemporary presidential politics.[59]

In short order, Trump developed an innovative campaign apparatus, replacing his 2016 improvised operation with a highly professionalized one.[60] At the center of this effort was an unprecedented fund-raising operation, which included maintaining his 2016 PCC, encouraging supportive Super PACs and tax-exempt groups,[61] and expanding joint fund-raising committees with the Republican national and state committees. The early and extensive integration of Trump's presidential campaign with the Republican Party marked a new level of White House dominance in national party affairs (see chapter 5).[62] Indeed, a key feature of the campaign was extensive and early spending on joint field operations between Trump's PCC and the RNC to contact voters (see below).

This approach was a marked contrast from Trump's campaign in 2016. As one insider reported:

> I was one of the few members of the original 2016 team with prior presidential campaign experience. While ultimately successful, the campaign was primarily staffed with inexperienced and untested political operatives and often lacked a cohesive organizational structure . . . For the 2020 reelection, we have a vastly different operation.[63]

Though not without liabilities, this approach allowed Trump to simultaneously hone his brand, develop and deploy his campaign strategy, raise an extraordinary amount of money, and discourage credible primary opponents. Trump was renominated with only token opposition from within his party. He formally began primary campaigning in June 2019, fielding an impressive effort,[64] receiving 18 million primary votes, and clinching the Republican nomination on March 5, 2020.

The Democratic presidential nomination campaign was unprecedented in its own right: a record twenty-nine candidates formally joined the race—substantially more than the record seventeen Republican candidates in 2016. The field included one former U.S. vice president, nine sitting or former U.S. senators, seven sitting or former members of the U.S. House of Representatives, five sitting or former mayors, three sitting or former governors, three candidates with nongovernmental backgrounds, and one state legislator. The field was unusually diverse in terms of gender, race, ethnicity, religion, and ideology.[65] Although many of the candidates were clearly longshots, many had good prospects for success as well. In one way or another, they all believed that they represented an excellent prospect for defeating President Trump in the general election.

In the end, however, the 2020 Democratic nomination campaign resembled many previous contests: a steady winnowing of the field before primaries began, with the early contests compacting the field into a two-candidate race, quickly followed by a resolution in favor of the now battle-tested front-runner.[66] But it included unique twists and turns along the way. Indeed, the "invisible primary" was starkly visible in 2020.

The Democratic Nomination Campaign

Most of the 2020 Democratic presidential candidates had special fundraising assets, ranging from past donors to special constituencies to personal funds. This large number of candidacies made the early quest for money very competitive, a pattern intensified by the need for contributions in small amounts from thousands of individuals across the country to qualify for the DNC-sponsored debates (see above). At the same time, this increased fund-raising expanded the Democratic donor pool with potential benefits for general election fund-raising.

Figures 3.1 and 3.2 chart the finances throughout the Democratic primary season, March 2019 through March 2020. The first figure shows the cumulative receipts of the top vote-getting candidates, Biden and Sanders, plus the mean cumulative receipts of all the other active non-self-financed candidates; the second figure shows cash on hand for Biden and Sanders, plus the mean cash on hand for all of the other active non-self-financed candidates. Taken

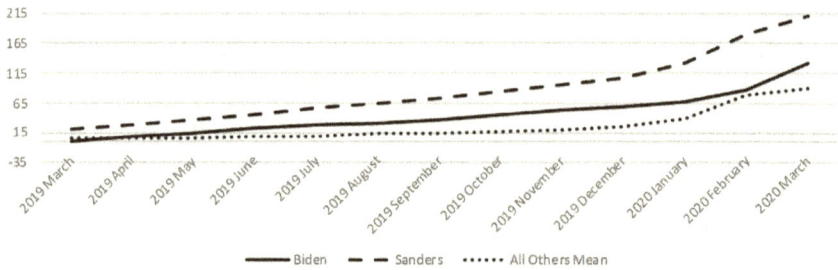

Figure 3.1 Democratic Presidential Nomination 2020: Cumulative Receipts. *Source*: OpenSecrets, compiled from candidate reports to the FEC

together, these figures provide an overview of the fiscal dynamics of the Democratic primary season.

Figure 3.1 shows that the receipts of the candidate field increased steadily over the nomination campaign, with an upward inflection once the early contests began in 2020. Sanders's receipts grew more rapidly than the rest of the field, peaking at the end of the primary season. Meanwhile, Biden's receipts grew even more slowly but with an upward inflection after the nomination was decided. Overall, these figures provide perspective to the two most prominent candidates in the very large and competitive candidate field. Although most of the Democratic candidates brought new donors into the pool, they found it difficult to raise additional funds in the face of intense competition from multiple rivals.

Figure 3.2 complements figure 3.1. Unlike the other candidates, Sanders's cash on hand showed considerable variation, starting high and trending downward to the end of 2019, then rising sharply once the primary contests began in 2020. Meanwhile, Biden's cash on hand was essentially constant—and low—rising in 2020, with a large uptick once the nomination was decided. The mean of all the other active non-self-financed candidates was low and constant as well. This figure reveals why the self-financed Bloomberg and Steyer campaigns were taken seriously by the other candidates and

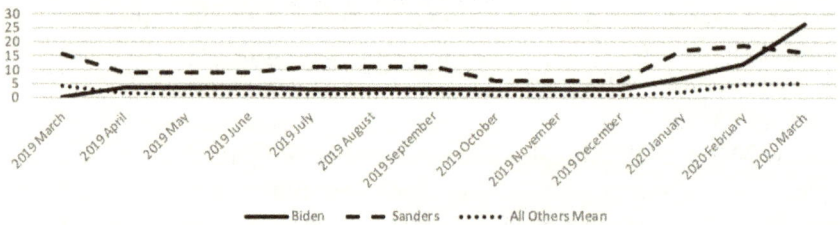

Figure 3.2 Democratic Presidential Nomination 2020: Cash on Hand. *Source*: OpenSecrets, compiled from candidate reports to FEC

analysts when the primary contests began. But these patterns also suggest that the role of money may well have been less important for the nomination outcome than the qualities of the candidates.

The fund-raising activities of the Democratic field in the first half of 2019 revealed three key features. The first feature was an unusual criticism of political money, including a bias for small donations and against large individual donations, especially Traditional PACs, Super PACs, and tax-exempt groups.[67] These concerns were largely symbolic, allowing the various candidates to show their support for grassroots democracy and draw distinctions with their rivals (see chapter 7). Such positions explain the small number of Super PACs closely aligned with candidates in the 2020 nomination campaign. Indeed, the activities of such Super PACs eventually produced some embarrassment for candidates—including Biden, Warren, and Sanders—when this suspect source of funding became crucial to their campaigns (see chapters 4, 6, and 7).[68]

The second feature was a dramatic expansion in spending on social media in pursuit of funds, name recognition, and ultimately votes.[69] Indeed, in the first half of 2019, the Democratic field had spent a record $15 million on Facebook and Google ads. (By way of comparison, Trump's spending was $18 million.) Expansion was similar in the use of other social media platforms, including Twitter and Instagram, as well as email, telephone, and texting.[70] Owners of all kinds of potential donor lists did a brisk business with the campaigns.[71] One reason for the increase was the growth of digital communications in general, but another reason was the small-donation fund-raising criteria for participating in the debates that the Democratic National Committee sponsored.

The third feature is related to the second: the aggressive pursuit of small donations, in aggregate and by most candidates (see chapters 4, 5, and 6). The candidates routinely bragged about the number of individual contributors, with an emphasis on the average donation size. In the second quarter, for example, Sanders claimed 690,000 individual donors and $1 million in donations, with an average donation of $18. Analogous figures for other candidates were: Buttigieg (294,000 donors, 400,000 donations, $15 average), Biden (256,000 donors, 436,000 donations, $49 average), and Warren (384,000 donors, 683,000 donations, $28 average). (Comparable figures for Trump were 250,000 donors, 725,000 donations, $41 average.)[72] These patterns persisted throughout the primary season and during the bridge period and general election for Biden, and especially for Trump.

Such efforts were not always cost effective, however, with some candidates suffering a net loss of funds rather than a net gain. Of course, such a fiscal deficit might have been productive if the symbolic value of small donations and the communication value of participating in the debates were included in the calculation. Indeed, a complex interaction among media—social, earned, and paid—and fund-raising emerged during the primary campaign.[73]

To understand these factors better, it is worth looking at the details of the campaigns of the six candidates who did best in the money race.

As the former vice president, Biden had long been seen as the front-runner due to his name recognition and governmental experience. But although well liked, he generated little enthusiasm among the party's activists. Indeed, when Biden finally announced his candidacy on April 25, 2019, he already faced twenty rivals, including the 2016 runner-up Sanders. And these candidates had already raised a total of $89 million in the first quarter of 2019 and had $64 million in cash on hand. (By way of comparison, Trump raised $30 million in the first quarter of 2019.) Although Biden led in national poll standing throughout the primary season, he was severely tested in the quest for campaign funds. In retrospect, the primary season became a contest over who would be the final challenger to the front-runner.

The first major event of the nomination campaign was the initial DNC-sponsored debate. Held on June 26 and 27, fourteen candidates qualified by both the poll standing and donations criteria (58 percent of the declared candidates), although another six candidates (25 percent) met the donation criteria. The debate favorably showcased some less well-known candidates, such as Buttigieg, but Warren and Harris benefited as well—especially the latter's criticism of Biden. The perceived debate results generally matched the second-quarter fund-raising figures: Sanders was first in a top tier of candidates, raising $26 million, followed closely by Buttigieg ($25 million), Biden ($22 million), and Warren ($19 million). Harris came next in line ($11 million), at the top of a second tier of candidates. Only one of the other second-tier candidates would be competitive when the primary season began, and that was Klobuchar ($3.8 million). The receipts of the top-tier candidates were closely grouped, with spending about half of receipts, and cash on hand growing. On the last count, Biden was an exception, with only $11 million cash on hand, about half that of his top-tier rivals. (The comparable figures for Trump were $26 million raised, with $57 million cash on hand.)

On July 9, liberal activist and billionaire Tom Steyer entered the nomination race, reversing his previous decision not to seek the nomination. He was already the top federal donor to liberal and Democratic causes, with lifetime contributions of $248 million.[74] In line with his strong progressive ideals, Steyer had promoted the impeachment and removal of President Trump and may have sensed an opportunity in a large, competitive field. Indeed, due to the late start of his campaign, his chances were predicated on his personal wealth.

The second and third DNC-sponsored debates followed on July 30–31 and September 12, involving twenty-one and ten candidates, respectively (Steyer did not qualify for either). It was widely perceived that Warren benefited from these debates, mostly at Biden's expense. Meanwhile, numerous candidates complained to the DNC about the unfairness of the criteria for debate participation (see chapter 7). The third-quarter fund-raising totals showed some shifts among the top-tier candidates as well as a growing gap with the second-tier candidates: Sanders was still in first place, raising $28 million, but Warren rose to second place ($25 million), while Buttigieg fell to third ($19 million), and Biden slipped to fourth ($16 million). Harris was still in fifth place ($11 million); Klobuchar raised $5 million. Similarly, cash on hand continued to grow for Sanders, Warren, and Buttigieg but declined sharply for Biden and Harris ($9 and $11 million, respectively). All of these efforts, however, were dwarfed by Steyer's self-financed contribution of $48 million. Due in large measure to financial necessity, seven candidates suspended their campaigns in the third quarter.[75] (The comparable figures for Trump were $40 million raised and $83 million cash on hand.)

Although some candidates had earlier paid broadcast expenditures, television ads began in earnest in September. Buttigieg spent $1 million (1,960 airings), followed by Sanders at $800,000 (1,623 airings) and Biden at $600,000 (883 airings). Such spending grew in October: Buttigieg spent $1.5 million (2,056 airings), Sanders spent $1.8 million (4,400 airings), and Biden spent $400,000 (700 airings). It grew again in November, with Sanders at $2.7 million (5,874 airings), Buttigieg at $1.9 million (3,348 airings), and Biden at $1.8 million (1,730 airings). Warren was less active, spending $1.3 million in October and November (3,496 airings). All of the top-tier candidates also expanded their social media buys. Once again, Steyer's ad buys were gigantic in comparison: $27 million (59,618 airings).[76] These efforts helped Steyer meet both the polling and donation criteria to qualify for the October debate.

As the field was winnowed, the intensity of the next set of debates increased, including the fourth debate on October 15 (twelve candidates, including Steyer), the fifth on November 20 (ten candidates), and the sixth on December 19 (seven candidates). Although Biden maintained his lead in the national poll standing throughout the fourth quarter of the year, Warren's poll standing rose—and then fell—between the third and fourth debates.

Then in November, former New York mayor Michael Bloomberg declared his candidacy; like Steyer, he reversed his earlier decision not to seek the nomination. The announcement came too late for Bloomberg to participate in the four initial contests (Iowa, New Hampshire, Nevada, and South Carolina), so he focused his efforts on Super Tuesday and beyond. Bloomberg's decision may have been influenced by the competitiveness of the race, but defeating Trump was also an important factor. His personal wealth allowed him to quickly create a national campaign infrastructure, including campaign offices in thirty states, hundreds of staffers, and massive advertising buys.[77] When fully operational, the Bloomberg campaign was spending $7 million a day.[78] The campaign eventually exceeded the financial resources of all previous major party presidential *general election campaigns* and improved Bloomberg's poll standing.[79]

The fourth-quarter fund-raising reports revealed the potential for the self-financed campaigns to shake up the race: Bloomberg and Steyer spent of their own money, $200 and $157 million, respectively. Among the top-tier candidates not self-financing, Sanders remained in first place, raising $35 million; Buttigieg took back second place ($25 million), with Biden rising to third ($23 million), and Warren a close fourth ($22 million); Klobuchar raised $11 million. All of these candidates were engaged in heavy spending, with cash on hand shrinking in all cases; Biden was in the most difficult straits with only $9 million.[80] Harris and five other candidates suspended their campaigns as 2019 ended and 2020 began. (The comparable figures for Trump were $46 million raised and $103 million cash on hand.)

Bloomberg and Steyer dominated broadcast spending at the very end of the fourth quarter, with $76 million (77,736 airings) and $25 million (23,003 airings), respectively. Bloomberg's advertising was national in scope, including the Super Tuesday states, whereas Steyer's was concentrated in the first four nomination contests, especially South Carolina.

Among the top-tier candidates, Sanders spent $2.7 million (5,874 airings); Buttigieg, $1.9 million (3,348 airings); Biden, $1.8 million (1,730 airings); and Warren, $1 million (2,407 airings). During the fourth quarter, the Biden aligned Super PAC Unite the Country had $3.9 million in independent expenditures. (Trump made a $5 million ad buy attacking Biden.)[81]

As 2020 began, the next set of debates was timed in advance of the initial nomination contests: January 14 (held in Iowa with six candidates); February 7 (held in New Hampshire with six candidates); February 19 (held in Nevada with six candidates, including Bloomberg); February 29 (held in South Carolina with seven candidates). In January and February combined, Sanders raised $73 million, followed by Warren ($40 million), Biden ($25 million), Klobuchar ($25 million), and Buttigieg ($24 million). Operating in the shadow of these self-financed campaigns, the top-tier candidates felt financial pressure: Bloomberg and Steyer continued spending their own money, $735 million and $113 million, respectively.

The results of the Iowa caucuses were close, with Sanders coming in first with 27 percent of the ballots, followed by Buttigieg (25 percent), Warren (23 percent), Biden (14 percent), and Klobuchar (12 percent). The caucuses were marred by technical difficulties, which may have limited the momentum the top finishers received.[82] The total spending in Iowa broke records—for example, $50 million in broadcast expenditures (137,193 airings).[83] There was a rough correlation between the caucus results and the total broadcast spending by the top-tier candidates: Buttigieg spent $7 million; Sanders, $6.5 million; Warren, $4 million; Biden, $3 million; and Klobuchar, $2 million. Unite the Country Super PAC assisted Biden with $2.3 million in independent expenditures.

Unlike Iowa, the campaign spending declined in New Hampshire, largely because the state was seen as favorable to Sanders. And Sanders did indeed finish first with 26 percent of the vote, followed by Buttigieg (24 percent), Klobuchar (20 percent), Warren (9 percent), and Biden (8 percent). Here, too, there was a rough correlation between the results and total broadcast expenditures by the top-tier candidates: Sanders spent $4 million; Buttigieg, $1.5 million; Warren and Klobuchar, $400,000 each. Biden spent very little in the primary but received $1 million in assistance from Unite the Country Super PAC, while Buttigieg benefited from $500,000 in independent expenditures from VoteVets.org. Another three candidates soon left the race.

Candidate spending increased in the next contest, the Nevada caucuses. Sanders finished first with an impressive 41 percent of the ballots, followed by Biden (19 percent), Buttigieg (17 percent), Warren (11 percent), and Klobuchar (7 percent). The rough correlation between results and broadcast expenditures continued: Sanders, $1.8 million; Buttigieg, $1.2 million; Warren, $1.2 million; Biden, $1.1 million; and Klobuchar, $800,000. Two new Super PACs entered the fray: Persist PAC made $1 million in independent expenditures to assist Warren, and Kitchen Table Conversation made $300,000 in independent expenditures to assist Klobuchar. Unite the Country ($700,000) and VoteVets.org ($300,000) continued to help Biden and Buttigieg, and the Nurses Super PAC ($700,000) assisted Sanders. In addition, there were independent expenditures against Sanders, led by the Super PAC Democratic Majority for Israel ($600,000).

Sanders's success in the first three nomination contests roiled the race. His national poll standing shot up, and Biden's plunged. "Joe Biden is collapsing" was the meme of the moment.[84] The prospect of Sanders becoming the Democratic nominee worried moderate Democratic leaders, who feared that he would be unable to defeat Trump. Some redoubled their efforts for Biden, including an endorsement by South Carolina Congressman Jim Clyburn, while others looked toward Bloomberg as an alternative to Biden.[85] But there was already a preview of things to come: Steyer and Bloomberg debate performances and heavy spending in the initial contests had only modest effects on their poll standings.

Sanders's early momentum came to an abrupt halt in the South Carolina primary, where Biden finished first with 40 percent of the vote, followed by Sanders (20 percent), Steyer (11 percent), Buttigieg (8 percent), Warren (7 percent), and Klobuchar (3 percent). These results were a special disappointment for Steyer, who had spent $23 million on broadcast ads, dwarfing Sanders ($3 million), Buttigieg ($2 million), Biden ($800,000), and Warren ($500,000).[86] The Super PACs aligned with Warren, Klobuchar, and Biden continued to make independent expenditures. But after South Carolina, Steyer, Buttigieg, and Klobuchar ended their campaigns and endorsed Biden.

The stage was set for the fifteen primaries and caucuses on Super Tuesday. Buoyed by his South Carolina success, Biden prevailed in ten of the contests, Sanders won four, and Bloomberg claimed just one. As in South Carolina, the correlation between results and broadcast expenditures was very weak: Bloomberg spent $215 million (and was active in all fifteen contests), followed by Sanders ($18 million), Warren ($2.4 million), and Biden ($2.2 million). Persist PAC spent $11.7 million to assist Warren, and United the Country spent a token amount for Biden. The results were a disappointment for Bloomberg, whose massive investment's yield was meager; and disheartening for Warren, who lost her home state of Massachusetts. After Super Tuesday, Bloomberg and Warren suspended their campaigns, endorsing Biden.

The pandemic set in after Super Tuesday, eventually cutting short the nomination contests, to the benefit of front-runner Biden and to the detriment of the major challenger, Sanders.[87] Biden won eight of the eleven primaries and caucuses in March, effectively ending the race (although Sanders did not suspend his campaign until after losing Wisconsin on April 7).

The Postprimary Campaign

Figure 3.3 charts the fund-raising and expenditures of Team Biden and Team Trump during the postprimary season campaign, including the bridge period (April through August 2020) and the general election (September through December 2020). The figure shows the cumulative receipts and cash

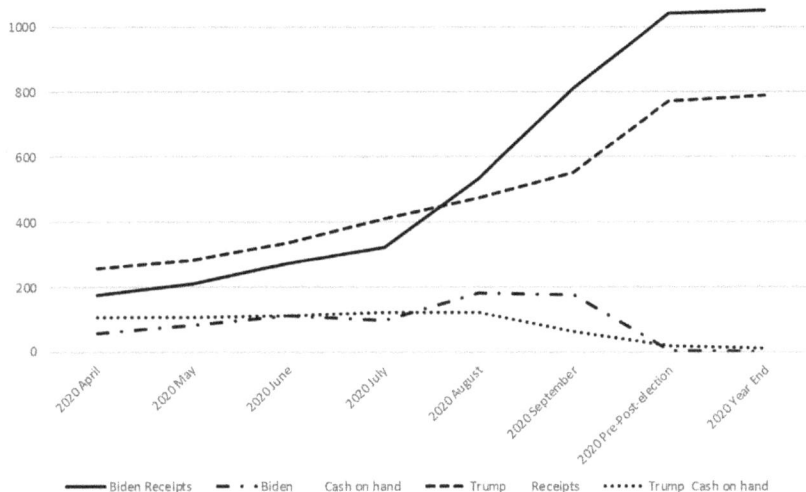

Figure 3.3 Presidential General Election 2020: Cumulative Receipts, Cash on Hand.
Source: OpenSecrets, compiled from candidate reports to FEC

on hand for Biden's and Trump's PCCs, providing an overview of the fiscal dynamics of the general election campaign.

Early in the bridge period, Team Biden began raising funds at a rate parallel to Team Trump, but from April through July Biden trailed in total receipts. Then in August 2020, Team Biden's fund-raising accelerated and moved past Team Trump in total receipts. Team Biden then outraised Team Trump through Election Day. The cash on hand of both campaigns was comparable—and low—through August, when Biden's cash on hand began to exceed Trump's, a pattern that continued through Election Day.

Figure 3.4 charts the net campaign expenditures by Team Biden and Team Trump during the bridge period and general election campaign, including the net expenditures by the candidates' PCCs, net independent expenditures by noncandidate committees (IEs), and net party expenditures for voter outreach. For each of these measures in the figure, a positive number (above the horizontal axis) indicates that Team Biden spent more than Team Trump, whereas a negative number (below the horizontal axis) indicates that Team Trump spent more than Team Biden.[88]

The expenditure patterns in figure 3.4 show that Team Biden gained a financial advantage over the bridge period and general election campaign. From April through August, the net expenditures of the Biden and Trump PCCs were roughly even (hovering around the horizontal axis). Then, beginning in August, Biden's PCC expenditures moved ahead of Trump's PCC in a dramatic fashion, so that the net expenditures advantaged Team Biden.

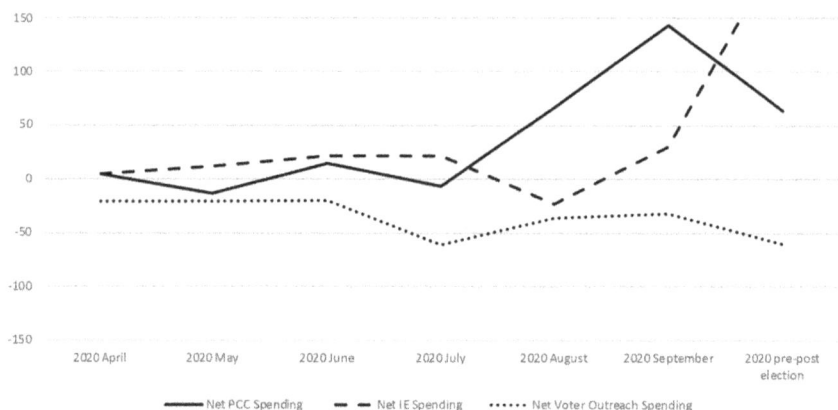

Figure 3.4 The General Election Campaign 2020: Net Candidate, Voter Outreach, and Independent Expenditures (positive figures, net advantage Team Biden; negative figures, net advantage Team Trump). *Source*: OpenSecrets, compiled from candidate, party, and PAC reports to FEC

This trend peaked in September and remained high through Election Day. Overall, the combined volume of advertising by the candidates' PCC was estimated to be a record-breaking $1.8 billion over the bridge period and general election.[89]

Record-breaking expenditures also occurred for independent expenditures and voter outreach efforts. The net independent expenditures (IEs) by non-candidate groups were also roughly even from April through August, with a small net advantage for Team Biden in net expenditures until August, when the net expenditures favored Trump. Then in September the net independent expenditures moved dramatically in favor of Team Biden, staying so through Election Day (see below). Unlike net PCC and net independent expenditures, net party expenditures for voter outreach consistently favored Team Trump over the bridge period and general election (see below).

The Bridge Period

Once Biden had become the presumptive Democratic presidential nominee in April 2020, his campaign began transitioning from seeking convention delegates (a task not completed until June 5) to seeking electoral votes in the general election. This new task was a daunting one. After all, Biden's primary fund-raising had been anemic, his opponent was well funded and well organized, and the pandemic posed tough fund-raising challenges.

But as the Democratic nominee, Biden could draw on the extensive organizational resources as well as help from many of his recent rivals, including access to the large pool of new donors generated during the nomination campaign. In addition, Biden could mobilize the deep antipathy many Democrats shared toward President Trump and their determination to defeat him. And there were creative ways to cope with the pandemic challenges: digital solicitation of small donors, virtual fund-raisers for larger donors, independent expenditures spending by sympathetic Super PACs and tax-exempt groups, and a new array of electronic communications to target voters.[90] And the polls consistently showing Biden with a solid lead over Trump nationally as well as in most battleground states, suggesting that the prospects of victory were good.

The Biden campaign took advantage of these opportunities in a methodical fashion. In April, Biden let it be known that Priorities USA Action was his preferred Super PAC, and it soon began independent expenditures that were helpful to the campaign.[91] Biden began organizing JFCs with the DNC (paralleling Trump's JFCs); these efforts added new funds, allowing Team Biden to shift fund-raising into general election mode.[92] The campaign engaged in extensive (low-cost) social media ads, but limited (high-cost) broadcast ads, while Biden himself retreated from the campaign trail into his basement in Delaware, leaving the public stage—and its problems—to the embattled President Trump.[93]

Meanwhile, the Trump campaign bought $31 million in broadcast ads and $23 million in social media ads, one goal of which was to improve Trump's poll standing.[94] Such expenditures took a toll on the campaign's war chest. When combined with the Biden campaign's cautious approach, the result was near parity in the cash on hand positions between the rival campaigns.[95] In a sign of things to come, Team Biden launched $40 million worth of ads in July, outspending Team Trump's $32 million in broadcast media.[96]

Then Team Biden raised $365 million in August—a record for one-month receipts.[97] These gains allowed Biden to pull ahead of Trump in total funds raised and cash on hand. One reason for these numbers was the $70 million raised during the Democratic National Convention. Additional gains were associated with Biden's choice of Kamala Harris as his vice-presidential running mate—the first woman of color to hold such a position. Party officials reported receiving $48 million in the first forty-eight hours after the announcement. Another reason was the maturation of the assembled fund-raising programs: more than half of the August funds came in small donations raised online ($205 million), while the remaining funds were in larger donations, including transfer from JFCs. Team Trump's August fund-raising ($154 million) was less than half of Team Biden's.

Yet another factor in this record fund-raising was the attention Biden gained from a continuing favorable balance in broadcast expenditures: in

August, Biden spent $46 million (92,360 airings) versus Trump's $14 million (26,159 airings); and although Biden still trailed Trump in digital ads, the margin decreased, $34 million to $45 million.

Financing the National Conventions

Due to the pandemic, the national party conventions—the traditional end of the nomination campaigns—were largely digital events. On balance, they were successful in accomplishing the prime goals of modern conventions: publicizing presidential tickets. One analyst described them thus: "As productions, a departure; as rhetorical exercises, business as usual."[98]

The Democratic Convention went smoothly, with a small group of party leaders meeting in Milwaukee, August 17–20, to conduct necessary business. But much of the traditional rituals and pageantry was adapted to digital and electronic media, including a well-received acceptance speech by Biden. The Republican Convention went less smoothly. President Trump unsuccessfully attempted to switch the convention site from Charlotte, North Carolina, to Jacksonville, Florida, adding confusion and costs. Eventually, a small group of party leaders met in Charlotte August 24–27 to conduct necessary business. But other activities were conducted in Washington, D.C., including Trump's acceptance speech broadcast from the White House—a controversial choice but fitting with Trump's disregard for political norms. Many traditional convention activities were presented via digital and electronic media. Neither convention produced a significant "bounce" in the polls for the nominees.

Overall, the conventions cost less in 2020 than in 2016. Both parties used funds from their special convention accounts (see chapter 5), $18.6 million by the Democrats (up slightly from $16 million in 2016); and $17.9 million by the Republicans (down slightly from $24 million in 2016), plus an estimated $14 million due to venue changes.[99] The Milwaukee Host Committee spent $44 million (down from $75 million in Philadelphia in 2016),[100] and the Charlotte Host Committee spent $37 million (down from $66 million in Cleveland in 2016).[101] As in 2016, the U.S. Department of Homeland Security provided $40 million for security for each convention (down from the $50 million in 2016).

The General Election Campaign

When the general election campaign formally began in September, Team Biden broke its own August fund-raising totals, again outpacing Team Trump.[102] The Biden campaign took advantage of these riches to make high-volume broadcast purchases with a two-to-one advantage over Trump, $95 million (135,382 airings) versus $41 million (59,714 airings), and for the first time took a lead in digital ad spending, $32 million versus $23 million.[103]

Team Trump was soon trailing Team Biden financially and facing a severe shortage of cash as Election Day approached. The campaign was forced to cut back on expenditures, including broadcast ads.[104] An incredulous Trump considered making a large donation from his own funds as he had done in 2016 (a figure of $100 million was discussed). However, in the end he doubted that more money would be needed to fund his campaign. Many observers also wondered how Team Trump had largely spent the $1.1 billion it had raised to date. One answer was poor financial management and profligate expenditures (see chapter 5).[105] This problem had been recognized back in July, when there was a shakeup in the campaign leadership.[106] Another reason was the extensive investment by Team Trump and the RNC in grassroots voter outreach (see below). In response, the campaign cut back on expenditures (including broadcast) and redoubled its fund-raising efforts. The latter response may have included aggressive online solicitation that ultimately produced a high level of complaints from, and refunds to, donors who felt overcharged by the campaign (see chapter 7).[107]

Biden's financial surge was not without its controversies, especially the prominence of Super PACs, fueled by very large donations (see chapter 6), and a close connection between these efforts and a network of tax-exempt groups. Indeed, it was soon discovered that the Democrats were benefiting from extensive support from "dark money" groups, reigniting the intra-party debate over money in politics from the primary season. One aspect of this phenomenon was an innovative coordinating mechanism for raising and distributing funds from tax-exempt groups to an array of Democratic and liberal political operations.[108]

As the general election campaign ended, the Biden campaign continued its high level of broadcast expenditures with an additional $54 million (90,352 airings) compared to $35 million by Trump (23,347 airings), but it fell back behind Trump in digital ads, $38 million to $44 million.[109] Because of its financial resources, Team Biden was able to purchase extensive advertising across the country, whereas the Trump ads became increasing focused on battleground states. Indeed, Team Biden faced the unusual challenge of spending $180 million in the last two weeks of the campaign.[110] To the surprise of many observers, the Biden ads were largely positive, touting the former vice president, eventually shifting toward more contrast ads with the president. Trump's broadcast spending was overwhelmingly for attack ads.

As in past elections, noncandidate groups made a surge of independent expenditures as Election Day neared. The final spending paralleled the tone of candidate broadcast spending: independent expenditures associated with Biden were on balance positive, whereas those associated with Trump were on balance negative. The contrast between these figures was stark: a net $134 million in positive ads for Biden and a net $87 million in negative ads against Trump.

Table 3.4 reports the top ten groups in terms of independent expenditures in the presidential campaign, the vast bulk of which were made during the general election campaign. Nine of the top ten entries were Super PACs associated with the presidential candidates (see above), but also included the Lincoln Project, an effort by anti-Trump Republicans. The tenth entry is an environmental group, the League of Conservation Voters (LCV), a reminder that a wide variety of interests groups also spent directly to influence the 2020 presidential election (see chapter 6).

According to a tally posted by OpenSecrets,[111] more than 580 entities engaged in such direct election activities, 221 associated with Trump, 206 associated with Biden, and 155 with both candidates. Spending by these groups nearly totaled $1 billion. However, the mean expenditure was $1.8 million, and the median $35,000, revealing that most of these entities spent only modest sums. These entities were extraordinarily diverse, organized at the national, state, and local levels, ranging from organized labor to cultural

Table 3.4   Top Ten Noncandidate Group Independent Expenditures, 2020 Presidential Election Campaigns

(millions of dollars) GROUP NAME	TOTAL	FOR BIDEN	AGAINST BIDEN	FOR TRUMP	AGAINST TRUMP
America First Action (Trump)	$134	$0	$134	*	$0
Future Forward USA (Biden)	$128	$74	$0	$0	$55
Priorities USA Action (Biden)	$110	$53	$0	$0	$58
Preserve America PAC (Trump)	$103	$0	$103	$0	$0
Independence USA PAC (Biden)	$56	$55	$0	$0	$2
American Bridge 21st Century (Biden)	$51	*	$0	$0	$51
Unite the Country (Biden)	$34	$38	$0	$0	$1
Lincoln Project (anti-Trump)	$36	$2	$0	$0	$34
Committee to Defend the President (Trump)	$18	$0	$4	$14	$0
LCV Victory Fund	$17	$7	$0	$0	$10

Source: OpenSecrets, compiled from FEC reports
*Less than $1 million

and citizens' groups. Overall, this spending showed the pro-Biden and anti-Trump pattern as well.

In contrast to independent expenditures, party expenditures for voter outreach on balance favored Trump and the Republicans. This measure reflects the extraordinary grassroots efforts that Team Trump implemented. As one analyst concluded in late October, "Dems beware—the RNC is Crushing it" regarding field operations.[112] The Trump Victory operation contacted more than 150 million voters in person or by telephone, nearly doubling the 71 million voters that the Republicans contacted in 2016—and surpassing the existing record that the Obama campaign set in 2012. Built over the election cycle, the effort relied on sophisticated data to design voter outreach with the help of 1,500 paid staffers and 2.5 million volunteers.[113] Team Trump spent $377 million to build and operate Trump Victory. Team Biden also funded a voter outreach program, spending about $137 million, and focused more on digital contacts due to the pandemic.[114]

CONCLUSION AND CONTINUANCE

The results of the 2020 presidential election have been aptly described as "an imperfect tie."[115] Biden reversed Trump's 2016 Electoral College tally by winning many of the battleground states by very close margins. At the same time, Republican candidates did better than expected in House and Senate races, resulting in tiny Democratic majorities in the House and the Senate. And all this happened with unexpectedly high voter turnout. These outcomes substantially contradicted common preelection predictions, raising new questions about the accuracy of public opinion polls.

The independent impact of the record-breaking expenditures on the 2020 presidential election results is unclear. It could well be that, in the end, the numerous efforts simply balanced out where it mattered, in key states and districts. It could also be that much of the expenditure was far less productive than anticipated, and in some cases, ineffective or even counterproductive. The pandemic may have played an unexpected role in such matters. On the Democratic side, the dramatic increase in early voting, including the record use of mail-in ballots, may have reduced the persuadable electorate more quickly than in past elections, leaving many fewer voters to persuade with Team Biden's late campaign advertising advantage.[116] For the Republicans, the pandemic may have made mass rallies as well as voter outreach at the grassroots much less productive than anticipated. It could also be that the electorate was so deeply divided that even the vast expenditures on behalf of two imperfect candidates could only end in some kind of draw.

Postelection Fund-Raising

Breaking yet another political norm, President Trump refused to concede the 2020 election until the electoral votes were officially counted by the Congress in January 2021—a process interrupted by Trump supporters rioting on Capitol Hill on January 6. The Trump campaign filed numerous challenges to the election outcome in many states, with many of these efforts paid for by Trump's PCC and the RNC (see chapter 5).[117] Ostensibly to pay for these activities, Team Trump continued to raise funds after Election Day under the guise of an "Election Defense Fund," raising $280 million. However, only about $13 million of these funds went to pay for such legal expenses.[118] The rest was spent on covering fund-raising expenses, postelection advertising, and $31 million to a new Leadership PAC, Save America, that Trump organized right after the election.[119]

Trump continued to raise funds after he left office in January 2021, and roughly one year later, Save America and other Trump aligned organizations had $105 million cash on hand.[120] These funds allowed Trump to pay for political activities in the 2022 election cycle as well as prepare for his 2024 White House bid. It is worth noting that the Democrats' innovative coordination of political funding by tax-exempt groups continued after the election into the 2022 election cycle—and likely in the 2024 election cycle as well.[121]

The reification of the "permanent campaign" by Trump continues at this writing.

NOTES

1. Herbert E. Alexander, *Financing the 1960 Election* (Princeton, NJ: Citizens' Research Foundation, 1962).

2. Unless otherwise noted, all figures here are in constant 2020 dollars.

3. For the remainder for this chapter, the term Super PAC includes Hybrid PACs as well. See chapter 2 for definitions of these groups.

4. In 2020, no major presidential candidates participated in the public financing system, although a few candidates eventually applied for and received $185,000 in public funds. Beginning in the 1976 election in response to the Supreme Court ruling in *Buckley v. Valeo*, a voluntary set of rules limited the funds candidates could expended in the nomination and general election campaign in return for matching public funds in the primaries and a lump-sum payment to the major party nominees for the general election. Simply put, candidates found that they could raise and expend more campaign funds by forgoing public financing (see chapter 2). For a description of the presidential public financing system when most candidates

participated in it, see John C. Green and Nathan S. Bigelow, "Financing the 2000 Presidential Nomination Campaigns: The Costs of Innovation," in *Financing the 2000 Election*, ed. David B. Magleby (Washington, DC: Brookings Institution, 2002), 49–78.

5. On the invisible primary in 2008, see Arthur C. Paulson, "The 'Invisible Primary' Becomes Visible: The Importance of the 2008 Presidential Nominations, Start to Finish," in *Winning the Presidency 2008*, ed. William J. Crotty (Boulder, CO: Paradigm, 2009), 87–109.

6. David B. Magleby, "Electoral Politics as Team Sport: Advantage the Democrats," in *The State of the Parties: The Changing Role of Contemporary American Parties*, ed. John C. Green and Daniel J. Coffey (Lanham, MD: Rowman & Littlefield, 2011), 81–101.

7. "Democratic Primary Rules, 2020," https://ballotpedia.org/Democratic delegate rules.

8. The twenty-nine Democratic candidates were, in alphabetical order, Michael Bennet, Joseph Biden, Michael Bloomberg, Cory Booker, Steve Bullock, Pete Buttigieg, Julian Castro, Willian de Blasio, John Delaney, Tulsi Gabbard, Kirsten Gillibrand, Michael Gravel, Kamala Harris, John Hickenlooper, Jay Inslee, Amy Klobuchar, Wayne Messam, Seth Moulton, Richard Ojeda, Beto O'Rourke, Deval Patrick, Timothy Ryan, Bernard Sanders, Joseph Sestak, Thomas Steyer, Eric Swalwell, Elizabeth Warren, Marianne Williamson, and Andrew Yang.

9. See Nik DeCosta-Klipa, "Pete Buttigieg Took a Dig at Elizabeth Warren's Small-Donation Fund-Raising Strategy," *Boston.com*, October 15, 2019, https:// www.boston.com/news/politics/2019/10/15/pete-buttigieg-elizabeth-warren-fund -raising-strategy/; Jonathan Allen, Lauren Egan, and Jeremia Kimelman, "Kamala Harris Blows Past Democratic Rivals in Fund-Raising in Communities of Color," *NBC News*, May 8, 2019, https://www.nbcnews.com/politics/2020-election/kamala -harris-blows-past-democratic-rivals-fund-raising-communities-color-n1000031; Brian Bakst, "Never Shy of Campaign Money, Klobuchar 2020 Bid Poses New Test," *MPR News*, April 4, 2019, https://www.mprnews.org/story/2019/04/04/klobuchar -2020-campaign-money-poses-new-test.

10. David S. Bernstein, "Warren Campaign Carries Big Payroll; Plus, Female Staffers Setting Salary High," WGBH.org, April 18, 2019, https://www.wgbh.org /news/commentary/2019/04/18/warren-campaign-carries-big-payroll-plus-female -staffers-setting-salary-highs; Maggie Severns, "Behind Bernie's Rise: A $50 Million Spending Surge—and More Where That Came from," Politico, February 1, 2020, https://www.politico.com/news/2020/02/01/bernie-sanders-fec-spending-110157.

11. Allied organizations are created by a candidate alongside his or her PCCs; aligned organizations are created independent of a candidate's PCC but for the purpose of supporting the candidate; and assisting organizations are issue-based organizations that support a candidate in pursuit of these goals. Because of independent expenditures, it is often a fine line between aligned and assisting organizations.

12. David B. Magleby, "A High Stakes Election," in *Financing the 2000 Election*, ed. David B. Magleby (Washington, DC: Brookings Institution, 2002), 9.

13. On 2016 nomination campaign finances, see John C. Green, "Financing the 2016 Presidential Nomination Campaigns," in *Financing the 2016 Election*, ed. David B. Magleby (Washington, DC: Brookings Institution Press, 2019), 131–86; and on 2012 finances, see John C. Green, Michael E. Koehler, and Ian P. Schwarber, "Financing the 2012 Presidential Nomination Campaigns," in *Financing the 2012 Election*, ed. David B. Magleby (Washington, DC: Brookings Institution Press, 2014), 77–122; for the general election finances, see David A. Hopkins, "Financing the 2016 Presidential General Election," in *Financing the 2016 Election*, ed. David B. Magleby (Washington, DC: Brookings Institution Press, 2019), 187–216.

14. Former congressman John Delaney also substantially self-funded his campaign with $22 million.

15. See Herbert E. Alexander and Anthony Corrado, *Financing the 1992 Election* (New York: Routledge, 1996).

16. Some of the other Democratic presidential candidates also participated in joint fund-raising committees, including Ryan, Hickenlooper, Booker, Klobuchar, Gillibrand, and Moulton. However, these committees were also involved in these candidates' 2020 congressional campaigns.

17. Donna Brazile, *Hacks: The Inside Story of the Break-ins and Breakdowns That Put Donald Trump in the White House* (New York: Hachette, 2017).

18. These figures include the cash on hand from the end of the 2018 election cycle.

19. Trump's PCC was active in the 2018 cycle, raising $67 million and disbursing $55 million.

20. Lachlan Markay, "Scoop: Trump Campaign Boosted by Unsuspecting State GOPs," *Axios*, April 11, 2021, https://www.axios.com/republicans-state-gop-trump-campaign-cd16bae3-ebf9-4ed5-94de-98a85d23e06c.html.

21. Trump's JFCs were active during the 2018 election cycle, raising $99 million, transferring $45 million to Trump's PCC and $31 million to Republican party committees, and spending an additional $26 million.

22. Multiple small contributions posed a challenge in estimating these figures: an itemized contribution in one reporting period often was part of unitemized contributions in a previous reporting period, necessitating complex adjustments in previous estimates of unitemized donations.

23. If all the Democratic candidates were included, unitemized donations were $381 million, accounting for 12 percent of all Democratic candidate donations in 2020. If self-financed candidates are excluded, and only primary receipts considered, unitemized donations were $377 million, accounting for 51 percent of Democratic candidate donations.

24. Castro (65 percent), Williamson (57 percent), O'Rourke (51 percent), Inslee (50 percent), and Wang (49 percent) all did better than Sanders in this regard but raised far less money.

25. Both candidates paid for 99 percent of their campaign with their own funds, with Bloomberg adding $7 million in Traditional PAC contributions and Steyer $3 million in small donations.

26. Warren also contributed some $400,000 to her campaign. Biden, Buttigieg, Harris, Klobuchar, and Sanders did not contribute to their campaigns.

27. Warren ($14 million), Sanders ($13 million), Klobuchar ($4 million), and Harris ($2 million) transferred funds from previous campaigns.

28. Hopkins, "Financing the 2016 Presidential General Election Campaign," 205.

29. Due to filing and reporting challenges, this figure understates the level of internal communications in 2020 (see chapter 6 for more details).

30. For the sake of completeness, it is worth noting that federal election activity by state and local party organizations in the 2020 cycle equaled $350 million for the Democrats and $244 million for the Republicans. These expenditures are likely to have been focused on congressional as well as presidential races.

31. Funds raised by exploratory committees are reported by the candidates once they have officially declared their candidacy. The candidates were Warren, Bloomberg, Buttigieg, Messam, Williamson, Castro, Gillibrand, and Gravel.

32. The candidates were Biden, Sanders, Klobuchar, Buttigieg, Patrick, Bennet, Booker, Castro, Harris, Bullock, Sestak, O'Rourke, Ryan, De Blasio, Gillibrand, Moulton, Inslee, Hickenlooper, and Swalwell.

33. The candidates were Biden, Warren, Klobuchar, Yang, Delaney, Booker, Harris, Patrick, Bullock, O'Rourke, DeBlasio, Inslee, and Hickenlooper.

34. The candidates were Biden, Sanders, Bullock, Harris, Yang, Booker, Gabbard, Buttigieg, Klobuchar, Warren, and DeBlasio.

35. The candidates were Biden, Sanders, Hickenlooper, Inslee, Gillibrand, O'Rourke, Bullock, Harris, Bennet, Patrick, Booker, Castro, Gabbard, Buttigieg, Klobuchar, Warren, and DeBlasio.

36. Theodore Meyer and Maggie Severns, "Ex-Biden Aide Forms Unite the Country Super PAC," Politico, October 29, 2019, https://www.politico.com/news /2019/10/29/ex-biden-aide-super-pac-unite-the-country-061096.

37. "Priorities USA Action," https://ballotpedia.org/Priorities_USA_Action.

38. "American Bridge to 21st Century," https://ballotpedia.org/American_ Bridge_21st_Century.

39. "Independence USA PAC," https://ballotpedia.org/Independence_USA _PAC.

40. Will Greenberg, "A Closer Look at the Top Democratic Super PAC Future Forward," *Blue Tent*, March 9, 2021, https://bluetent.us/articles/campaigns-elections /how-future-forward-became-a-leading-liberal-super-pac/.

41. Fredreka Schouten, "Joe Biden Discloses Names of Elite Fundraisers," *CNN*, November 11, 2020, https://www.cnn.com/2020/11/01/politics/joe-biden-bundlers -released/index.html.

42. The Super PACs were Nosotros PAC, Mid-Mo for Bernie, and Citizens against Plutocracy.

43. See https://ballotpedia.org/Our_Revolution; https://apnews.com/article/ bernie-sanders-iowa-us-news-elections-political-action-committees-345bbd1af52

9cfb1e41305fa3ab1e604; https://nationalinterest.org/blog/buzz/inside-dark-money-boosting-bernies-campaign-112561.

44. "Persist PAC," https://www.influencewatch.org/political-party/persist-pac/.

45. Maggie Severns, "Inside Warren's Secret Big-Donor Fan Club," Politico, November 18, 2019, https://www.politico.com/news/2019/11/18/big-democratic-donors-elizabeth-warren-2020-071333.

46. "VoteVets.org," https://ballotpedia.org/VoteVets.org.

47. Caroline Linton, "Pete Buttigieg Releases Names of Donor Bundlers," *CBS News*, December 13, 2019, https://www.cbsnews.com/news/pete-buttigieg-bundlers-buttigieg-releases-names-of-donor-bundlers-after-pressure-from-elizabeth-warren-2019-12-13/.

48. Gabe Schneider, "New Super PAC Has Spent More Than $1 Million Backing Klobuchar," *Minnesota Post*, February 21, 2020, https://www.minnpost.com/national/2020/02/new-super-pac-has-spent-more-than-1-million-backing-klobuchar/.

49. Tal Axelrod, "Klobuchar Releases Names of Bundlers," *The Hill*, January 10, 2020, https://thehill.com/homenews/campaign/477789-klobuchar-releases-names-of-bundlers.

50. Karl Evers-Hillstrom, "Presidential Contenders Still Not Disclosing Bundlers," *OpenSecrets*, October 9, 2019, https://www.opensecrets.org/news/2019/10/bundlers-remain-undisclosed-for-presidential-contenders/.

51. Save America raised $31.5 million and spent $0.3 million in 2020; https://ballotpedia.org/Save_America.

52. Green, "Financing the 2016 Presidential Nomination Campaign," 150–54.

53. "American First Action," https://ballotpedia.org/America_First_Action.

54. "Great America PAC," https://ballotpedia.org/Great_America_PAC.

55. "Committee to Defend the President," https://ballotpedia.org/Committee_to_Defend_the_President.

56. "Preserve America," https://ballotpedia.org/Preserve_America.

57. Brian Schwartz, "Trump's Business Allies and Over 400 Bundlers Give His 2020 War Chest a Boost," cnbc.com, July 7, 2019, https://www.cnbc.com/2019/07/18/trumps-business-allies-and-400-bundlers-give-2020-war-chest-a-boost.html.

58. David Levin, "Donald Trump Created a Permanent Presidential Campaign. Here's How," Center for Public Integrity, February 19, 2019, https://publicintegrity.org/politics/donald-trump-president-campaign-money-fund-raising/.

59. James Pindell, "Under Trump, 'Permanent Campaign' Takes on a Whole New Meaning," *Boston Globe*, March 16, 2017; also see Sidney Blumenthal, *The Permanent Campaign* (Chicago: Touchstone Books, 1980), and Brendan J. Doherty, *The Rise of the Permanent Campaign* (Lawrence: University of Kansas Press, 2012).

60. Michael E. Toner and Karen E. Trainer, "The $14 Billion Election," in *A Return to Normalcy?*, ed. Larry J. Sabato, Kyke Kondik, and J. Miles Coleman (Lanham, MD: Rowman & Littlefield, 2021), 219.

61. Michael Warren and Fredreka Schouten, "'It's Been a Disaster.' Inside the Trump Super PAC Struggles," *CNN*, June 8, 2019, https://www.cnn.com/2019/06 /07/politics/trump-super-pac-america-first/index.html.

62. Boris Heersink, "Trump and the Party-in-Organization: Presidential Control of National Party Organizations," *Journal of Politics* 80, no. 4 (2018): 1474–82.

63. Alex Isenstadt, "Trump Rolls out Massive Corporate-Style Campaign Structure for 2020," *Politico*, February 2019, https://www.politico.com/story/2019/02/19 /trump-campaign-2020-1175976.

64. Brad Parscale, "Campaigning in the Coronavirus Age: A New Frontier," *Realclearpolitics.com*, April 14, 2020, https://www.realclearpolitics.com/articles/2020 /04/14/campaigning_in_the_coronavirus_age_a_new_frontier_142930.html.

65. Andrew E. Busch and John J. Pitney, *Divided We Stand* (Lanham, MD: Rowman & Littlefield, 2021), 33–68.

66. A total of thirteen candidates (45 percent) entered the nomination race in the first quarter of 2019, another ten (34 percent) in the second quarter, and six candidates in the third and fourth quarters (21 percent). Three candidates (10 percent) announced their bids before 2019 and another three candidates (10 percent) entered later in 2019. Eighteen of these candidates (62 percent) ended their campaigns before the Iowa caucuses in 2020, eleven (38 percent) were still active for the Iowa caucuses, and just three were still active after Super Tuesday.

67. Karl Evers-Hillstrom and Yue Stella Yu, "Leading 2020 Democrats Want to Get Money out of Politics—Here's How They Plan to Do It," *OpenSecrets*, October 15, 2019, https://www.opensecrets.org/news/2019/10/2020-democrats-want-to-get -money-out-of-politics.

68. Kevin Robillard, "How Super PACs Took over the 2020 Democratic Primary," *Huffington Post*, February 2, 2020, https://www.huffpost.com/entry/super -pacs-took-over-2020-democratic-primary_n_5e4efc9fc5b6b82aa65044b7.

69. Wesleyan Media Project, "Wesleyan Media Project Publishes End-Of-Cycle Report," https://mediaproject.wesleyan.edu/2020-summary-032321/.

70. Toner and Trainer, "The $14 Billion Election," 217–18; Anna Massoglia and Karl Evers-Hillstrom, "Democrats Dominate Political Spending on Twitter," *OpenSecrets*, January 14, 2019, https://www.opensecrets.org/news/2019/01/demo- crats-dominate-political-spending-on-twitter.

71. Karl Evers-Hillstrom and Camille Erickson, "Your Email Is for Sale—and 2020 Candidates Are Paying Up," *OpenSecrets*, June 13, 2019, https://www.opense- crets.org/news/2019/06/email-list-for-sale-2020-candidates-are-paying.

72. These figures were culled from campaign press releases collected at www .democracyinaction.us.

73. Busch and Pitney, *Divided We Stand*, 50.

74. Vaughn Golden, "Tom Steyer, the Top All-Time Democratic Donor, Enters Presidential Field," *OpenSecrets*, July 9, 2019, https://www.opensecrets.org/news /2019/07/tom-steyer-enters-2020presidential-field.

75. Jessica Piper, "Debate Deadline Is Sink or Swim for Some 2020 Democrats," *OpenSecrets*, August 27, 2019, https://www.opensecrets.org/news/2019/08/debate-deadline-is-sink-or-swim-for-some-2020-democrats.

76. Wesleyan Media Project, "Candidates Have Spent $61 Million on Facebook and Google and Just $11 Million on TV," https://mediaproject.wesleyan.edu/releases-091919/.

77. Isaac Stanley-Becker and Michael Scherer, "Mike Bloomberg's Money Buys Him a Very Different Kind of Campaign. And It's a Big One," *Washington Post*, December 7, 2019, https://www.washingtonpost.com/politics/mike-bloombergs-money-buys-him-a-very-different-kind-of-campaign-and-its-a-big-one/2019/12/07/0593ec7c-184a-11ea-a659-7d69641c6ff7_story.html; Ali Vitali, "Bloomberg's Campaign Hires 500 Staffers in 30 States," NBC News, January 6, 2020, https://www.nbcnews.com/politics/2020-election/bloomberg-s-campaign-hires-500-staffers-over-30-states-n1110791; Paul Steinhauser, "Bloomberg Rising in Polls, Hiring Staff Army as Campaign Plows Millions into Unprecedented Ad Blitz," *Fox News*, January 6, 2020, https://www.foxnews.com/politics/bloomberg-rising-in-national-polls-as-campaign-plows-millions-into-unprecedented-ad-blitz.

78. Allan Smith, Maura Barrett, and Josh Lederman, "Bloomberg Spends about $7 Million Per Day on His Campaign, Latest Filing Shows," *NBC News*, February 20, 2020, https://www.nbcnews.com/politics/2020-election/bloomberg-spends-about-7-million-day-his-campaign-latest-filing-n1140001.

79. Steinhauser, "Bloomberg Rising in Polls."

80. Yue Stella Yu, "2020 Democrats Are Burning Cash Faster Than They Can Raise It," *OpenSecrets*, October 10, 2019, https://www.opensecrets.org/news/2019/10/2020-democrats-are-burning-cash-faster-than-they-can-raise-it.

81. Wesleyan Media Project, "Groups Mention Impeachment Issue in House Races; Total Ad Spending Approaches $300 Million in Presidential Race," https://mediaproject.wesleyan.edu/releases-121919/.

82. Busch and Pitney, *Divided We Stand*, 54–55.

83. Wesleyan Media Project, "Self-Funded Billionaires Drive Ad Spending Up 131% over 2016," https://mediaproject.wesleyan.edu/releases-012920/.

84. Busch and Pitney, *Divided We Stand*, 53–54.

85. Mollie Hemingway, "Panicked Democrat Establishment Turns to Bloomberg," February 19, 2020, https://thefederalist.com/2020/02/19/panicked-democrat-establishment-turns-to-bloomberg/.

86. Wesleyan Media Project, "Presidential Digital Ad Spending Nearly $200 Million," https://mediaproject.wesleyan.edu/releases-020520/.

87. Busch and Pitney, *Divided We Stand*, 58–60.

88. In figure 3.4, the net PCC expenditures were calculated by subtracting the Trump PCC expenditures from the Biden PCC expenditures in each time period; net party expenditures over outreach were calculated in the same fashion. The net independent expenditures were calculated in a similar way, except that expenditures against Trump were counted as pro-Biden (along with expenditures in support of

Biden) and expenditures against Biden were counted as pro-Trump (along with expenditures in support of Trump).

89. More than one-half (55 percent) of this extraordinary level of advertising was on broadcast TV, about one-quarter (24 percent) on digital media, almost one-fifth (19 percent) on cable and satellite TV, and the remaining (2 percent) on radio. Wesleyan Media Project, "Political Ads in 2020: Fast and Furious," https://mediaproject .wesleyan.edu/2020-summary-032321/.

90. Karl Evers-Hillstrom, "Political Campaigns Are Staying Home Amid the Coronavirus Pandemic," *OpenSecrets*, August 6, 2020, https://www.opensecrets.org/ news/2020/08/political-campaigns-stay-home-covid.

91. Ken Thomas, "Biden Campaign Indicates Priorities USA Is Preferred Super PAC," *Wall Street Journal*, April 15, 2020, https://www.wsj.com/articles/biden -campaign-indicates-priorities-usa-is-preferred-super-pac-11586986904; Paul Steinhauser, "Air Wars Heating Up as a Leading Pro-Biden Super PAC Announces Ad Blitz," Fox News, April 20, 2020, https://www.foxnews.com/politics/air-wars-heat-ing-up-as-a-leading-pro-biden-super-pac-announces-ad-blitz.

92. Brian Schwartz, "Biden and the DNC Start to Lay the Groundwork for a Joint Fund-Raising Effort to Take on Trump," *CNBC.com*, April 8, 2020, https:// www.cnbc.com/2020/04/08/biden-dnc-start-to-lay-the-groundwork-for-fund-rais-ing-committee-to-battle-trump.html.

93. Busch and Pitney, *Divided We Stand*, 90–91.

94. Wesleyan Media Project, "Senate Ads Spike; Eight Races See 10,000 Spots since May," https://mediaproject.wesleyan.edu/releases-070220/.

95. Karl Evers-Hillstrom, "Trump's Cash Advantage over Biden Is Shrinking," *OpenSecrets*, June 22, 2020, https://www.opensecrets.org/news/2020/06/trump-cash -advntg-over-biden-shrinks.

96. Wesleyan Media Project, "Record Breaking Volume of US House and US Senate Airings," https://mediaproject.wesleyan.edu/releases-090920/.

97. Sarah Ewall-Wice and Bo Erickson, "Joe Biden Shatters Record with $364.5 Million Haul in August," CBS News, September 2, 2020, https://www.cbsnews.com /news/biden-2020-campaign-364-5-million-fund-raising-committees-august/.

98. Theodore F. Sheckels, "The 2020 Conventions: As Productions, a Departure; as Rhetorical Exercises, Business as Usual," in *The 2020 Presidential Campaign*, ed. Robert E. Denton Jr. (Lanham, MD: Rowman & Littlefield, 2021), 23–46.

99. Karl Evers-Hillstrom, "Familiar Faces Bankroll DNC Convention Account," *OpenSecrets*, August 8, 2020, https://www.opensecrets.org/news/2020/08/familiar -faces-bankroll-dnc-convention-account; Kristen Welker, Carol E. Lee, Shannon Pettypiece, and Monica Alba, "Trump's Convention Cancellation Is Costing GOP Donors Millions," NBC News, July 24, 2020, https://www.nbcnews.com/poli-tics/2020-election/trump-s-convention-cancellation-costing-gop-donors-millions -n1234896.

100. Daniel Bice and Bill Glauber, "Milwaukee Host Committee Raised $42.7 Million for 2020 DNC, Projecting a Small Deficit," *Milwaukee Journal Sentinel*, October 15, 2020, https://www.jsonline.com/story/news/politics/elections/2020/10

/15/milwaukee-2020-dnc-host-committee-raised-less-than-convention-cost-virtual
/3652079001/.

101. Karl Evers-Hillstrom, "Who's Funding the Virtual Republican National
Convention?," *OpenSecrets*, August 20, 2020, https://www.opensecrets.org/news
/2020/08/virtual-republican-national-convention.

102. Sarah Mucha, "Biden Announces Record $383 Million Fund-Raising Haul
for September," CNN.com, October 15, 2020, https://www.cnn.com/2020/10/14/
politics/biden-september-fund-raising/index.html.

103. Wesleyan Media Project, "Biden Up Big in Ad War, Overtakes Trump in
Recent Digital Spend," https://mediaproject.wesleyan.edu/releases-100120/.

104. Eliana Miller, "As His Campaign Pulls Ads, Trump Considers Opening His
Own Wallet," *OpenSecrets*, September 9, 2020, https://www.opensecrets.org/news
/2020/09/920-donald-trump-considers-his-wallet.

105. Shane Goldmacher and Maggie Haberman, "How Trump's Billion-Dollar
Campaign Lost Its Cash Advantage," *New York Times*, September 7, 2020, sec. U.S.,
www.nytimes.com/2020/09/07/us/politics/trump-election-campaign-fund-raising
.html.

106. Busch and Pitney, *Divided We Stand*, 90.

107. Shane Goldmacher, "How Trump Steered Supporters into Unwitting Donations," *New York Times*, April 3, 2021, https://www.nytimes.com/2021/04/03/us/
politics/trump-donations.html.

108. Kenneth P. Vogel and Shane Goldmacher, "Democrats Decried Dark Money.
Then They Won with It in 2020," *New York Times*, January 29, 2022, https://www
.nytimes.com/2022/01/29/us/politics/democrats-dark-money-donors.html; Emma
Green, "The Massive Progressive Dark-Money Group You've Never Heard Of," *The
Atlantic*, November 2, 2021, https://www.theatlantic.com/politics/archive/2021/11/
arabella-advisors-money-democrats/620553/.

109. Wesleyan Media Project, "Pro-Dem Ad Advantage Up and Down the Ballot; Republican Airings More Negative," https://mediaproject.wesleyan.edu/releases
-102920/.

110. Nicole Goodkind, "The Biden Campaign Has Less Than Two Weeks to
Spend $180 Million—Here's What It Will Do," *Fortune*, October 23, 2020, https://
fortune.com/2020/10/23/biden-campaign-cash-on-hand-fund-raising-spending-lef
tover-money-2020-election/.

111. See https://www.opensecrets.org/2020-presidential-race/joe-biden/candi-
date?id=N00001669; https://www.opensecrets.org/2020-presidential-race/donald
-trump/candidate?id=N00023864.

112. A. B. Stoddard, "Dems Beware—the RNC Is Crushing It," RealClearPolitics, October 25, 2019, https://www.realclearpolitics.com/articles/2019/10/25/dems
_bewarethe_rnc_is_crushing_it_141582.html; Alex Thompson, "Trump's Campaign Knocks on a Million Doors a Week. Biden's Knocks on Zero," Politico, August
4, 2020, https://www.politico.com/news/2020/08/04/trump-joe-biden-campaign
-door-knockers-391454; Joshua Darr, "In 2020, the Ground Game Is All Trump,"

Mischiefs of Faction, October 9, 2020, https://www.mischiefsoffaction.com/post /2020-ground-game.

113. Tal Axelrod, "Republicans Surpass 150 Million Voter Contacts," *The Hill*, October 23, 2020, https://thehill.com/homenews/campaign/522399-republicans -surpass-150-million-voter-contacts?amp.

114. Charlotte Alter, "Inside Joe Biden Campaign's Plan to Get Out the Vote Online," Time, November 2, 2020, https://time.com/5906237/inside-joe-biden -campaigns-plan-to-get-out-the-vote-online/; Alex Roarty, "How the DNC Exorcised the Ghosts of 2016 and Helped Deliver a Biden Victory," McClatchydc.co m, November 23, 2020, https://www.mcclatchydc.com/news/politics-government/ election/article247323479.html.

115. Busch and Pitney, *Divided We Stand*, 147.

116. Zachary Scherer, "Majority of Voters Used Nontraditional Methods to Cast Ballots in 2020," April 29, 2021, https://www.census.gov/library/stories/2021/04/ what-methods-did-people-use-to-vote-in-2020-election.html.

117. Trump's PCC spent $36 million on postelection litigation.

118. Soo Rin Kim and Will Steakin, "How Trump, RNC Raised Hundreds of Millions Pushing Baseless Election Fraud Claims," ABCNews, February 3, 2021, https://abcnews.go.com/US/trump-rnc-raised-hundreds-millions-pushing-baseless -election/story?id=75633798.

119. Zach Montellaro and Elena Schneider, "Trump's Post-Election Cash Grab Floods Funds to New PAC," Politico, December 4, 2020, https://www.politico.com /news/2020/12/03/trump-pac-fund-raising-442775.

120. Karl Evers-Hillstrom, "Trump Has $105 Million in the Bank to Influence Intra-GOP Battles," *OpenSecrets*, February 1, 2021, https://www.opensecrets.org/ news/2021/02/trump-has-105-million-for-intra-gop-battles.

121. Susan Crabtree, "Democrats Dark Money Devotion," RealClearPolitics, January 13, 2023, https://www.realclearpolitics.com/articles/2023/01/13/democrats _dark-money_devotion_148723.html.

4

Financing the 2020 Congressional Elections

Molly E. Reynolds

In *Financing the 1960 Election*, Herbert E. Alexander paid little attention to the financing of congressional campaigns, largely due to the lack of detailed information on individual candidates.[1] Then, as in 2020, much of the attention was on the race at the top of the ticket. But the outcome of the contests for control of the U.S. House and U.S. Senate were no less consequential for governing, and in some ways, the overall results of these contests were more surprising than that of the presidential race. Thus, understanding the broader landscape of campaign finance in 2020 requires exploring congressional races as well.[2]

In 2020, spending in congressional campaigns set records; this cycle included nine of the ten most expensive Senate races and five of the ten most expensive House races in history.[3] Candidates raised significantly more money for their campaigns in 2020 than in 2016, thanks in large part to a large increase in contributions from individuals. For many individual contributors, these donations represented an expressive political act during a global pandemic, often directed to candidates beyond the district or state in which they lived, when other forms of political activity were more limited. Spending by outside groups, especially by Super PACs, also increased dramatically between 2016 and 2020, suggesting that congressional campaigns will likely continue to be big-money affairs in the years to come.

THE CONTEXT OF THE 2020
CONGRESSIONAL ELECTIONS

As has been documented widely in the political science literature, congressional elections in the twenty-first century are highly nationalized, with declining levels of ticket splitting. This pattern has resulted in a decrease of the incumbency advantage for current officeholders.[4] In 2016, for example, there were no states in which a Senate candidate of one party won while the presidential candidate of the other party received the state's Electoral College votes. Indeed, it was the first presidential election since the universal implementation of direct election of senators in 1914 in which there were no split states.[5]

Against this structural backdrop, Democrats entered the 2020 congressional campaign season defending a majority in one chamber—the House—for the first time since 2014, when the party controlled (but ultimately lost) the Senate. The party's success in the 2018 election was in line with the strong historical pattern: the party that controlled the White House lost seats in each first midterm election of each presidential term but one—2002, when Republicans gained seats two years into George W. Bush's term.

In 2018, Democrats won 42 seats in districts previously held by Republicans.[6] Of these, 30 were in races where an incumbent lost and 12 were open races. Hillary Clinton won a majority of these districts in 2016, with Donald Trump winning only 11 of the 42. Notably, the districts that fueled Democrats' majority were largely suburban, with only two classified "pure rural" and just one "pure urban."[7]

The population of these districts was also both slightly whiter than the average congressional district (75 percent versus 72 percent, respectively) and better educated, as measured by the share of the population over eighteen with at least a bachelor's degree (36 percent versus 30 percent, respectively).[8] Indeed, the Democrats' overall electorate in 2018 was well educated, with half of Democratic voters having at least a four-year degree.[9] Voter turnout among groups central to the Democratic coalition, including white voters with college degrees and black voters, was up from the previous midterms in 2014 by twelve percentage points and eleven percentage points, respectively.[10] Strong turnout for Democrats in 2018 was consistent with the history of midterm elections dating to the 1970s, when a Republican was in the White House; Democrats were generally able to close their midterm turnout gap with Republicans.[11]

Whether this turnout advantage could be maintained in 2020 was one factor that stood to affect Democrats' fortunes. Another was the degree to which the 2018 results had left the party "overextended": heading into 2020, thirty-one House Democrats represented districts that Trump had carried in

2016 as compared to only three House Republicans elected from districts that Clinton had won.[12]

Even with questions about turnout and the distribution of the seats in the Democrats' majority, however, forecasters still predicted a successful election night. The *Cook Political Report*, for example, had five Republican-held seats rated as "likely" or "lean" Democratic in its last preelection update. (Two of these were in North Carolina, which had undergone a court-ordered redistricting that advantaged Democrats before the 2020 cycle.) In addition, no seats held by Democrats were forecasted by *Cook* as "lean" or "likely" Republican.[13] The competitive seats were also largely clustered in states that Joe Biden was expected to win. Of the twenty-seven seats that *Cook* rated as toss-ups, sixteen were states also categorized as either "lean," "likely," or "solid" Democrat in the presidential race, whereas only five were in "lean," "likely," or "solid" Republican states.[14] The strength of straight-ticket voting, the overall trends toward the nationalization of congressional elections, the overlap between competitive congressional races and areas where Biden was expected to do well were all positive signs for Democratic congressional candidates.[15] At the same time, decisions on where and how to invest resources at the presidential level are often connected to expectations about how spending will affect down-ballot races.[16]

In the Senate, meanwhile, of the thirteen states that *Cook* rated as "toss-up" or "lean" in its final preelection rating, eight also had Senate races. Democrats entered the cycle defending fewer seats than Republicans—twelve versus twenty-three, respectively—but given the Republicans' 53-47 margin in the chamber following the 2018 elections, Democrats needed a three-seat net gain and to win the presidency (and with it, the tie-breaking vote of the vice president) to take control of the chamber. Of races with Democratic incumbents, the seat held by Doug Jones in Alabama—which Jones had won unexpectedly in a special election in 2017—was considered the most vulnerable throughout the entire cycle; Democrats were also defending one seat in a state that Trump won in 2016 (Michigan).

For Republicans, meanwhile, the most competitive races at the start of the cycle included two in states that Clinton won in 2016 (Colorado and Maine). The contest in Arizona was also expected to be competitive. Not only had Clinton received 48 percent of the two-party vote there in 2016, but the Republican-controlled seat was held by Martha McSally. McSally had lost a Senate race in the state in November 2018 to Kyrsten Sinema, but when Jon Kyl, who was serving as an appointed successor after the death of John McCain earlier in the year, resigned in December, Arizona Governor Doug Ducey appointed McSally to the seat until the scheduled special election in 2020.

Because Democrats would need to *net* three Senate seats while also winning the White House to gain a majority, however, coverage for much of the cycle focused on what other seats appeared winnable for the party's candidates. Given how narrowly Republican Thom Tillis had won his seat in an otherwise pro-Republican year in 2014, North Carolina was also a top target for a Democratic pickup. After Montana Governor Steve Bullock withdrew from the Democratic presidential primary and entered the Senate race, it was also seen as competitive.

Shifts over several previous cycles in voting patterns in Georgia, where Clinton received 47 percent of the vote in 2016 and Democratic gubernatorial candidate Stacey Abrams won 49 percent of the vote in 2018, also suggested that that state's Senate race between Republican David Perdue and Jon Ossoff could be competitive. When Georgia's other Republican senator, Johnny Isakson, resigned due to health issues in December 2019, that set up a second special election in 2020, in which Kelly Loeffler, the Republican appointed to fill the vacancy, would have to defend the seat for the balance of Isakson's term. Under Georgia election law, the regularly scheduled contest between Perdue and Ossoff would go to a runoff in January 2021 if neither candidate got more than 50 percent of the vote. In the special election, meanwhile, there would be no primary; rather, all candidates would be on the ballot in November, and if none received at least 50 percent of the vote, then that contest, too, would go to a runoff. While Democrats largely coalesced behind Raphael Warnock, Loeffler faced a significant challenge from Representative Doug Collins. It was widely expected that at least the special election would not be decided until after the runoff.[17]

Beginning in early 2020, another contextual factor loomed over this distribution of competitive seats in the House and Senate: the COVID-19 pandemic. Campaigns found themselves facing widespread limits on in-person activities at the time when they would generally be ramping up those types of functions—including fund-raisers.[18] The economic consequences of the pandemic were also expected, at least initially, to make it more difficult for candidates to raise funds, especially from small donors who were more likely to be hit hard by the downturn. And incumbents, with established fund-raising bases, were expected to be penalized less relative to challengers.[19]

THE STRUCTURE OF CONGRESSIONAL CAMPAIGN FINANCE

In total, House and Senate candidates raised about $4 billion during the 2020 cycle, almost twice the $1.6 billion raised during the 2015–16 period.[20]

Table 4.1   Average Source of House and Senate Candidates' Receipts, 2020 Congressional Elections (hundreds of thousands of dollars)

	House			Senate		
	Incumbents	*Challengers*	*Open*	*Incumbents*	*Challengers*	*Open*
Party Committees	0.2	0.2	0.3	4.9	4.4	1.1
Candidates	0.2	0.9	3.5	7.6	3.1	9.9
PACs	8.4	0.8	2.4	21.6	3.7	7.6
Individuals	18.3	9.9	15.1	212.8	327	67.2
Transfers	1.7	0.3	0.8	23.5	11.1	2.1
Total	28.7	12.1	22.1	270.4	349.3	87.9

Source: OpenSecrets, analysis of FEC, www.fec.gov/campaign-finance-data/congressional-candidate-data -summary-tables/?year=2020&segment=24

As in the past, the congressional campaigns were funded by what one party campaign operative has described as a "three-legged stool" of money raised by candidates, funds from party groups, and financial resources from non-party organizations[21] As shown in table 4.1, individual candidates received funds for their principal campaign committees (PCCs) from a number of different sources in 2020.

In the House, on average, incumbents raised the most, followed by open-seat candidates and then challengers. This pattern represents a change from 2016, where individuals running in open seats brought in slightly more on average than incumbents.[22] As can be seen in the first row of table 4.1, a relatively small share of these funds came from the four major party congressional campaign committees (CCCs, including the Democratic Congressional Campaign Committee [DCCC], the National Republican Congressional Committee [NRCC], the Democratic Senatorial Campaign Committee [DSCC], and the National Republican Senatorial Committee [NRSC]). Legal limits set how much the CCCs can give to candidates' PCCs as well as CCCs coordinated expenditures to assist their candidates (see chapter 2).

The third and fourth rows on table 4.1 report that House candidates raised the most money, by far, from individual contributions, which also represents a departure from 2016. In 2020, House incumbents raised twice as much, on average, from individuals as they did from Traditional PACs (see chapter 2); in 2016, these figures were roughly equal. For House challengers, the average total that individuals contributed was twelve times the amount raised from Traditional PACs as compared to approximately four times in 2016. Open-seat candidates, meanwhile, raised, on average, six times more from individuals than from Traditional PACs in 2020 versus approximately 3.5 times more in 2016.

Importantly, the widening of this gap between individual donations and those from Traditional PACs was largely driven by increases in the amounts raised from individuals, as opposed to reductions in the amounts from Traditional PACs. (Only open-seat candidates saw a small reduction in the average amount raised from Traditional PACs between the two cycles.) This pattern occurred despite a record number of Democratic candidates pledging not to take any donations from Traditional PACs of corporations in 2020.[23] Contributions from Traditional PACs, while perhaps diminishing somewhat in influence especially in comparison to Super PACs, continue to be an important source of funds, but they were simply outpaced by individual donations in 2020. (See chapter 6 on PAC spending.)

The Traditional PAC donations listed in table 4.1 include those from Leadership PACs (LPAC in this chapter), which are committees created by individual House members and senators to raise funds and then direct them to their colleagues. Originally largely a tool of House and Senate leaders, many rank-and-file members now also sponsor LPACs and distribute funds strategically to aid their personal and partisan goals.[24]

Indeed, table 4.2 displays the various forms of party-connected giving directly to candidate PCCs. LPAC contributions represent by far the largest form of such giving. In the House, LPAC contributions to Republicans enjoyed a very slight advantage (roughly $1.1 million) over Democrats. Importantly, this gap between House Republicans and Democrats was much larger in both 2012 and 2016, with Republican candidates receiving almost twice as much as their Democratic counterparts in LPAC contributions.[25] In a similar departure from the 2012 and 2016 cycles, House Democratic candidates also received more from other candidates' PCCs in 2020 than did their Republican peers.

On the Senate side, as table 4.1 indicates, challengers raised, on average, roughly one and one-half times their incumbent counterparts—a difference

Table 4.2   Party-Connected Contributions, 2020 Congressional Elections

	House		Senate	
	Democrats	Republicans	Democrats	Republicans
Leaderships PACs (LPACs)	19,954,489	21,033,961	8,414,137	9,164,763
Other Candidates (PCCs)	8,337,632	5,634,753	526,854	437,208
Congressional Retirees and Members Not Up for Reelection	535,331	653,388	179,680	113,850
PACs Sponsored by Nonfederal Politicians	9,400	2,000	2,800	0
Total	28,836,852	27,324,102	9,123,471	9,715,821

Source: OpenSecrets, analysis of FEC bulk data, https://www.fec.gov/data/browse-data/?tab=bulk-data, "Any transaction from one committee to another"; OpenSecrets industry coding of FEC bulk data, https://www.opensecrets.org/industries/methodology.php

driven largely by significant differences in the average level of individual contributions. The average Senate challenger raised roughly $11.4 million more from individual donors than the typical Senate incumbent, thanks in part to significant amounts of "expressive" small donations from individuals in several high-profile Senate races. Notably, the individual contributions in many of these races tended to come from outside of the state in which the contest was happening.[26] The overall lower spending levels in open-seat races, meanwhile, are likely because 2020 had only four such contests—in Kansas, New Mexico, Tennessee, and Wyoming. Of these, only the Kansas race was considered at all competitive,[27] and although that race set records for spending in the state, it saw a lower total amount of spending compared to other Senate races.[28]

Unlike in the House, Senate Republicans maintained the advantage in LPAC giving in 2020 that they enjoyed in 2016, though the gap shrank by about 40 percent between the two cycles ($1.8 million versus $750,000, respectively). Table 4.2 also shows a slight Democratic edge in contributions from other candidates in the Senate—a category where Republicans had a significant advantage in 2016. Together, across both chambers, 2020 saw the two parties come much closer to parity in these forms of party-connected contributions; Democrats had a roughly $1 million advantage as compared to the $14 million lead Republicans enjoyed in 2016.

It is also worth noting that, depending on the candidate, funds from joint fund-raising committees (JFCs) can also represent a significant source of funds; some congressional candidates participate in several.[29] JFCs are structures that allow a donor to make a single contribution that is then shared across multiple individual candidates, parties, or Traditional PACs. Although their use predates the Supreme Court's 2014 decision in *McCutcheon v. Federal Election Commission*, the court's abolition of aggregate individual limits on federal political giving made them a more attractive tool; in the absence of overall individual limits, a single JFC could collect contributions for more individual candidate or party committees post-*McCutcheon* (see chapter 2).

In the House, although the average amount received by an incumbent in transfers from other committees (most of which represent transfers from JFCs) was only about 6 percent of total receipts, the amount was much higher for some candidates, especially members of the House leadership. For Republican whip Rep. Steve Scalise (R-LA), for example, transfers from other committees represented approximately 27 percent of all receipts by his PCC in 2020. In the Senate, meanwhile, incumbents and challengers both received more, on average, via transfers from other committees than they did in Traditional PAC contributions. For incumbents, the average total transfers ($2.35 million) were only slightly larger than the average total Traditional PAC contributions ($2.16 million), but for challengers, the average received via transfers was approximately three times the average raised from Traditional PACs ($1.1 million versus $370,000, respectively). Although some of the funds a candidate received via transfers are themselves sourced from Traditional PACs, most come originally from individuals.

Although contributions or transfers directly to candidates' PCCs are an important source of funding for their campaigns, the largest part of the second leg of the three-legged stool—party independent expenditures—also represent a key investment of resources. Party independent expenditures can take a variety of forms, including advertising and direct mail, that advocate for the election or defeat of a given candidate. But they must be "independent"—that is, undertaken without any consultation or coordination with the candidate's campaign (see chapter 2). CCCs may engage in unlimited amounts of independent expenditures on behalf of a candidate, and as a result, they comprise a significant majority of party spending in congressional elections. Figure 4.1 displays the expenditures by party and chamber in 2020 and demonstrates how independent expenditures by the party CCCs were the primary form of their spending in 2020.

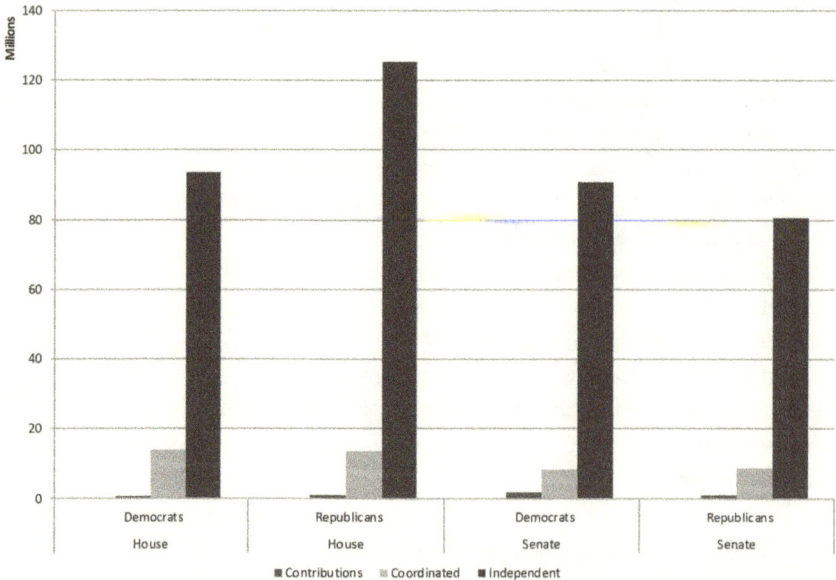

Figure 4.1 Party Contributions, Coordinated Expenditures, and Independent Expenditures, 2020 Congressional Elections. *Source*: OpenSecrets, compiled from FEC reports (including national, state, and local parties)

All told, Republican CCCs outspent Democratic ones by roughly $21 million in 2020, though this advantage is not consistent across the chambers. In the House, Republican committees spent approximately $31 million more than their Democratic counterparts—almost all in independent expenditures. In the Senate, meanwhile, Democratic committees spent roughly $10 million more than Republican ones with the difference coming, again, largely from independent expenditures. The Republican advantage in party independent expenditures gave the party an overall edge over Democrats that it did not enjoy in 2016.

The final leg of the stool is independent expenditures by nonparty organizations for or opposed to candidates, which is displayed in table 4.3. These expenditures are not associated with candidates' PCCs, but unlike the expenditures captured in figure 4.1, were made by a variety of groups: the parties' CCCs ($385 million), Traditional PACs ($65 million, plus nearly $5 million in internal communications to their members),[30] and tax-exempt groups ($33 million). However, the most significant—both in size and substance—within this category is independent expenditures by Super and Hybrid PACs (a combined total of $1.66 billion; see chapters 5 and 6). In 2020 nearly 80 percent of all nonparty spending in congressional races came from Super PACs—a figure that is up from the first full cycle, 2012, involving such organizations when it was about half of all nonparty spending. In addition, the amount of Super PAC spending has also continued to rise dramatically. In 2016, Super PACs spent approximately $487 million in congressional races; in 2020, that number had increased to $1.4 billion—an increase of 189 percent.

Super PACs, which can raise unlimited amounts but are restricted to making independent expenditures only, take several forms (chapter 6). One type of Super PAC is affiliated with issue-based organizations already involved in politics by other means. In 2020, for example, issue groups with opposite

Table 4.3 Noncandidate Spending in 2020 Congressional Races, Independent Expenditures and Internal Communications

Super PACs (IEs)	1,408,254,497
Tax-Exempt Groups (IEs)	33,477,777
Traditional PACs (IEs)	65,040,542
Hybrid PACs (IEs)	250,380,219
Internal Communications	4,637,012
Party Committees (IEs)	385,414,614
Other IEs	3,687,695
Total	2,150,892,356

Source: OpenSecrets, compiled from FEC reports

positions on gun control—Everytown for Gun Safety and the National Rifle Association—both had issue-based Super PACs that spent more than $19 million on independent expenditures across a range of races.[31]

A second type of Super PAC may be more consequential for congressional elections: Super PACs aligned with each of the major party leaders in each chamber: Senate Majority PAC (SMP; Senate Republicans) and Congressional Leadership Fund (CLF; House Republicans), Senate Leadership Fund (SLF; Senate Democrats) and House Majority PAC (HMP; House Democrats). These party-aligned Super PACs represent a different way for party-connected resources to be spent on behalf of candidates beyond the spending done by the parties' CCCs. Approximately 60 percent of all Super PAC spending in 2020 was done by one of these four groups, or by one of two entities funded entirely by the SLF and SMP, the PeachTree PAC and The Georgia Way, respectively. By comparison, in 2012—the first full cycle in which Super PACs were involved—these entities represented roughly one-third of all Super PAC spending in congressional elections. By 2016, that share had increased to approximately half. The 2020 figure, then, marks a continued increase in the share of Super PAC spending in congressional elections that flows through party-aligned committees.

In 2020, as shown in table 4.4, there was an increase in the advantage in this type of spending for congressional Republicans, who outraised Democratic-aligned groups by roughly $90 million. Indeed, spending by the House Republicans' CLF was credited for helping minimize Democrats' gains in the chamber even as Biden won the presidency. CLF's total spending was a record for a House-focused Super PAC, helping Republican candidates keep pace with the high levels of fund-raising and spending by Democratic campaigns—including by, in some races, engaging in most of the ad spending.[32]

A third type of Super PAC is aligned with a single candidate. In 2020, twenty-eight candidate-aligned Super PACs spent at least $1 million either for or against twenty-three different candidates in a primary and/or general election. Although such candidate-aligned Super PACs can represent valuable support for a candidate, they can have several potential disadvantages

Table 4.4   Major Party-Aligned Super PACs, 2019–20 Congressional Elections

Senate Majority Project	246,208,165
House Majority PAC	138,867,515
Senate Leadership Fund	331,577,046
Congressional Leadership Fund	142,524,130
Total	859,176,856

Source: OpenSecrets, compiled from FEC reports

as well, including less adherence to a common party message. Candidate-aligned Super PACs have been used more heavily by Republicans than by Democrats—especially in the Senate, where the party did not have an aligned Super PAC until the 2016 cycle. This trend generally continued in 2020, where six Super PACs aligned with individual Senate candidates spent more than $10 million in total. Of these, the top spender was Georgia Honor, a Super PAC associated with Warnock that spent $19.2 million. The other five, however, were all connected to Republicans: incumbents McSally (AZ), Graham (SC), McConnell (KY), and Collins (ME), plus challenger John James of Michigan. And whereas the three other candidate-aligned Super PACs spending more than $5 million were associated with Democrats, they were not among the party's top priority races (Al Gross of Alaska and Barbara Bollier of Kansas, who had two). In total, candidate-aligned Super PACs in Senate races spent roughly $148 million in 2020—a small fraction of the overall Super PAC spending in these races.[33]

SMALL DONATIONS IN 2020

The health, social, and economic consequences of the COVID-19 pandemic in 2020 were profound and widespread, leaving few aspects of American life untouched—including, in its earliest months, campaign fund-raising. Contributions to the six major political party committees—including the CCCs—were lower in parts of April 2020 than they were at the equivalent point in the 2016 cycle, despite overall levels of fund-raising being higher in 2020 than 2016. Individual contributions to all federal candidates were similarly affected in the early days of the pandemic: based on a seven-day rolling average, contribution levels in 2020 were three to four times higher than they were in 2016 but declined steeply starting in the middle of March.[34]

As the year wore on, however, it became clear that initial concerns on the part of campaigns about their ability to raise funds in the wake of pandemic disruption were largely unfounded, thanks, in part, to an increased share of small donations. By the end of October, small donations comprised 22 percent of all 2020 fund-raising, as compared to 15 percent over the equivalent period in 2016.[35] This trend was aided by several technological developments that predated the COVID-19 pandemic but proved increasingly important for connecting with potential donors of small contributions during the public health crisis. These include the use of email and text message solicitations, including texts sent by volunteers to voters, and of the fund-raising platforms ActBlue and WinRed. The former, used by Democratic candidates, was founded in 2004, while the 2020 election marked the first cycle for the latter, created in 2019 for Republican candidates. In both cases, the platforms allow users to save payment information and are thus explicitly designed to ease the process of repeated giving.[36]

As a result, tabulating the share of a candidate's fund-raising that comes in individual small donations of less than $200 captures something different than the true number of individual small donors. A given individual often makes a series of small, discrete contributions of less than $200 to a specific candidate, but over the course of the full cycle, ultimately donates a much larger sum to that campaign. In one of the two Georgia Senate races, for example, Jon Ossoff raised $42 million in itemized contributions of $200 or less, indicating that he received a significant number of donations from contributors who gave more than $200 in total but broke up that giving into smaller distinct pieces.

But examining the kinds of candidates whose campaigns raised large sums through small contributions—even if the donors who made them contributed larger sums in total—does illustrate several interesting dynamics. On the House side, of the top five candidates who raised the most in small donations, three were members of the House leadership: Scalise, at $21.3 million; Speaker of the House Nancy Pelosi (D-CA), at $19.2 million; and House minority leader Kevin McCarthy (D-CA), at $15.7 million. Other top fund-raisers via small donations include individuals whose own seats are safe but who have significant national profiles, such as Reps. Alexandria Ocasio-Cortez (D-NY), Devin Nunes (R-CA), Jim Jordan (R-OH), Adam Schiff (D-CA), and Dan Crenshaw (R-TX). Indeed, of the top ten raisers of small donations, only three—Nunes, Crenshaw, and Katie Porter (D-CA)—ultimately won their races with less than 60 percent of the vote.

A second notable trend in small dollar contributions involves the challengers who raised large total amounts via small discrete donations. In House races, of the five challengers who collected the largest sums in small contributions, only one, Wendy Davis in Texas's 21st congressional district, was running in a competitive race, ultimately receiving 47 percent of the two-party vote. Davis had, however, risen to national prominence in 2013 when she engaged in a talking filibuster to delay passage of antiabortion legislation in the Texas state senate and subsequently ran for governor in 2014.[37] The other four top challengers—none of whom got more than 29 percent of the two-party vote in their districts—were all running against high-profile House Democratic incumbents of color and, in some cases, relied on dubious tactics as part of their fund-raising efforts. Kimberly Klacik, a Republican running against Kweisi Mfume in Maryland's Baltimore-based 7th congressional district, for example, attracted substantial contributions after a three-minute video from her campaign was promoted by President Trump and went viral. Of the $8.3 million she raised by the end of her campaign, almost $3.7 million was paid to Olympic Media, a company hired to promote her now-famous video. Another unsuccessful challenger, Lacy Johnson (who ran against Democrat Ilhan Omar in Minnesota's Minneapolis-based 5th congressional district), reported working with a vendor that retained 80 percent of any funds raised from new donors.[38]

On the Senate side, the small donation landscape looked somewhat different. Of the top ten campaigns that raised the most in small donations, four were the Democratic and Republican candidates in the two Georgia races that were not resolved until runoff elections in early January 2021 (Ossoff, Warnock, Perdue, and Loeffler). Indeed, these two races were both the most expensive congressional elections ever and ultimately quite close, with Ossoff winning 50.6 percent of the vote in one race, and Warnock winning 51 percent of the vote in the other one.[39] But the other six candidates who brought in the largest amounts via small donations were a mix of winners and losers, in competitive and uncompetitive races alike. Mark Kelly, a Democrat who defeated incumbent Republican Martha McSally in Arizona with 51 percent of the vote, was the highest-raising successful challenger outside of Georgia, with more than $53 million in small contributions.

Three other unsuccessful Democratic challengers—Sara Gideon in Maine, Jaime Harrison in South Carolina, and Amy McGrath in Kentucky—also brought in more than $30 million each via small donations. Of these, Gideon's race was considered the most competitive, but ultimately, she only won roughly 45 percent of the two-party vote against incumbent Republican Susan Collins. Harrison—who also raised more than $83 million via small contributions—fared similarly against Lindsey Graham in South Carolina, winning approximately 45 percent of the two-party vote. McGrath managed to raise more than $58 million via small donations en route to just 40 percent of the two-party vote against Republican leader Mitch McConnell.

Together, these examples tell an important story about contemporary campaign donations: that many small contributions are not made strategically by the individuals who make them. As political scientist Eitan Hersh has described it, "rather than stopping and thinking and planning a strategy . . . many online donors are just acting expressively."[40] The circumstances of the 2020 election—including a global pandemic that restricted a wide range of other traditional political activities; and discrete events, such as the death of Supreme Court Justice Ruth Bader Ginsburg, that prompted surges in online giving[41]—appear to have only encouraged more of this behavior.

Data that OpenSecrets compiled on the share of candidates' contribu-tions composed of donations from out-of-state individuals (of all sizes, not just small donations) also illustrates this nationalization of congressional races. For House general-election candidates, the median percent raised from in-district donors was comparable in 2012 and 2016 (36 percent and 34 percent, respectively) before dropping to 29 percent in 2020.[42] For Senate incumbents, the median share of in-state contributions fell slightly between 2012 and 2016 (from 47 percent to 44 percent) and then declined more substantially, to 38 percent, in 2020.[43]

WHO GIVES TO WHOM?

Funds raised by members of Congress from their colleagues are important because they represent a key investment by legislators in the shared party goal of maintaining or gaining majority party control of Congress. Although parties that hold majorities, even unified ones across the House, Senate, and White House, are often frustrated in pursuit of their policy goals,[44] majority status remains a key aim of legislative parties. In addition to legislative power, for example, members of the majority party appear to bring home more fed-eral funds to their states.[45]

One element of this effort involves the resources expended directly by the four party CCCs in the form of direct contributions and coordinated expen-ditures (see figure 4.1 for overall amounts of coordinated expenditures by parties). Generally, these groups have targeted their direct contributions to competitive races and on potentially vulnerable incumbents,[46] and in 2016, this held across three of the four CCCs, with the DCCC giving to roughly equal numbers of vulnerable and nonvulnerable candidates. In 2020, the Senate committees continued this focus. Three-quarters of the campaigns to which the DSCC made direct transfers were in competitive races; for the NRSC, it was 70 percent. In the House, however, both the DCCC and the NRCC gave to candidates in competitive and noncompetitive races at much more similar rates: roughly half of the campaigns to which both committees made direct contributions were competitive and roughly half were not. For the NRCC, these direct investments in noncompetitive races represented a change from the committee's strategy in 2016, where most of its transfers were to campaigns in competitive contests. One consequence of this change for House Republicans was to narrow the gap with House Democrats in the number of races in which the committee made direct contributions. In 2016, the DCCC made direct contributions to roughly five times more candidates than the NRCC (108 versus 22) as compared to approximately one and one-half times more in 2020 (127 versus 79).

A second component of fund-raising as a means of pursuing majority status involves contributions by members to their CCCs; the parties communicate expectations to their members about these donations, often referred to as "party dues." House members and senators who are invested in having their party maintain or obtain the majority may see their party's chamber-specific campaign operation as an important tool in this effort and contribute from their own operations accordingly. At the same time, during a period of intra-party conflict, legislators may decide purposefully to withhold contributions from their party's committee as a signal of their displeasure of various kinds with the leadership. In 2020, for example, some House Democrats from the progressive wing of the caucus—including the cochairs of the Congressional Progressive Caucus, Reps. Pramila Jayapal (D-WA) and Mark Pocan (D-WI)—initially refused to make their expected contributions to the DCCC. At issue was a policy that the Democrats' campaign arm adopted stipulating that it would not work with any consultants who also worked for Democratic candidates challenging Democratic incumbents.[47] The disputes may also be more personal in nature, such as when, in 2019, House Republican Conference Vice Chair Mark Walker (R-NC) withheld his dues from the NRCC after the committee declined to pay his legal expenses related to a criminal case against the chair of the North Carolina state Republican Party.[48] In addition, members may be pursuing personal goals in addition to (or, potentially, in lieu of) collective aims with their contributions to party committees. Recent research documents, for example, the expectations that the NRCC and DCCC place on House members from each party who are seeking committee leadership positions: legislators who serve as committee leaders, or who are hoping to ascend to these positions in the future, are expected to raise large sums for their party's chamber-specific campaign arm.[49]

In 2020, 162 House incumbents seeking reelection gave to the DCCC. The overall average contribution was roughly $172,000, but this was inflated by an exceptionally large donation from Speaker Pelosi; she gave $1.9 million, which is more than twice more than the next largest contribution ($895,000, from DCCC Chair Cheri Bustos of Illinois). Without Pelosi's contribution included, the average donation was roughly $162,000. On the Republican side, 115 incumbents seeking reelection contributed to the NRCC with an average donation of approximately $285,000—but like Democrats, this figure is inflated by a particularly large contribution of $12.5 million from Republican Whip Steve Scalise (R-LA). The average across other Republicans was much lower—roughly $178,000—but still higher than for Democrats.[50] On the Senate side, meanwhile, only ten Democratic incumbents gave to the DSCC, with an average contribution of roughly $132,000. Nine of their Republican colleagues donated an average of $320,000 each. This represents a shift from earlier years, when Democrats were more successful in terms of both participation and typical size of contribution.[51]

Both House members and senators also make contributions directly to their colleagues' campaigns, either via their PCCs or LPACs. The latter vehicle allows larger contributions than the former ($2,000 versus $5,000). Both approaches are common in the House. Roughly two-thirds of House members made contributions to other candidates from their PCCs. Democrats were more likely to do so than Republicans, but the average size of the total donations made to other House candidates by members of both parties was roughly the same.[52] Contributions to colleagues from PCCs, on the other hand, were much less frequent in the Senate. Only nine senators (six Republicans and three Democrats) used this approach, and their investments were in a small number of races. All six GOP senators gave to their two colleagues running for reelection in Georgia, Perdue and Loeffler, and all three Democrats contributed to Doug Jones.

Roughly 80 percent of House members and nearly all senators gave to colleagues via their LPACs. In both chambers, Democrats gave slightly larger average totals (approximately $101,000 in the House and roughly $158,000 in the Senate) than Republicans (roughly $95,000 in the House and approximately $149,000 in the Senate). As we would expect, incumbent legislators from both parties in both chambers tended to give more from their LPACs to candidates running in competitive races than in safe ones. The typical amount a House member received from colleagues' LPACs was slightly higher for Republican incumbents ($62,000) than their Democratic counterparts ($57,000). In the Senate, this pattern was reversed, with Democratic incumbents receiving, on average, approximately $313,000 from colleagues, and Republican incumbents netting, on average, roughly $266,000. This difference may reflect the fact that nearly twice as many incumbent Republicans as Democrats were running for reelection in 2020, requiring sitting GOP senators to spread around their resources to more races; more of the Republican-held seats than Democratic ones were competitive as well.

Importantly, donations among colleagues can also perform other important functions. Recent sessions of Congress have seen intra-party caucuses, such as the Freedom Caucus and the Progressive Caucus among House Republicans and Democrats, respectively, play an important role in structuring legislative negotiation.[53] Membership in these groups also helps individual legislators establish their brands and reputations within the broader party. There is evidence, for example, that party factions do establish distinct voting records and that these brands also appear to attract distinctive sets of donors to members themselves.[54] This relationship between intra-party caucus membership and campaign financing extends to giving among members themselves. In recent Congresses, legislators donated to their fellow faction members more frequently than to other colleagues. In addition, party leaders, especially Republican ones, appear to withhold contributions from members who join intra-party caucuses—likely because active factions can make leaders' legislative lives more difficult.[55]

SPENDING BY INCUMBENTS VERSUS CHALLENGERS

In 2020, as in other recent election years, incumbents were overwhelmingly successful in winning reelection to the House and Senate: approximately 95 percent of House members and 84 percent of senators who ran for reelection won. Indeed, incumbents continue to outraise and outspend their challengers on average, and research suggests that interest groups, seeking access to lawmakers once in office, create a financial advantage for the incumbent's party.[56] But it is difficult to discern whether the financial advantages that incumbents enjoy—both in the form of their campaigns' own spending and of spending by outside groups on their behalf—are responsible for their success in elections.

One reason it is difficult to definitively determine the exact relationship between incumbents' financial advantages and their electoral success arises from the possibility of strategic behavior by potential challengers. A substantial literature explores whether incumbents successfully "scare off" challengers by recruiting individuals who would mount the strongest candidacies (often referred to as "high-quality" challengers). Recent empirical work on the size of such scare-off effects suggests that the degree to which experienced challengers avoid entering races varies.[57]

To the extent that scare off occurs, it could be driven, at least in part, by the deterrent effect on challengers of an incumbent raising large sums. If an incumbent has amassed a significant war chest, it may lead experienced potential challengers to sit out the race. If a less-experienced or lower-quality candidate enters instead, that may, in turn, lead the incumbent to enjoy an even larger fund-raising advantage. Attempts to establish a causal effect of larger war chests that incumbents held on successfully deterred challengers have found limited evidence,[58] though it is possible this work understates the relationship.[59]

Although many discussions of scare-off effects involve the general election, the prospect of primary challenges to incumbents may also distort the perceived relationship between incumbent spending and electoral success. Notably, candidates are not required by the FEC to specify whether their spending is for the purposes of a primary- or general-election campaign, and we cannot assume that spending that occurs before a primary was explicitly spent on contesting that nominating contest. But incumbents who are concerned about the possibility of primary challengers have an incentive to raise large sums. There is reason to believe that this effect could have been especially pronounced in 2020, which was one of the most competitive primary cycles in at least a decade. Eight incumbents were defeated in primaries, and the cycle featured more competitive primary challengers than any year since 1992. This increase in competitiveness of primaries was especially notable on the Democratic side, as members of the party have generally faced fewer serious primary challengers than their Republican colleagues in the past several decades.[60]

Despite these limitations, exploring the difference in spending between incumbents and challengers, as well as in open-seat races, is still of potential interest—especially because combining outside spending on behalf of a candidate with the spending by that candidate's campaign can help illustrate how different forms of raising and spending may offset each other. As can be seen in table 4.5, incumbents significantly outspent challengers in both the House and Senate. In the House, this advantage was roughly $1.3 million on average—approximately the same size as in 2016. In the Senate, though, it was approximately $6.5 million, which represents a larger gap than four years earlier.[61]

Open-seat races often have sizable inequities in spending between candidates. The right side of table 4.5 displays, for the House and Senate, a

Table 4.5 Average House and Senate General Election Candidate Campaign Expenditures, 2020 Congressional Elections

	Incumbent	Challenger	Gap (I–C)	Open Seat— High (H)	Open Seat— Low (L)	Open Seat Gap (H–L)
House	2,443,905	1,141,360	1,341,193.98	2,710,107	1,149,648	1,777,696
N	(385)	(329)	(329)	(50)	(44)	(44)
Senate	31,353,238	24,895,972	6,457,266	12,958,624	3,263,399	9,695,225
N	(31)	(31)	(31)	(8)	(8)	(8)

Source: OpenSecrets, compiled from FEC reports

Table 4.6   Average Nonparty Spending on Behalf of Candidates, 2020 Congressional Elections

	Incumbent (I)	Challenger (C)	Gap (I–C)	Open Seat— High (H)	Open Seat— Low (L)	Open Seat Gap (H–L)
House	722,605	681,312	41,293	2,230,970	2,382,871	688,750
N	(385)	(329)	(329)	(50)	(44)	(44)
Senate	24,488,553	21,034,205	3,454,348	7,918,730	2,653,375	5,265,355
N	(31)	(31)	(31)	(8)	(8)	(8)

Source: OpenSecrets, compiled from FEC reports

comparison of what was spent by the "high" spending candidate who laid out more than his or her "low" spending opponent. In the House, the average high spending candidate looked similar in expenditures to the typical incumbent, whereas the average "low" spending candidate spent approximately the same as a typical challenger. For Senate candidates, however, the averages were much lower; a typical Senate incumbent spent more than twice what the average "high" spending open-seat candidate did, and a typical Senate challenger would spend almost eight times the average "low" spending open-seat candidate.

Spending by candidates' own campaigns is not, of course, the only way in which resources are expended on behalf of candidates. Table 4.6 describes the amounts of outside spending on behalf of contestants in House and Senate races—both those where an incumbent was running and those in open-seat races. Across both chambers and both types of races, we see that the gaps between types of candidates (incumbents and challengers and high and low spending open-seat contestants) are smaller than the differences in the spending by candidates' campaign committees. This pattern suggests that outside spending can help compensate for the advantages that incumbents often have over challengers and can serve to lessen the differences between candidates in open-seat contests. In the open-seat Senate race in Kansas, for example, the Republican candidate (and eventual winner) Roger Marshall was outraised for his own campaign account by his Democratic opponent, Barbara Bollier, by a margin of approximately 4:1. The independent spending in the race, however, broke overwhelmingly for Marshall by roughly 3:1.

A NOTE ON 2021 AND BEYOND

As Congress convened to count the electoral votes and certify Joe Biden's election as president on January 6, 2021, it was met with shocking violence when a mob, acting at President Trump's encouragement, stormed the

Capitol.[62] After the House and Senate returned to their business late in the evening, each chamber considered two objections to slates of electors, from Arizona and Pennsylvania. Across the two votes, 139 House members and 8 senators voted to sustain one or both objections.[63]

Immediately following the insurrection, many corporate PACs responded by making changes in their political giving—especially those that generally are concerned about socially responsible behavior (see chapter 7).[64] Some companies, such as AT&T, Marriott, Dow, Airbnb, and Morgan Stanley, announced that they would cease giving from their PACs to the Republicans who voted for either of the electoral vote objections. Others, including Facebook, Microsoft, Coca-Cola, Citigroup, JP Morgan Chase, and Goldman Sachs, chose to stop PAC contributions to all congressional candidates for varying periods.[65] By the end of the first quarter in April, however, it became clear that although PAC contributions to the Republican legislators who objected to Arizona and/or Pennsylvania's electoral votes were down significantly since the analogous period in the prior cycle, not all corporations were approaching the question of whether to alter their giving in response to members' behavior in the same way. In the eyes of some—including Toyota, Cigna, and the Chamber of Commerce—different objectors should be judged differently, and, as a result, not every member who voted for one of the objections should be cut off from PAC contributions.[66]

By the summer of 2021, it became clear that even if corporations had ceased contributing to the PCCs of the individual candidates who had objected to the certification of the electoral votes, they were comfortable continuing to give to party committees. Walmart, for example, gave $30,000 each to the NRCC and the NRSC in the months after January 6 despite having pledged to halt donations to objectors.[67] And by the end of the third quarter of 2021, Republican committees (the RNC, the NRSC, and the NRCC) had, collectively, raised roughly $9 million more than their Democratic counterparts despite the corporate pledges, and similar ones from some individuals, to redirect their giving.[68] In total, reporting suggests that, by the end of the 2022 midterm cycle, fewer than half of the corporations that had pledged to stop political donations entirely or to cease contributing to Republicans who rejected the outcome of the 2020 election ultimately kept their promise.[69]

Even as many corporations appear to have backed off these pledges—and the subsequent reneging on them by some companies and individual donors—they remind us that donations are, ultimately, an expression of *something*, whether that is shared preferences or a strategic position; the DCCC and NRCC raised roughly equivalent amounts in 2021 ($146 million versus

$140 million).[70] And even as individual giving outpaces Traditional PAC spending in terms of their relative shares of candidates' fund-raising, PACs remain important group-based actors in American politics. Examining the landscape of congressional campaign financing, then, matters for our broader understanding of the contemporary American political system.

NOTES

1. Alexander did, however, report on the financial activities of the national parties in congressional campaigns.

2. Thanks are due to Emily Larson for helpful research assistance.

3. Karl Evers-Hillstrom, "Most Expensive Ever: 2020 Election Cost $14.4 Billion," *OpenSecrets*, February 11, 2021, https://www.opensecrets.org/news/2021/02/2020-cycle-cost-14p4-billion-doubling-16/.

4. Gary C. Jacobson, "It's Nothing Personal: The Decline of the Incumbency Advantage in US House Elections," *Journal of Politics* 77, no. 3 (2015): 861–73; Gary C. Jacobson and Jamie L. Carson, *The Politics of Congressional Elections* (Lanham, MD: Rowman & Littlefield, 2015); Daniel J. Hopkins, *The Increasingly United States: How and Why American Political Behavior Nationalized* (Chicago: University of Chicago Press, 2018). For a discussion of how nationalization is not sufficient to explain all the outcomes we see in congressional elections, however, see, for example, Charles R. Hunt, "Beyond Partisanship: Outperforming the Party Label with Local Roots in Congressional Elections," *Congress and the Presidency* 48, no. 3 (2021): 343–72.

5. Harry Enten, "There Were No Purple States on Tuesday," *FiveThirtyEight*, November 10, 2016, https://fivethirtyeight.com/features/there-were-no-purple-states-on-tuesday/.

6. Table 2.4, *Vital Statistics on Congress*, https://www.brookings.edu/wp-content/uploads/2019/03/2-4-Full.pdf.

7. David Montgomery, "CityLab's Congressional Density Index," *Bloomberg*, November 20, 2018, https://www.bloomberg.com/news/articles/2018-11-20/city-lab-s-congressional-density-index.

8. Estimates of educational attainment by congressional district are taken from the 2018 American Community Survey.

9. Scott Keeter and Ruth Igielnik, "Democrats Made Gains from Multiple Sources in 2018 Midterm Victories," *Pew Research Center*, September 8, 2020, https://www.pewresearch.org/wp-content/uploads/sites/10/2020/09/PM__09.08.20_vote.report_Full.Report.pdf.

10. William H. Frey, "2018 Voter Turnout Rose Dramatically for Groups Favoring Democrats," Brookings Institution, May 2, 2019, https://www.brookings.edu/research/2018-voter-turnout-rose-dramatically-for-groups-favoring-democrats-census-confirms

11. Nate Cohn, "For a Change, Democrats Seem Set to Equal or Exceed Republicans in Turnout," *New York Times*, October 19, 2018.

12. Kyle Kondik, "The House: A Blue Wave Reduced to a Blue Trickle," in *A Return to Normalcy? The 2020 Election That Almost Broke America*, ed. Larry J. Sabato, Kyle Kondik, and J. Miles Coleman (New York: Rowman & Littlefield, 2021), 101–14.

13. All references to competitive House seats are based on the *Cook Political Report*'s final preelection House race ratings. "2020 House Race Ratings," *Cook Political Report*, November 2, 2020, https://cookpolitical.com/ratings/house-race-ratings/230686.

14. "2020 Electoral College Ratings," *Cook Political Report*, October 28, 2020.

15. Joel Sievert and Seth C. McKee, "Nationalization in U.S. Senate and Gubernatorial Elections," *American Politics Research* 47, no. 5 (September 2019): 1055–80.

16. See, for example, Seth Masket, John Sides, and Lynn Vavreck, "The Ground Game in the 2012 Presidential Election," *Political Communication* 33, no. 2 (2016): 169–87; and Joshua P. Darr and Matthew S. Levendusky, "Relying on the Ground Game: The Placement and Effect of Campaign Field Offices," *American Politics Research* 42, no. 3 (May 2014): 529–48.

17. Greg Bluestein, "Jimmy Carter Backs Warnock in Crowded U.S. Senate Race in Georgia," *Atlanta Journal-Constitution*, September 29, 2020.

18. Carl Hulse, "With Campaigns in Remote Mode, Pandemic Upends Battle for Congress," *New York Times*, April 5, 2020.

19. Ally Mutnick, Sarah Ferris, and James Arkin, "Congressional Campaigns Brace for Fund-Raising Disaster," *Politico*, April 6, 2020; Daniel Marans, "Coronavirus Pandemic Forces House Primary Challengers to Get Creative with Campaigning," *HuffPost*, April 14, 2020.

20. "Statistical Summary of the 24-Month Campaign Activity of the 2019–20 Election Cycle," *Federal Election Commission*, April 2, 2021, https://www.fec.gov/updates/statistical-summary-24-month-campaign-activity-2019-2020-election-cycle/#:~:text=United%20States%20House%20and%20Senate,2019%20and%20December%2031%2C%202020.

21. Interview with Preston Elliot, deputy executive director for the Democratic Senatorial Campaign Committee in the 2015–16 election cycle, quoted in Molly E. Reynolds and Richard L. Hall, "Financing the 2016 Congressional Election," in *Financing the 2016 Election*, ed. David Magleby (Washington, DC: Brookings Institution Press, 2019), 220.

22. All comparison data for 2016 is from Reynolds and Hall, "Financing the 2016 Congressional Election."

23. Kate Ackley, "'No Corporate PAC' Pledges Hit Record in 2020, But May Face Uncertainty in 2022," *Roll Call*, December 2, 2020.

24. Kristin Kanthak, "Crystal Elephants and Committee Chairs: Campaign Contributions and Leadership Races in the U.S. House of Representatives," *American Politics Research* 35, no. 3 (May 2007): 389–406.

25. All 2012 figures are from Paul S. Herrnson, Kelly D. Patterson, and Stephanie Perry Curtis, "Financing the 2012 Congressional Elections," in *Financing the 2012 Election*, ed. David Magleby (Washington, DC: Brookings Institution Press, 2014).

26. Kenneth L. Miller, "Nationalized Financing in the 2018 and 2020 Congressional Elections," prepared for presentation at the State of the Parties: 2020 and Beyond Virtual Conference, November 4–5, 2021.

27. Ella Nilsen and Dylan Scott, "A Former Republican Could Win the Kansas Senate Race for the Democrats," *Vox*, October 12, 2020, https://www.vox.com/2020/10/12/21503061/kansas-senate-race-bollier-marshall.

28. Cat Reid, "Kansas U.S. Senate Race Breaks Spending Records for Campaigns," *KSHB*, October 30, 2020, https://www.kshb.com/news/election-2020/kansas-u-s-senate-race-breaks-spending-records-for-campaigns.

29. Jessica Piper, "What Are Joint Fund-Raising Committees, and How Are They Helping Trump?," *OpenSecrets*, August 29, 2019, https://www.opensecrets.org/news/2019/08/what-are-joint-fund-raising-committees-and-how-are-they-helping-trump/.

30. Due to filing and reporting challenges, this figure understates the level of internal communications in 2020 (see chapter 6 for more details).

31. Data from "2020 Outside Spending, by Super PAC," *OpenSecrets*, https://www.opensecrets.org/outsidespending/summ.php?cycle=2020&chrt=V&disp=O&type=S.

32. Bridget Bowman, "How a Super PAC Helped House Republicans Survive the 'Green Wave,'" *Roll Call*, November 11, 2020.

33. "2020 Outside Spending, by Super PAC."

34. Karl Evers-Hillstrom, "Political Donations Dropped Off as Coronavirus Pandemic Peaked," *OpenSecrets*, June 9, 2020, https://www.opensecrets.org/news/2020/06/political-donations-dropped-off-as-coronavirus-pandemic-peaked/.

35. Ollie Gratzinger, "Small Donors Give Big Money in 2020 Election Cycle," *OpenSecrets*, October 30, 2020, https://www.opensecrets.org/news/2020/10/small-donors-give-big-2020-thanks-to-technology/.

36. Jim Zarroli, "Getting Lots of Political Messages on Your Phone? Welcome to the 'Texting Election,'" *National Public Radio*, October 7, 2020, https://www.npr.org/2020/10/07/920776670/getting-lots-of-political-messages-on-your-phone-welcome-to-the-texting-election; Gratzinger, "Small Donors Give Big Money in 2020 Election Cycle."

37. Matt Stevens, "Wendy Davis, Who Rose to Fame with Filibuster, Will Run for Congress in Texas," *New York Times*, July 22, 2019.

38. Meagan Flynn and Michael Scherer, "Donors Gave a House Candidate More Than $8 Million. A Single Firm Took Nearly Half of It," *Washington Post*, March 2, 2021.

39. Karl Evers-Hillstrom, "Georgia Senate Races Shatter Spending Records," *OpenSecrets*, January 4, 2021, https://www.opensecrets.org/news/2021/01/georgia-senate-races-shatter-records/.

40. Eitan Hersh, "Rage-Donating Only Made Democrats Feel Better," *The Atlantic*, November 12, 2020, https://www.theatlantic.com/ideas/archive/2020/11/folly-just-throwing-money-political-candidates/617074/.

41. Elena Schneider, "Dem Donors Smash ActBlue's Daily Record after Ginsburg's Death," *Politico*, September 19, 2020.

42. "In-District vs. Out-of-District," *OpenSecrets*, March 21, 2021, https://www.opensecrets.org/elections-overview/in-district-vs-out-of-district?cycle=2020.

43. "In-State vs. Out-of-State," *OpenSecrets*, March 22, 2021, https://www.opensecrets.org/elections-overview/in-state-vs-out-of-state?cycle=2020.

44. James M. Curry and Frances E. Lee, *The Limits of Party: Congress and Lawmaking in a Polarized Era* (Chicago: University of Chicago Press, 2020).

45. James M. Curry and Christopher P. Donnelly, "State Congressional Delegations and the Distribution of Federal Funds," *Political Research Quarterly* 74, no. 3 (September 2021): 756–71.

46. Paul S. Herrnson, "The Roles of Party Organizations, Party-Connected Committees, and Party Allies in Elections," *Journal of Politics* 71, no. 4 (October 2009): 1207–24.

47. Ally Mutnick, Sarah Ferris, and Heather Caygle, "Top Progressives, DCCC Reach Ceasefire over 'Blacklist,'" *Politico*, January 22, 2020.

48. Juliegrace Bufke, "Tensions Rise during GOP Leadership Meeting over Dues," *The Hill*, June 11, 2019.

49. Amisa Ratliff and Michael Beckel, *The Continuing "Price of Power": How the Political Parties Leaned on Legislative Leaders for Cash during the 115th Congress* (Washington, DC: Issue One, 2019).

50. Notably, the second largest contribution, $1.7 million, from a member to the NRCC was from then-Republican Conference chair Liz Cheney of Wyoming. Following the insurrection at the Capitol on January 6, 2021, Cheney was stripped of her leadership post for her vocal criticism of President Trump, including encouraging a serious investigation and accountability for the event.

51. Reynolds and Hall, "Financing the 2016 Congressional Election."

52. The average for Democrats was approximately $45,000, whereas for Republicans, it was approximately $42,000, but a difference of means test suggests that these quantities are not statistically distinguishable.

53. Ruth Bloch Rubin, *Building the Bloc: Intraparty Organization in the U.S. Congress* (New York: Cambridge University Press, 2017).

54. Andrew J. Clarke, "Party Sub-Brands and American Party Factions," *American Journal of Political Science* 64, no. 3 (July 2020): 452–70.

55. SoRelle Wyckoff Gaynor, "The (Financial) Ties That Bind: Social Networks of Intraparty Caucuses," *Legislative Studies Quarterly*, forthcoming.

56. Alexander Fouirnaies and Andrew B. Hall, "The Financial Incumbency Advantage: Causes and Consequences," *Journal of Politics* 76, no. 3 (July 2014): 711–24.

57. Andrew B. Hall and James M. Snyder Jr., "How Much of the Incumbency Advantage Is Due to Scare-Off?," *Political Science Research and Methods* 3, no. 3

(February 2015): 493–514; Pamela Ban, Elena Llaudet, and James M. Snyder Jr., "Challenger Quality and the Incumbency Advantage," *Legislative Studies Quarterly* 41, no. 1 (February 2016): 153–79.

58. Jay Goodliffe, "The Effect of War Chests on Challenger Entry in the U.S. House Elections," *American Journal of Political Science* 45, no. 4 (October 2006): 830–44; Jay Goodliffe, "Campaign War Chests and Challenger Quality in Senate Elections," *Legislative Studies Quarterly* 32, no. 1 (February 2007): 135–56.

59. David Epstein and Peter Zemsky, "Money Talks: Deterring Quality Challengers in Congressional Elections," *American Political Science Review* 89, no. 2 (June 1995): 295–308; Jay Goodliffe, "War Chests for Deterrence and Savings," *Quarterly Journal of Political Science* 4, no. 1 (March 2007): 129–50.

60. Robert G. Boatright, "What Do the 2020 Congressional Primaries Tell Us about the Direction of the Democratic and Republican Parties?," paper prepared for the 2021 State of the Parties Conference, Ray C. Bliss Institute, University of Akron, November 4–5, 2021.

61. Reynolds and Hall, "Financing the 2016 Congressional Election."

62. Nicholas Fandos and Emily Cochrane, "Rampage in Capitol Forces Evacuations; It's 'Part of His Legacy,' A Republican Says," *New York Times*, January 7, 2021, A1.

63. Roll Call Vote #10, 1st session, 117th Congress; Roll Call Vote #11, 1st session, 117th Congress.

64. Florian Gawehns and Amy Meli, "Are U.S. Companies Punishing Republicans for Jan. 6? Here's What Our Research Finds," *Washington Post*, January 5, 2021.

65. Kate Kelly, Emily Flitter, and Shane Goldmacher, "Companies Suspending Campaign Donations," *New York Times*, January 12, 2021, B1.

66. Andrew Ross Sorkin et al., "How Corporate Donations Changed after the Capitol Riot," *DealBook Newsletter, New York Times*, April 19, 2021, https://www.nytimes.com/2021/04/19/business/dealbook/corporate-donations-capitol-riot.html.

67. David Klepper, "6 Months After Capitol Assault, Corporate Pledges Fall Flat," *Associated Press*, July 4, 2021.

68. Josh Dawsey, Issac Stanley-Becker, and Michael Scherer, "Donors Threated to Shun the GOP after Jan. 6. Now, Republicans Are Outraising Democrats," *Washington Post*, November 9, 2021.

69. Jessica Piper and Zach Montellaro, "Corporations Gave $10M to Election Objectors after Pledging to Cut Them Off," *Politico*, January 6, 2023.

70. Tal Axelrod, "House Democratic Campaign Arm Outraises GOP Counterpart in Final Quarter of 2021," *The Hill*, January 14, 2022.

5

Party Money in the 2020 Election

Robin Kolodny and Diana Dwyre

In *Financing the 1960 Election*, Herbert Alexander focused considerable attention on the financial role of the national committees of the major political parties in a historic election.[1] The 2020 election was also historic—even outdoing the 2016 election. With COVID-19 hovering over all events after lockdowns began in March 2020, the major political parties and other political actors found ways to adapt to this truly unique environment. They managed to declare candidacies, hold presidential nominating conventions, and register and contact voters in primaries and the general election. All this activity involved raising and spending record amounts of money, including by the national party committees. Compared to 1960, party committees are a much bigger factor in campaign finance and are at the center of expanded networks of allied organizations.

In the 2020 election, the national party organizations spent more than in any other election cycle, adjusted for inflation. The three national Democratic committees spent $1.09 billion, and the three national Republican committees spent $1.4 billion. Yet, this record party spending represents a shrinking share of all noncandidate spending relative to nonparty groups such as Super PACs and tax-exempt groups. As they have always done, the parties continue to work to adapt to the ever-changing campaign finance landscape to maintain influence in the mix with these formidable organizations that can raise and spend money with fewer restrictions than the parties face.

In this chapter, we explain how several adaptations that parties made contributed to their higher totals, not necessarily an increase in the cost of campaigns.

- First, President Trump used his impeachment events in 2019–2020 to raise an extraordinary amount of money, both for his personal campaign account and for the Republican National Committee. Then, both committees spent much of this money to pay for legal fees for his impeachment defense.
- Second, both presidential candidate campaigns cooperated with their national party organizations to create joint fund-raising committees (JFCs), which were more numerous and more active than in previous cycles (see figure 5.3). This helped them secure more maximum contributions from wealthy donors.
- Third, the national party committees raised and spent record amounts for the new accounts for conventions, headquarters, and recount/legal fees, some of it raised using JFCs (see figure 5.5).
- Finally, the unusual situation of not one but two U.S. Senate runoff elections in Georgia, which would determine control of the chamber, ramped up spending and campaign activity significantly, as did the start of President Trump's lawsuits over recounts of his election in several states.

We also examine the declining financial role of formal party organizations relative to other campaign spenders and discuss how parties have adapted by becoming the center of wider partisan networks and guiding the activities of many allied partisan Super PACs and other nonparty groups.

MAJOR PARTY FINANCES IN A HISTORIC ELECTION

In 2020, the Republicans controlled the presidency and the U.S. Senate, while the Democrats controlled the U.S. House of Representatives. The Democratic Party had to first select its presidential nominee, while also watching how Senate and House races were shaping up. The Republicans sought to protect their incumbents but also make gains in Congress. Given the controversial events of the Trump presidency, both parties were anticipating a huge electoral effort and hoping for high turnout. Yet focusing solely on the year 2020 does not provide the entire picture: one must look back to January 2017 and forward to January 2021.

Trump and the Republican National Committee (RNC)

As the "unconventional" candidate, Trump and the RNC had an arms-length relationship as he secured the party's nomination in 2016. Unlike recent Republican nominees, Mitt Romney (2012) and John McCain (2008), Trump lacked a strong personal organization to run the general election campaign; for this reason, he made more use of the RNC's infrastructure in the 2016 general election.[2]

In a recent analysis of presidential relationships with national party committees, Boris Heersink argued that whereas both George W. Bush and Barack Obama had strong candidate-focused organizations that ran their presidential campaigns, Trump did not.[3] Thus, Bush and Obama did not rely on the Republican National Committee (RNC) and the Democratic National Committee (DNC), respectively, in their general election bids, and mostly continued their own campaign organizations in a low-key fashion alongside the national committees during their presidencies and reelection campaigns. In contrast, Trump followed a different path.

Almost immediately after Trump took office in 2017, the ties between the presidency and the RNC changed dramatically. As president-elect, Trump exercised his right to appoint his own person as chair of the RNC, nominating Ronna Romney McDaniel, who was chair of Michigan's Republican Party and Trump's Michigan campaign in 2016. McDaniel put the RNC firmly behind Trump and his policies, setting the stage for a new relationship.[4] Previously, just weeks after the 2016 election, Trump named then-RNC Chair Reince Priebus to be his first White House chief of staff. This pick was surprising to many because Priebus had remained neutral in the 2016 Republican primaries. Although that might have put his loyalty in question, Priebus's position was also seen as an asset in Trump's adjustment to the Washington establishment. Priebus also brought RNC staff members with him to the White House.[5]

Trump declared that he was running for reelection in 2020 on inauguration day 2017. Presidents George W. Bush and Barack Obama both waited until the third year of their first term to establish formal campaign committees for a second term.[6] Within two months of his presidency, Trump managed to co-opt the past and current personnel of the RNC. *The Economist* stated: "As is usual when a party's candidate wins the presidency, the Republican National Committee (RNC) has become a subsidiary of the White House. In keeping with the tenor of its new ownership, it now has a website, LyinComey.com, dedicated to attacking the former head of the FBI."[7]

Trump Impeachment 2019–2020

Donald Trump was first impeached by the U.S. House of Representatives in 2019. The basis for the 2019 impeachment has special relevance for the 2020 election, as the focus of the inquiry was on a telephone call the president had with the leader of Ukraine, Volodymyr Zelenskyy, during which Trump asked Zelenskyy for help getting potentially compromising information on Hunter Biden, son of the front-runner for the 2020 Democratic presidential nomination, former vice president Joe Biden. Trump suggested that foreign aid to Ukraine depended on the leader's willingness to help with the investigation of Hunter Biden's Ukrainian business dealings.

Thus, even though the Democratic nomination process had not begun yet, and Biden had only announced that he would run three months previously, Trump had clearly identified Biden as the most likely general election opponent. In fact, Trump began testing his penchant for pejorative nicknames of rivals on Biden as early as March 2018 (settling ultimately on "Sleepy Joe"). Still, Trump's campaign communications director speculated that Trump would still triumph in 2020 because the Democratic Party's nominee "will be beat up, broke, without a national operation, with a DNC that's in debt, and saddled with all of the socialist policies they will have adopted in order to win the nomination."[8]

When President Bill Clinton was impeached in late 1998, both parties used the event to raise money for candidate campaign committees (particularly of the House impeachment managers) as well as for a legal defense fund for the president. However, Clinton was only able to raise about $6.3 million this way, and he left the White House in early 2001 owing several million dollars to attorneys.[9] In the same vein, the Trump impeachment proceedings in 2019–20 proved to be a fund-raising boon, with the Trump campaign and the RNC bringing in $125 million combined in the third quarter of 2019 alone. The success was unexpected—about fifty thousand new, small-dollar donors responded to a message about the Democrats' impeachment efforts as partisan intimidation and false charges. A Trump campaign official noted that donors normally respond to pleas that things are "great and we have to continue that," but this new set of donors responded to a "panic style of messaging."[10]

A careful analysis by *Time* magazine revealed that the Trump campaign placed ads on Facebook within twenty-four minutes of the announcement by Democratic Speaker Nancy Pelosi that the House would move forward with articles of impeachment against Trump. The campaign kept up this strategy of targeting Facebook users (at that time, the content of communications was not yet being checked for accuracy by social media vendors). The Trump campaign, the White House, and the RNC all coordinated fund-raising messages. Overall, two *Time* reporters "analyzed hundreds of digital campaign ads and found that nearly all of Trump's Facebook messages about impeachment fit into three categories: 'The Democrats Are Against You,' 'The Democrats Are Against Me,' and 'The Democrats Are Against America.'"[11] Because the RNC and the Trump campaign committee were intimately coordinated by Trump loyalists, the party prospered from impeachment fund-raising. However, the spending that followed went in larger part to pay the legal fees related to Trump's impeachment defense, not direct support for the president, other candidates, or party operations at large (see below). This close partnership between the RNC and the Trump campaign continued during the 2019–2020 election cycle, resulting in record receipts and expenditures (see chapter 3).

Biden and the Democratic National Committee (DNC)

The 2016 campaign was difficult for the DNC. Accusations that the then-DNC chair, Rep. Debbie Wasserman-Schultz (D-FL), covertly supported Hillary Clinton's nomination for the presidency (to the disadvantage of Bernie Sanders) left the organization with a lack of funds, leadership, or infrastructure going into 2017.[12] Competition for DNC chair began in earnest in early 2017, with Rep. Keith Ellison (D-MN) endorsed by Bernie Sanders and former Obama labor secretary Tom Perez endorsed by Joe Biden, the main candidates.[13]

Perez won the chairmanship and began to rebuild the organization, which was in a shambles. For example, he discovered that the DNC's finance department had a staff of three people, though it was meant to have twenty-five.[14] He described his task as a "turnaround job."[15] Against this backdrop, the successes of the DNC in 2018, but particularly in 2020, were notable. As soon as Biden effectively secured the Democratic nomination, his campaign and the DNC made record gains in fund-raising (see chapter 3), dubbed by Mike Allen of *Axios* a "green tsunami."[16]

U.S. Senate Runoff Elections in Georgia

Beyond the presidency, the 2020 election featured an unusual situation in Georgia: both incumbent U.S. senators, Republicans David Purdue and Kelly Loeffler, were forced into runoff elections with Democratic challengers, Jon Ossoff and Raphael Warnock, respectively (see chapters 4 and 6). Georgia is one of ten states that requires a runoff election be held if no candidate wins a primary election with 50 percent of the vote. However, Georgia is the only state that requires a runoff of this type for a *general* election. Although the Georgia law dates from the 1960s, the law was modified in 2012 to require nine weeks between the regularly scheduled general election and the eventual runoffs—which explains why the Georgia runoff elections were held in January 2021. In the election held on November 3, 2020, Senator Perdue received 49.73 percent of the vote with three candidates on the ballot, not the 50 percent or more needed to win the seat outright. On the same night, Democratic challenger Raphael Warnock received 32.90 percent of the vote in a twenty-person race for Georgia's other Senate seat (Kelly Loeffler was second), far short of the 50 percent needed. Meanwhile, competitive U.S. Senate races in other states split more in favor of Republicans than predicted with the curious result that the winners of the two Georgia runoff races would determine which party controlled the U.S. Senate. So, the complexity of Georgia election law and political trends in the nation created a perfect storm when the typical campaign period did not produce a definitive result.

From Election Day on November 3, 2020, through the runoff election day on January 5, 2021, all eyes were on these two Senate contests. The Democrats won both these races, bringing the Senate to a 50-50 tie and giving the Democrats control of the chamber because of the tie-breaking vote of newly elected Vice President Kamala Harris. Because much of the big money in Georgia was raised and spent after Election Day in November, the national parties' fund-raising and spending totals were higher than they would otherwise have been (see below).

PARTY FUND-RAISING IN 2020

Overall, the receipts for the national party committees reached an all-time high in 2020. Figure 5.1 provides an overview of the fund-raising totals from 1992 to 2020 (in constant 2020 dollars)[17] for the six national party organizations: the Democratic National Committee (DNC), the Republican National Committee (RNC), the Democratic Senatorial Campaign Committee (DSCC), the National Republican Senatorial Committee (NRSC), the Democratic Congressional Campaign Committee (DCCC), and the National Republican Congressional Committee (NRCC). Early in this period (until after the 2002 election), these committees raised both "hard" and "soft" money (see chapter 2), and the totals displayed here contain both types of funds. But beginning in 2004, the 2002 Bipartisan Campaign Reform Act banned soft money (see chapter 2), so the amounts displayed for 2004 and beyond are hard money totals only.

Figure 5.1 shows that from 2004 to 2016, most national party committees either collected roughly the same amounts each cycle, or sometimes (as with

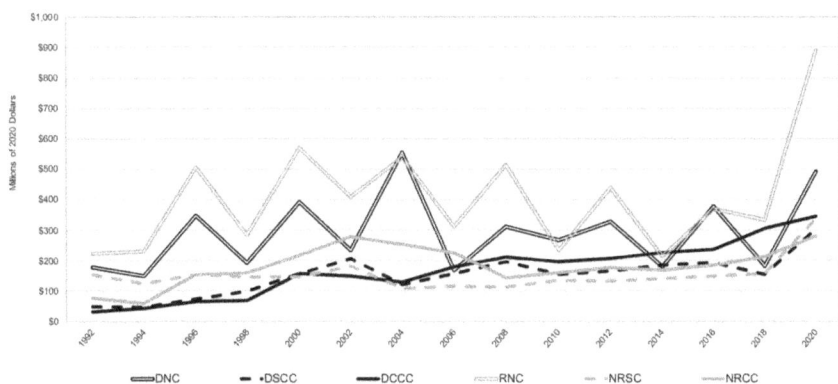

Figure 5.1   Hard and Soft Money Receipts of National Party Committees, 1992–2020 (millions of 2020 dollars). *Source*: OpenSecrets, analysis of FEC data, https://www.fec.gov /campaign-finance-data/political-party-data-summary-tables/?year=2020&segment=24

the DNC and RNC in midterm election years) significantly less. Clearly, 2020 tells a different story, with party receipts markedly higher for most of the committees. On the Republican side, both the RNC and the NRSC raised more money than they ever had before, with the RNC raising significantly more than its previous high in 2000 (56 percent more) and 81 percent more than the DNC's 2020 receipts. Only the NRCC's receipts were about the same as their previous high in 2002 ($280 million in 2020 compared to $278 million in 2002). Among the Democratic committees, the DSCC and DCCC also beat their organizational bests. However, the DNC raised more in 2004 ($554 million, in 2020 dollars) than in 2020 ($491 million).

Of course, the campaign finance landscape in 2020 was quite different than the early election cycles when soft money was allowed. Figure 5.2 shows the various sources of national party committees' receipts from 2000 to 2020. In 2000 and 2002, soft money was the largest source of the Democrats' receipts and a close second (behind individual contributions) for the Republicans. After party soft money was banned, from 2004 to 2018, both parties saw their overall receipts decline.

Party Fund-Raising and Joint Fund-Raising Committees (JFCs)

Starting in 2008, transfers from other committees became more important during presidential election cycles, with a significant uptick for Democrats in 2016 and a dramatic gain for Republicans in 2020. This increased transfer activity is due in part to both parties' use of joint fund-raising committees (JFCs), a fund-raising mechanism that allows its participants to efficiently

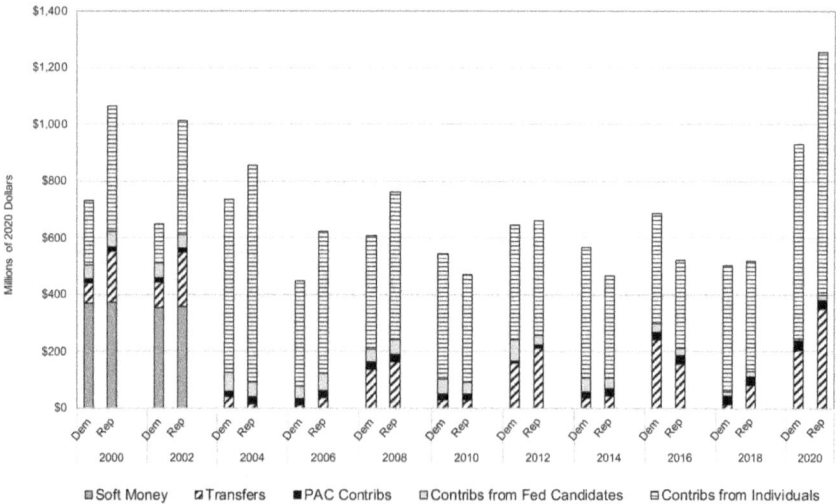

Figure 5.2 Sources of National Party Committee Money, 2000–2020 (millions of 2020 dollars). *Source*: OpenSecrets, analysis of FEC data, https://www.fec.gov/campaign -finance-data/political-party-data-summary-tables/?year=2020&segment=24

maximize fund-raising from wealthy donors, with parties, candidates, and Traditional PACs (but not Super PACs) raising money together. A donor may write one big check to give up to the maximum contribution to each entity participating in the JFC. Candidate committees, other party committees, and Traditional PACs also may contribute to JFCs (see chapter 2).

Parties and their candidates have used JFCs to raise money since the 1970s, and after the 2014 *McCutcheon* decision (see chapter 2), they were able to raise even more from their wealthy supporters through JFCs. After *McCutcheon*, donors may give to as many candidates, parties, and Traditional PACs as they wish, and thus to as many JFCs as they wish, provided their contributions "comply with the limits and prohibitions of the Federal Election Campaign Act" (i.e., a contributor may not exceed the contribution limit for any recipient in the JFC) (see table 2.2).[18] Moreover, beginning in the 2015–2016 election cycle, the national party committees were allowed new opportunities to raise funds with JFCs (see below).

According to the FEC, the 2019–2020 election cycle saw one thousand federal JFCs, many in which national party committees participated, including nine of the top ten JFCs that raised the most in 2019–2020.[19] As figure 5.3 shows, the DNC and RNC have taken advantage of the ability to raise money through JFCs during presidential election years, and their JFC hauls really took off in 2020, especially for the RNC. The DCCC and especially the NRSC raised more through JFCs in 2020 as well.

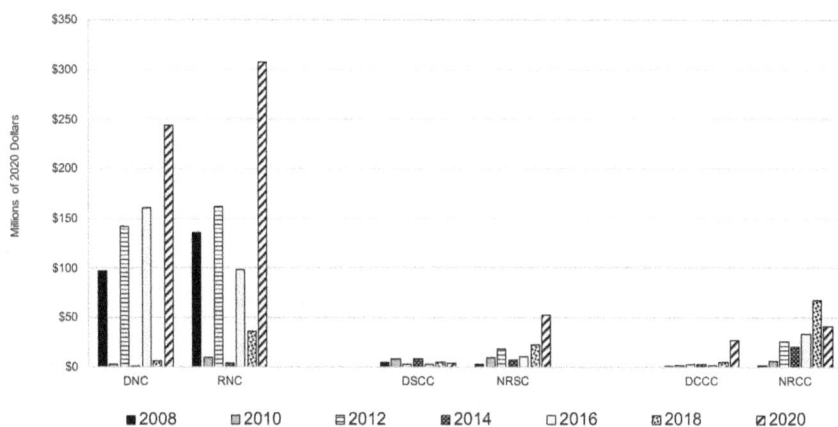

Figure 5.3   National Party Share of Joint Fund-Raising Receipts, 2008–2020 (millions of 2020 dollars). *Source*: OpenSecrets, "Joint Fundraising Committee Receipts, 2020," https://www.opensecrets.org/jfc/top.php?type=R&cycle=2020

The presidential nominees' JFCs were among the top ten overall in 2020. As in recent presidential elections, each party's presidential nominee created JFCs with their national party committees (see chapter 3). Biden and Trump each had two large JFCs, each type with a different organizational structure. The first type raised money for the candidate and their national party committee. The Biden Action Fund raised $5.9 million for the Biden campaign and $46.5 million for the DNC, and the Trump Make American Great Again Committee raised $233.7 million for the Trump campaign and $108.5 million for the RNC (and after Election Day, $30.5 million for a new Trump Leadership PAC, Save America).[20]

The second type of presidential nominee JFC included the nominee's campaign committee, their national party committee, and various state party organizations. The Biden Victory Fund JFC raised $237.5 million for the Biden campaign, $103 million for the DNC, and $115.2 million for forty-six state parties and the District of Columbia parties. The Trump Victory JFC raised $40.9 million for Donald J. Trump for President, Inc., $198.1 million for the RNC, and $72.5 million for forty-five state and the District of Columbia parties.[21] In these types of JFCs, each state party receives its cut of each donor's contribution, but because party committees may transfer unlimited amounts to and from one another, often all or some of a state party's JFC allocation is transferred right back to the national party committee or transferred from a state party without a competitive presidential contest to a state party in a battleground state. For instance, in 2020 the Alaska Republican Party's share of the JFC proceeds was $2.7 million, and the D.C. Republican Party received $2.3 million, and both transferred all of their Trump Victory JFC money back to the RNC.[22] This kind of activity occurred in previous presidential campaigns as well.[23]

State party transfers of JFC funds *back* to a national party committee are controversial because they allow a single donor to direct more than the allowable contribution limit to a national party committee. A single donor could, for example, write one big check for $498,300 to the Trump Victory JFC, and if any of that donor's state party JFC donations were later transferred back to the RNC, the donor would end up giving more to the RNC than allowed under the $35,500 contribution limit (see chapter 2).[24]

There were other JFC models used in 2020 as well. Donald Trump had four smaller JFCs for the 2020 election with GOP House and Senate incumbents from battleground states.[25] The Biden Fight Fund JFC raised $15 million for the DNC, and the Democratic Grassroots Victory Fund raised $6.7 million for the DNC and $11.3 million for all fifty states' and District of Columbia Democratic Party committees.[26]

The parties' congressional campaign committees and congressional party leaders also establish JFCs to aid their party's collective pursuit of majority control of the House and Senate. For example:

- **Take Back the House 2020** raised $19.4 million for the NRCC, $7.4 million for twenty-one state party committees, $11.5 million for 111 Republican House candidates, $2.5 million for House Minority Leader Kevin McCarthy's Leadership PAC (Majority Committee PAC), and $215,925 for the McCarthy Victory Fund JFC.
- **Nancy Pelosi Victory Fund**: Democratic Speaker of the House Nancy Pelosi raised $20.6 million for the DCCC, $1.8 million for her own campaign committee, and $1 million for her Leadership PAC (PAC to the Future).
- **Hold the House Victory Fund** raised $4.5 million for the DCCC and $2.7 million for thirty Democratic House candidates.
- **NRSC Targeted State Victory** raised $5.3 million for the NRCC and $12.1 million for twenty-two state Republican parties.
- **The McConnell Victory Committee** raised $4 million for the NRSC, $908,368 for Senate Minority Leader Mitch McConnell's campaign, and $207,250 for McConnell's Leadership PAC (Bluegrass Committee).
- **The House Senate Victory Fund** raised $628,000 each for the DCCC and DSCC.[27]

The two runoff Senate races in Georgia also featured a lot of joint fund-raising committee activity that included party committees. Table 5.1 shows the JFCs that raised the most for these special Georgia races.

Party Receipts from Transfers

The national party committees brought in quite a lot of money via transfers from other party committees. Figure 5.4 shows transfers from affiliated party committees to each of the national party committees from 2000 to 2020. The DNC and RNC raise the most from party transfers primarily during presidential election years, and sometimes they transfer funds to the congressional campaign committees in midterm election years. The DNC had its best year for party transfers in 2016, when it raised $225.7 million; and the RNC beat all records in 2020, raising $288.7 million from party transfers. The congressional campaign committees raise much less than the DNC and RNC via transfers today, but the DCCC, and especially the NRCC, raised more through transfers than their national party committees in 2000 and 2002, before BCRA banned soft money contributions.

Table 5.1   Georgia Senate Runoff Joint Fund-Raising Committee Receipts, 2020–2021

Joint Fund-Raising Committee	Participating Recipients	Amount Received
Senate Georgia Battleground Fund	NRSC	$24.6 million
	Purdue	$12.3 million
	Loeffler	$12 million
Team Perdue JFC	NRSC	$2 million
	Perdue	$1.5 million
	Republican Party of Georgia	$114,131
Team Loeffler JFC	NRSC	$432,046
	Loeffler	$567,088
	Republican Party of Georgia	$318,842
Ossoff-Warnock Victory Fund	DSCC	$1.2 million
	Ossoff	$670,000
	Warnock	$645,000
Ossoff Victory Fund	Ossoff	$1.2 million
	Georgia Federal Elections Committee	$1.5 million
Warnock Victory Fund	DSCC	$3,713
	Warnock	$393,000
	Georgia Federal Elections Committee	$370,381

Source: OpenSecrets, "Joint Fund-Raising Committees 2020," OpenSecrets.org, 2021, www.opensecrets.org /jfc/top.php?type=C&cycle=2020 (accessed December 30, 2021)

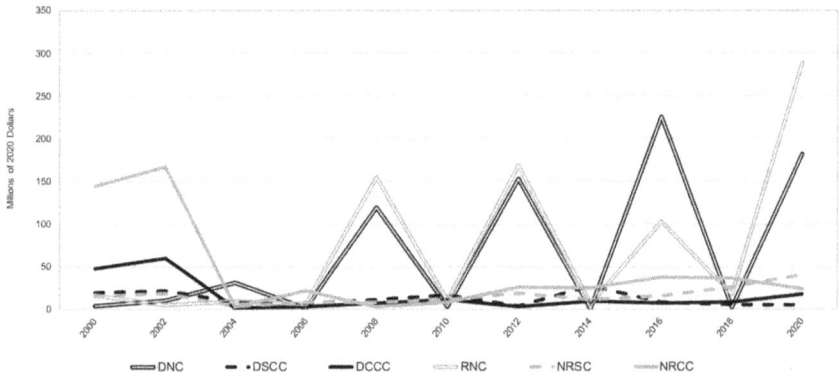

Figure 5.4   National Party Receipts: Transfers from Affiliated Party Committees, 2000–2020 (millions of 2020 dollars). *Source*: OpenSecrets, analysis of FEC data, https://www.fec.gov/campaign-finance-data/political-party-data-summary-tables/?year=2020&segment=24

Special Party Accounts

Public funding of political campaigns has never been particularly popular.[28] Yet, even after presidential candidates began declining federal public funds for their own campaigns in the early 2000s (see chapter 3), the DNC and RNC continued to receive public funds for the national presidential nominating conventions. Established as part of the 1976 FECA amendments, the convention public funding had long been eclipsed by the private funds raised by convention host committees, mostly from big corporations.[29] Thus, it is no surprise that Congress passed legislation to end the public funding for the national parties' conventions in 2014, devoting the money to pediatric cancer research.[30] Later that year, the Consolidated and Further Continuing Appropriations Act of 2015 (see chapter 2) was enacted.[31] The major purpose of the law was to prevent a looming government shutdown, but it also allowed the national party committees to establish three new special accounts with separate contribution limits: a convention account, a building account, and a recount/legal account (see chapter 2).

The convention account was meant to replace the public funds eliminated in 2014, and only the DNC and RNC were allowed to establish a convention account. Each of the national party committees established their own building account to raise and spend funds for the construction, renovation, and operation of their national party headquarters, and each established a recount/legal account to pay for election recounts and legal expenses (see chapter 2). The limits for donations to these special accounts are significantly higher than the contribution limits to the main party committee

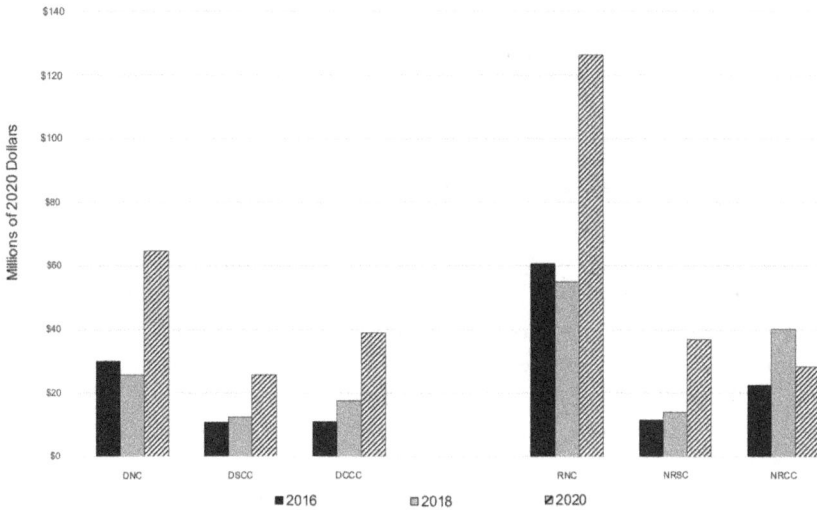

Figure 5.5   Contributions to Party Special Accounts, 2016–2020 (millions of 2020 dollars). *Source*: OpenSecrets, FEC data, https://www.fec.gov/resources/campaign-finance -statistics/2020/tables/party/Prty10_2020_24m.pdf

accounts. Moreover, contributions to all the party accounts, traditional and new, are now indexed to inflation, so the limits increase each election cycle.

For the 2019–2020 election cycle, a single individual donor could give a total of $1,704,000 to a party's three national committees by giving the maximum traditional contribution to each party committee and the maximum to each committee's special party accounts—almost twenty-five times more than the maximum allowed individual donation in 2012.[32] A single Traditional PAC could give $720,000 to one party's national committees and their special accounts in 2019–2020.[33] Contributors may give directly to the various party committees or to each account via a JFC. Given the new party account limits, a single individual or PAC can contribute very large amounts that are reminiscent of the big soft money contributions the parties raised in the 1990s and early 2000s. Figure 5.5 shows the totals each national party committee raised for these new special accounts since they began operation in 2016. Notice that the Republicans generally raised more than the Democrats, and in 2020, the RNC raised far more than the DNC—and more than double what it had raised in previous cycles.

Party Receipts from Individual Contributors

When soft money was banned in 2004, individual contribution limits were increased and indexed to inflation. Since that time, the national parties have raised most of their funds from individual contributors, either as direct contributions or through JFCs. As table 5.2 shows, the national Democratic committees raised 73 percent, while the national Republican committees raised 68 percent of their receipts from individuals in 2020. Indeed, these figures are the highest since 2000.

Both parties' national committees raised a good deal of money from individuals giving $200 or less. Table 5.2 shows that 35 percent of the DNC's and 65 percent of the RNC's individual contribution receipts came from these small-dollar donations in 2020. These tables also show that all of the national party committees have fluctuated over time in how much they rely on small donations. The parties also receive larger donations, and these contributions over $200 constitute a large portion of each party's individual contribution receipts. Of course, a few contributors give the maximum permitted by law ($35,500 to each party committee in 2020), providing 18 percent of the DNC's individual contributions and 11 percent of the RNC's.

Party Receipts from Traditional PACs

In contrast, the national party committees raise very little of their money from Traditional PACs (see figure 5.2), accounting for about 3 percent of the Democratic committees' receipts and about 2 percent of the Republican committees' receipts in 2020.[34] Indeed, Traditional PACs direct most of their contributions to congressional candidates (see chapters 4 and 6 for details). Most Traditional PACs pursue policy goals, and congressional donations help the lobbyists representing these organizations gain access to lawmakers.[35]

However, many Super PACs (and the Super PAC portion of Hybrid PACs; see chapter 2) have partisan goals, and some are even aligned with the national party committees and/or party leaders. Super PACs can raise unlimited funds from virtually any source, including corporations and unions, and make unlimited independent expenditures to influence campaigns—so long as they do not coordinate with the candidate beneficiaries (see chapter 2). Table 5.3 lists the fund-raising and spending of the top party-aligned Super PACs in 2020 (see chapters 4 and 6).

Party Receipts from Party Candidates and Officeholders

A final source of funds for the national parties is their own candidates and officeholders. Over time, the national parties have received a declining portion of their contributions from this source (see figure 5.2). Only the DCCC

Table 5.2 National Party Committee Receipts, by Source, Election Years, 2000–2020 (in 2020 dollars, except as indicated)

	2004	2006	2008	2010	2012	2014	2016	2018	2020
DNC									
All individual contributions plus other receipts	554,082,990	167,946,315	317,242,515	266,859,930	368,750,614	178,549,063	423,659,705	182,300,164	518,683,485
Total contributions from individuals	543,802,053	153,317,031	292,314,142	236,076,149	315,248,062	170,394,809	276,335,972	133,441,947	394,907,743
Individuals as share of total receipts (percent)	98%	91%	92%	88%	85%	95%	65%	73%	76%
Unitemized	226,724,256	93,971,851	99,440,727	123,092,011	85,710,945	76,918,021	62,376,704	70,816,284	138,126,992
Unitemized as share of total from individuals (percent)	42%	61%	34%	52%	27%	45%	23%	53%	35%
Contributions at the maximum permitted	61,640,382	4,822,152	51,001,684	26,276,243	86,623,240	21,444,908	65,368,360	10,122,310	71,241,209
Maximum as a share of individual total (percent)	11%	3%	17%	11%	27%	13%	24%	8%	18%
DSCC									
All individual contributions plus other receipts	121,629,357	155,357,883	195,688,037	153,743,787	164,474,502	183,271,490	194,903,964	153,885,788	303,985,715
Total contributions from individuals	87,313,566	117,079,436	133,860,966	107,535,830	121,178,561	136,276,786	130,532,268	107,469,674	244,343,319
Individuals as share of total receipts (percent)	72%	75%	68%	70%	74%	74%	67%	70%	80%
Unitemized	26,499,084	31,501,418	29,589,065	40,639,556	55,929,856	54,899,196	47,589,435	39,353,153	93,070,387
Unitemized as share of total from individuals (percent)	30%	27%	22%	38%	46%	40%	36%	37%	38%
Contributions at the maximum permitted	15,415,970	12,379,408	32,719,361	14,973,950	10,982,283	20,405,571	20,853,843	18,098,950	26,775,000
Maximum as a share of individual total (percent)	18%	11%	24%	14%	9%	15%	16%	17%	11%

(continued)

Table 5.2 (Continued)

	2004	2006	2008	2010	2012	2014	2016	2018	2020
DCCC									
All individual contributions plus other receipts	127,742,446	179,593,400	211,818,829	194,528,473	207,237,998	226,074,822	238,313,211	306,132,974	346,505,869
Total contributions from individuals	69,822,726	108,123,412	109,798,778	108,727,109	151,349,964	165,419,869	160,314,086	217,149,101	220,493,556
Individuals as share of total receipts (percent)	55%	60%	52%	56%	73%	73%	67%	71%	64%
Unitemized	34,524,983	40,902,454	37,078,346	44,506,226	80,076,451	82,578,437	71,986,043	98,927,921	100,677,164
Unitemized as share of total from individuals (percent)	49%	38%	34%	41%	53%	50%	45%	46%	46%
Contributions at the maximum permitted	9,179,638	6,826,900	18,876,832	13,458,751	9,999,203	15,486,168	18,627,378	23,723,371	18,558,899
Maximum as a share of individual total (percent)	13%	6%	17%	12%	7%	9%	12%	11%	8%
RNC									
All individual contributions plus other receipts	537,643,755	311,968,860	523,980,041	233,065,061	499,858,450	213,031,411	405,199,681	343,058,086	1,057,171,185
Total contributions from individuals	480,058,776	274,028,198	492,645,326	198,111,284	467,534,193	200,531,884	244,854,099	254,763,465	666,596,169
Individuals as share of total receipts (percent)	89%	88%	94%	85%	94%	94%	60%	74%	63%
Unitemized	215,230,808	144,874,073	182,970,485	135,104,682	141,388,891	94,812,047	111,448,606	140,642,855	436,345,259
Unitemized as share of total from individuals (percent)	45%	53%	37%	68%	30%	47%	46%	55%	65%
Contributions at the maximum permitted	84,200,649	1,028,312	45,121,440	4,438,062	114,266,690	36,664,564	54,872,877	27,615,735	75,876,649
Maximum as a share of individual total (percent)	18%	0%	9%	2%	24%	18%	22%	11%	11%

NRSC

All individual contributions plus other receipts	108,231,990	114,016,005	113,505,921	136,021,245	131,929,383	142,016,350	150,706,728	159,136,503	342,821,617
Total contributions from individuals	85,969,616	85,243,886	88,395,588	103,661,703	110,866,070	108,087,504	87,753,040	102,182,247	259,977,670
Individuals as share of total receipts (percent)	79%	75%	78%	76%	84%	76%	58%	64%	76%
Itemized	34,907,488	31,527,907	34,787,500	40,271,576	29,628,559	30,024,236	26,814,542	31,658,751	79,802,714
Itemized as share of total from individuals (percent)	41%	37%	39%	39%	27%	28%	31%	31%	31%
Contributions at the maximum permitted	8,494,591	2,737,799	15,486,972	19,200,981	20,519,199	27,239,350	24,455,416	21,260,183	37,060,900
Maximum as a share of individual total (percent)	10%	3%	18%	19%	19%	25%	28%	21%	14%

NRCC

All individual contributions plus other receipts	254,453,415	230,502,837	142,235,603	158,782,642	175,541,362	167,800,481	189,391,993	222,944,067	294,376,574
Total contributions from individuals	199,856,567	143,893,841	91,396,356	90,427,742	96,153,364	94,489,767	88,175,460	108,126,673	187,634,505
Individuals as share of total receipts (percent)	79%	62%	64%	57%	55%	56%	47%	48%	64%
Itemized	68,216,851	54,393,154	38,598,449	40,440,242	28,129,081	27,366,135	18,230,886	28,558,604	77,106,208
Itemized as share of total from individuals (percent)	34%	38%	42%	45%	29%	29%	21%	26%	41%
Contributions at the maximum permitted	5,069,353	239,939	3,186,108	8,587,945	10,832,470	18,178,189	22,394,802	23,488,479	19,844,500
Maximum as a share of individual total (percent)	3%	0%	3%	9%	11%	19%	25%	22%	11%

Source: OpenSecrets analysis of national party committee, and related joint fundraising committees, reporting to the Federal Election Commission
Note: To show a true view of individual donors, amounts include contributions attributable to the party committees via joint fund-raisers that, although itemized in memo entries, do not appear on the summary portion of FEC reports. Thus, in some cases, totals may differ from FEC reported totals. Contributions to the parties' special convention, building, and recount/legal accounts are included.

Table 5.3 Top Party-Aligned Super PACs, 2020 (millions of dollars)

Super PAC	Supports	Receipts	Independent Expenditures
Senate Majority PAC	Democratic Senate candidates	$372.3	$250.2
House Majority PAC	Democratic House candidates	$160.3	$139.9
Senate Leadership Fund	Republican Senate candidates	$475.4	$293.7
Congressional Leadership Fund	Republican House candidates	$165.7	$142.8
Unite the Country	Democratic presidential nominee Biden	$49.9	$38.9
America First Action	Republican presidential nominee Trump	$150.1	$133.8

Source: OpenSecrets, "2020 Outside Spending, by Group," OpenSecrets.org, 2021, https://www.opensecrets .org/outsidespending/summ.php?cycle=2020&chrt=V&disp=O&type=A (accessed December 30, 2021)

and NRCC raise much money from their own candidates and members (see chapter 4).[36] In 2020, the DCCC raised $28.9 million, and the NRCC raised $34.5 million from this source of funds, whereas the Senate committees raised relatively little.[37]

Indeed, House party leaders assess dues on their members, and party and committee leaders are expected to contribute more than other lawmakers. Party leaders and committee chairs, who can generally raise much more than rank-and-file members, often do give large sums to their chamber's party campaign committee. Speaker of the House Nancy Pelosi (D-CA) gave $1.9 million to the DCCC, and Minority Whip Steve Scalise (R-LA) gave a whopping $12.5 million to the NRCC.[38]

PARTY SPENDING IN 2020

With such successful fund-raising, the national party committees spent big in the 2020 election, especially the RNC, which expended $833.5 million, almost twice the $461.5 million that the DNC spent. Figure 5.6 shows total disbursements by each of the national party committees from 2002 to 2020.[39] The House and Senate campaign committees all spent more in 2019–2020 than in recent election cycles, especially the Senate committees, the NRSC and DSCC, as we discuss below. The big news, however, is the RNC's record spending for 2020. This increased spending included what RNC spokesperson Mike Reed called "the largest ground game operation in history"; by October 2020 the RNC had spent $300 million on targeting data, knocking on doors, calling voters, digital voter contact, and other GOTV activities.[40] Modeling their strategy after Barack Obama's successful

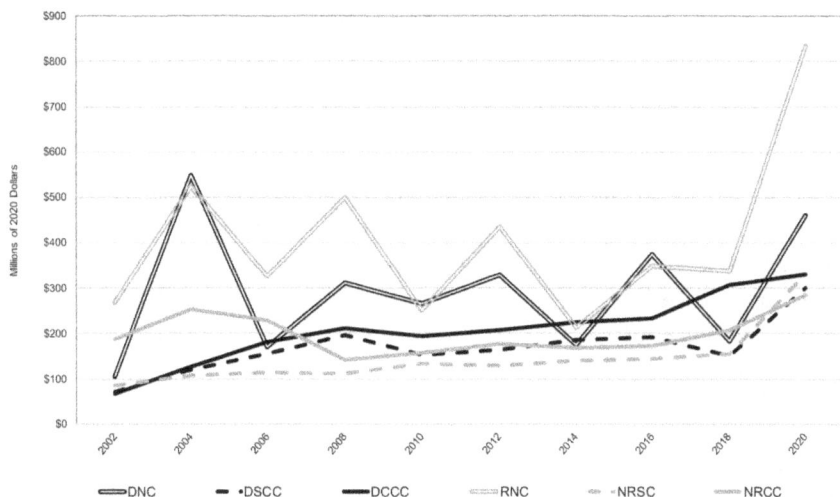

Figure 5.6 National Party Committee Disbursements, 2002–2020 (millions of 2020 dollars). *Source*: https://www.fec.gov/campaign-finance-data/political-party-data-summary-tables/?year=2020&segment=24

mobilization efforts,[41] the RNC deployed paid staff early in the campaign season to nineteen states and expanded its "fellows" program of trained grassroots volunteers to sixty thousand fellows for door-to-door party campaigning using detailed targeting data.[42]

However, the RNC's increased spending was not particularly efficient. The *New York Times* published a detailed article about how the Trump campaign and the RNC spent away their earlier cash lead over Biden and the Democrats on items that likely fed the president's ego rather than persuading voters to reelect him. About $350 million of the $800 million spent up to September of 2020 was for fund-raising—actively finding those new donors. Because Michael Bloomberg, a candidate for the Democratic presidential nomination ran an ad during the Superbowl in February, so did Trump—for more than $11 million. They also ran $1.6 million on TV ads in the Washington, D.C., media market, which was never competitive for Trump (reaching Maryland, Virginia, and the District) but where Trump was a regular TV watcher. Trump also directed the RNC to spend $30 million on mementos (swag) for donors.[43]

More money was squandered around the 2020 Republican National Convention. The convention was first scheduled for Charlotte, North Carolina, but Trump insisted it move to Jacksonville, Florida, when North Carolina Democratic Governor Roy Cooper rejected the RNC's plan to have fifty thousand people in attendance with no COVID prevention protocols other than daily temperature checks. Instead, Cooper wrote in a letter to the RNC:

"The people of North Carolina do not know what the status of COVID-19 will be in August, so planning for a scaled-down convention with fewer people, social distancing and face coverings is a necessity." Then, the RNC canceled in-person plans in both locations and went online from the White House in Washington, D.C.[44] Although some convention spending was done before the decision to move the convention to Florida and before the in-person event was canceled, some occurred around the online event. For instance, at least half a million dollars was spent on fireworks in the month of August for the RNC online convention,[45] and more than $1 million was paid to the Ritz-Carlton, Amelia Island, near Jacksonville, Florida, before the convention was moved online.[46]

Another reason for the big jump in RNC spending was the odd situation of having a president who owned resort properties insisting that his properties be the destinations for meetings and events where he appeared. The controversy surrounding Trump's mixing his business interests with his public and political roles has been widely reported.[47] The RNC was part of this pattern. Both parties' national committees routinely hold "winter" meetings. In January 2018 and 2020, the RNC held these meetings at Trump National Doral Miami. The RNC paid a deposit to the Doral in November 2019, just weeks after Trump received significant criticism for his plan to host the G7 Summit there in the summer of 2020.[48] But the real issue was evidence of price gouging by the Doral for both government employees such as Secret Service agents and press covering the RNC meeting. Writing for the *Huffington Post*, S. V. Date explained:

> For the latter half of December [2019] and the first days of January [2020], Doral's website advertised rates as low as $254 per night for nonrefundable rooms for the days of the RNC meeting . . . Those numbers suddenly jumped to $459 a night on Jan. 13, soon after the White House first began planning for a potential Trump trip to the meeting. The next day it jumped to $539 a night, before falling to $499 per room on Jan. 15, but with rooms only available for the final night of the RNC meeting, and the first two nights sold out.[49]

It did not end there. When his administration was only a year old, Trump had already directed the RNC to pay him rent for his 2020 reelection headquarters in Trump Tower in New York. Throughout 2017, the RNC held events at Trump's Washington, D.C., hotel as did other members of Congress for their fund-raisers.[50] Other reporting found that more than $7.4 million was spent at Trump-branded properties since 2017.[51]

Republican state parties benefited from donor enthusiasm for Trump. State GOP parties in many battleground states spent much more in 2020 than in

2016 due in part to the increased funding they received from the RNC and Trump joint fund-raising committees and their own Trump-themed fund-raising.[52] The Florida Party raked in $35 million, North Carolina almost $25 million, and Arizona almost $17 million, and all spent more in 2020 than they had in 2016—the North Carolina GOP, for example, built a new television studio, invested in other infrastructure, and expanded its email list.[53]

The DNC was flush with cash for the first time in many election cycles, as the party committee usually ended presidential elections with significant debt. Under the leadership of DNC Chair Tom Perez and a beefed-up staff, the DNC expanded spending beyond traditional battleground states and engaged in some much-needed party-building activities after years of neglect and Democratic losses at the state level.[54] For instance, by the end of 2020, the DNC's program for regular small donors was bringing in more than $1 million per month, and after going into the 2020 election with no text messaging fund-raising, the DNC expected to raise $2 million through text messaging in January 2021.[55] After the 2020 election, the new DNC chair, Jaime Harrison, former South Carolina state party chair and incoming President Joe Biden's choice to lead the party, "pledged a '50-state' investment strategy, pushing to embed the party into communities and states that are off the traditional battleground map."[56]

Both parties may face a more challenging fund-raising landscape with Trump out of office. One Democratic strategist noted, "when you're in power, it's very hard to fundraise, especially when you lose the motivation of getting the bad guy out of his seat."[57] Many Republican party leaders attributed their 2020 fund-raising success to enthusiasm for Trump, which may be diminished after the January 6 riot and occupation of the Capitol, the second Trump impeachment, and discord within the party.

Party Adaptation: New Use of the Party Recount/Legal Account

As noted above, the 2019–2020 impeachment proceedings increased fund-raising for the Trump campaign and the RNC. Those dollar amounts are part of the overall totals showing that the 2020 election featured unusually high spending. However, much of the new fund-raising around impeachment and other investigations was spent not for campaign expenses but to pay off the legal bills these same scandals produced for Trump and his family. The RNC paid for legal fees for the president's son, Donald Trump Jr., to defend him against allegations that he colluded with Russia during the 2016 campaign[58] and for Trump's impeachment defense.[59] One estimate published in September 2020 concludes that legal fees alone cost $58.4 million.[60]

More than $26 million was spent for "legal and compliance services" from the RNC's Recount/Legal account (one of the special accounts created in 2015).[61]

Party Contributions to Candidates and Coordinated Expenditures

National party committees may give their candidates limited contributions in primary and general elections and make limited coordinated expenditures to assist their candidates; both types of spending allow direct consultation with the candidate (see chapter 2). Typically, party committees have used coordinated expenditures to pay for standard campaign products and activities such as polls, campaign ads, opposition research, and targeted voter lists. Figures 5.7 and 5.8 show that the national party committees have never spent much on direct contributions for their House and Senate candidates, due to the very low limits that are not adjusted for inflation. Before 2004, the parties' major tool to help their candidates was coordinated expenditures, which have higher limits than direct contributions. The parties only started investing heavily in House and Senate races with independent expenditures, which are not limited at all, in 2004, after soft money was banned. (Soft money had been used to buy "issue advocacy advertisements." As these activities were technically not campaign ads, the spending was not disclosed to the FEC; see chapter 2.)

In 2020, the DCCC and the NRCC each spent similar amounts on coordinated expenditures, $8.2 million and $8.9 million, respectively. Meanwhile,

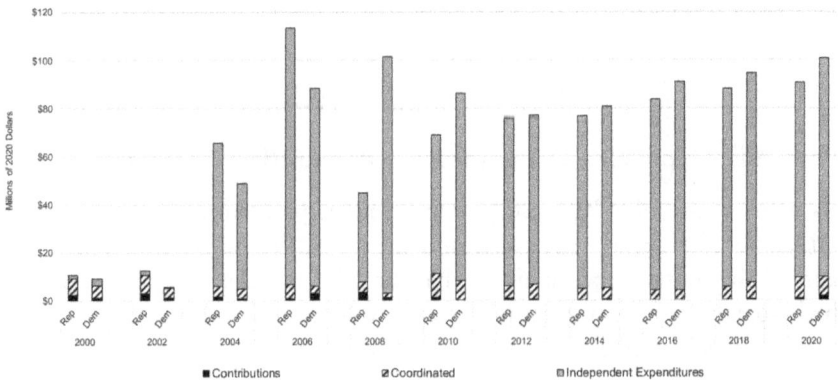

Figure 5.7 Party Spending on U.S. House Races, 2000–2020 (millions of 2020 dollars). *Source*: OpenSecrets, compiled from Campaign Finance Institute, "Table 3-6: Political Party Contributions, Coordinated and Independent Expenditures for Congressional Candidates, 1976–2018," http://www.cfinst.org/pdf/federal/HistoricalTables/pdf/CFI_Federal-CF_18_Table3-06.pdf; Federal Election Commission, "Any Transaction from One Committee to Another," in Bulk Data, https://www.fec.gov/data/browse-data/?tab=bulk-data

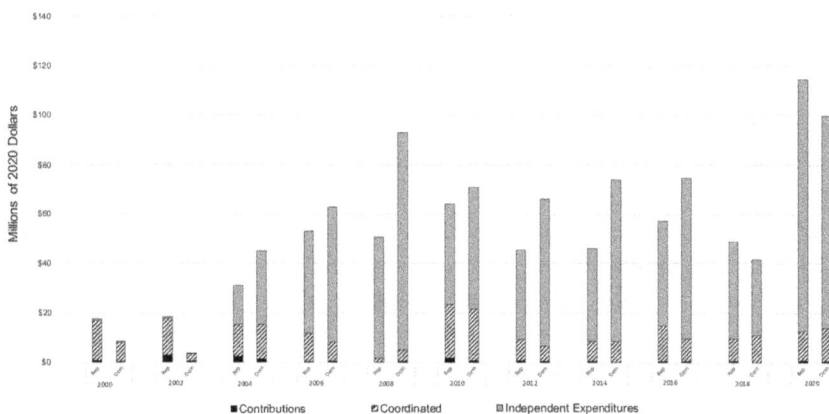

Figure 5.8 Party Spending on U.S. Senate Races, 2000–2020 (millions of 2020 dollars). *Source*: Campaign Finance Institute, "Table 3-6: Political Party Contributions, Coordinated and Independent Expenditures for Congressional Candidates, 1976–2018," http://www.cfinst.org/pdf/federal/HistoricalTables/pdf/CFI_Federal-CF_18_Table3-06.pdf; Federal Election Commission, "Any Transaction from One Committee to Another" in Bulk Data, https://www.fec.gov/data/browse-data/?tab=bulk-data

the NRSC spent $13.6 million in coordinated expenditures, and the DSCC spent $14.2 million. Both Senate committees spent a significant proportion of this total on the Georgia runoff Senate races. On the Republican side, $1.8 million, or 18 percent of the total coordinated expenditures, were spent in the runoffs.[62] On the Democratic side, the DSCC spent $1.4 million in coordinated expenditures to help Ossoff defeat Perdue in the regular election but nothing in the runoff. Before November 3, the DSCC spent $731,000 to help Warnock against Loeffler and $741,000 to defeat her in the runoff, with the latter constituting about 5 percent of all coordinated expenditures.[63]

The national party committees may also make limited coordinated expenditures for their presidential candidate in the general election. In 2020, the RNC spent $25.3 million in the presidential election for Trump, compared to $20 million they spent for him in 2016. The DNC spent $18.8 million on Joe Biden's presidential campaign, compared to $22 million in coordinated expenditures for Hillary Clinton in 2016.[64]

Party Independent Expenditures

Since 1996, the national party committees could make unlimited independent expenditures to help their candidates, spending that may not be coordinated with the candidates (see chapter 2). Figure 5.7 shows that in 2020, the House party committees spent about the same on such independent expenditures as they did in 2018: $90 million by the DCCC and $80 million by the NRCC. The two Senate party committees spent substantially more on independent expenditures than in 2018—about 300 percent more for each committee—and more than they had spent in any election cycle since 2000 (see figure 5.8). With control of the U.S. Senate in active contention, it is no wonder that spending soared. Yet again, the Georgia Senate runoffs account for a considerable portion of the increased spending, with the NRSC spending $17 million of the $120 million total conventional independent expenditures in the Georgia runoffs (about 14 percent of all such funds), and the DSCC spending $8.2 million of their $93 million total in the Georgia runoffs (about 9 percent of such funds).[65]

The RNC and DNC have used independent expenditures inconsistently in recent presidential election cycles. In 2020, neither committee made any independent expenditures for their presidential candidates. However, the RNC did use $7.1 million in independent expenditures to help their candidates in the Georgia Senate runoffs.

Party-Aligned Super PACs

One reason that party-coordinated expenditures and independent expenditures make up a modest proportion of the overall total spent in 2020 was the increased reliance on party-affiliated and candidate/officeholder Super PACs (see chapters 2 and 6). Wealthy donors who once spent through political party soft money accounts and tax-exempt groups now often turn to one or more Super PACs aligned with the national party committees.[66] Table 5.3 reports the large amounts raised and spent by the top party-aligned Super PACs (see chapters 4 and 6).

Although parties are not permitted to coordinate their independent expenditures with their targeted candidates, and Super PACs may not coordinate with candidates or parties, party and Super PAC strategies do appear to complement one another. For instance, the party congressional and senatorial committees often publicly highlight which House and Senate races they plan to target and what type of spending they plan to do for the most competitive contests. This signaling enables Super PACs to focus on the same races as the parties (those most consequential for control of each chamber) and to spend in different ways than the parties (such as running mostly negative ads against the opposing candidate). We contend that this process amounts to party "orchestration" of "outside" groups' partisan electoral efforts, thus assisting the parties' pursuit of electoral victory for their candidates and majority control of the Congress.[67]

The formal party committees sit at the center of wider extended party networks that include these party-aligned groups, and the party-aligned groups look to the parties for strategic direction on where to focus their campaign spending and other efforts. This orchestration of party-aligned Super PACs allows the formal national party organizations to extend their campaign finance influence as the parties' share of overall noncandidate spending has

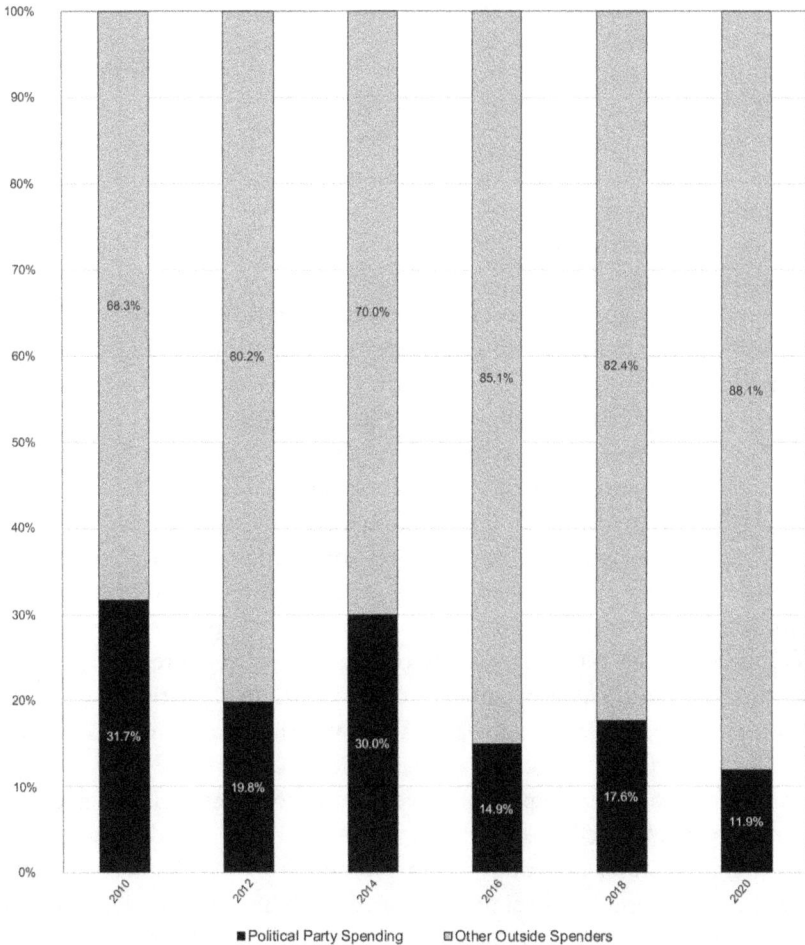

Figure 5.9   Noncandidate Spending: Party and Nonparty Sources, 2010–2020. *Source*: 2012–2020 Data: Center for Responsive Politics, "Outside Spending: Total by Type of Spender," https://www.opensecrets.org/outside-spending/summary?cycle=2012. 2010 Data: Nonparty: CRP, "2010 Outside Spending, by Group," https://www.opensecrets.org/outside-spending/by_group/2010?chart=V&disp=O&type=I (accessed December 29, 2022)

declined significantly relative to nonparty spenders since 2010, as figure 5.9 shows.

HOW WAS 2020 HISTORIC FOR PARTIES?

Although the 2020 elections certainly featured some new and unique national party campaign finance activities—such as impeachment-fueled fund-raising and the GOP's spending for legal fees to defend Trump and support his challenges to the election results, and the pandemic-altered voter mobilization and convention activities—the parties' fund-raising and spending during this election cycle confirmed much of our understanding of party behavior and party adaptation. For instance, party spending was directed efficiently where it was likely to make the most difference. Early in 2021, we saw increased investment by both parties in legal challenges to vote counting procedures in many states. Indeed, all of the national party committees now have special party accounts specifically created to raise money for the parties' legal and recount activities, and we expect increased legal spending will be a permanent central strategy for both parties.

Both parties' Senate campaign committees significantly increased their spending in 2019–2020 as control of the chamber was seriously in contention during the entire election season and into 2021 because of the two Georgia Senate runoffs. In addition, both parties continue to raise more each election cycle through joint fund-raising committees for all of their party entities, including the special convention, legal/recount, and headquarters committees. Joint fund-raising committees offer the parties economies of scale, whereby they have successfully been able to raise more from big contributors for multiple party-connected recipients (e.g., national and state party committees, the special party accounts, candidates, and Leadership PACs). Moreover, the national party committees continuously look for ways to raise and spend more in pursuit of electoral victory, particularly since party soft money was banned with BCRA in 2002 and because of the fund-raising and spending limits on contributions to and from parties. Party-aligned Super PACs help the national parties overcome these limits and have become institutionalized features of the campaign finance landscape as additional organizations in pursuit of the parties' electoral goals.

We expect continued use of JFCs and party-aligned Super PACs in the future. We also expect competition for control of both chambers of Congress and the White House to continue to be realistically up for grabs, and that the parties will be motivated to look for new ways to raise and spend more and more effectively to win control of each part of the federal government.

However, the unique circumstances of the 2020 elections—the pandemic, a presidential impeachment, two postelection Senate runoffs that decided control of the chamber—might not occur again . . . at least we can hope that they will not.

NOTES

1. Herbert E. Alexander, *Financing the 1960 Election* (Princeton, NJ: Citizens' Research Foundation, 1962).

2. David A. Hopkins, "Financing the 2016 Presidential General Election," in *Financing the 2016 Election*, ed. David B. Magleby (Washington, DC: Brookings Institution Press, 2019), 187–216.

3. Boris Heersink, "Trump and the Party-in-Organization: Presidential Control of National Party Organizations," *Journal of Politics* 80, no. 4 (October 2018): 1474–82.

4. Heersink, "Trump and the Party-in-Organization," 1480.

5. Michael D. Shear, Maggie Haberman, and Alan Rappeport, "Donald Trump Picks Reince Priebus as Chief of Staff and Stephen Bannon as Strategist," *New York Times*, November 13, 2016, www.nytimes.com/2016/11/14/us/politics/reince-prie-bus-chief-of-staff-donald-trump.html.

6. James Pindell, "Under Trump, 'Permanent Campaign' Takes on a Whole New Meaning," *Boston Globe*, March 16, 2017, https://www.bostonglobe.com/metro/2017/03/16/under-trump-permanent-campaign-takes-whole-new-meeting/DhZCLgG2DMCsiAgbC96bcM/story.html.

7. "Donald Trump's Takeover of His Party Is Near Complete," *The Economist*, April 19, 2018, www.economist.com/briefing/2018/04/19/donald-trumps-takeover-of-his-party-is-near-complete.

8. Eliana Johnson and John Bresnahan, "Trump's Biden Insults Fueled by Belief He Can Win," Politico, April 25, 2019, https://www.politico.com/story/2019/04/25/donald-trump-joe-biden-2020-1290338.

9. Don Van Natta Jr., "Raising Funds: Impeachment Is Powerful Tool," *New York Times*, July 20, 1999, sec. A; Don Van Natta Jr., "Fewer Donations Coming in for Clinton Defense Fund," *New York Times*, August 13, 1999, sec. A.

10. Noah Bierman, "The Nation: Campaign Profits from Impeachment Woes; Trump's Reelection Team Raises Millions from Riled Supporters: 'Money Is Flying In,'" *Los Angeles Times*, October 1, 2019, www.latimes.com/politics/story/2019-10-01/trumps-reelection-campaign-cashes-in-on-impeachment-woes.

11. Brian Bennett and Chris Wilson, "Quid Pro Dough: How Trump 2020 Profits from Impeachment," *Time*, December 5, 2019, https://time.com/magazine/us/5744386/december-16th-2019-vol-194-no-26-u-s/.

12. Donna Brazile, *Hacks: The Inside Story of the Break-Ins and Breakdowns That Put Donald Trump in the White House* (New York: Hachette, 2017), chap. 10.

13. Daniel Strauss, "Biden Endorses Perez in DNC Chair Race," *Politico*, February 1, 2017, www.politico.com/story/2017/02/joe-biden-endorses-tom-perez-dnc-chair-234495.

14. Soma Biswas and Reid J. Epstein, "Restructuring Pro Prepares His Toughest Turnaround Yet: The Democratic Party," *Wall Street Journal*, May 26, 2017, sec. Markets, www.wsj.com/articles/restructuring-pro-prepares-his-toughest-turnaround-yet-the-democratic-party-1495827628.

15. Kendall Karson, "The DNC's Road from 'on the Ropes' to Securing a Democrat in the White House," ABC News, November 13, 2020, https://abcnews.go.com/Politics/dncs-road-ropes-securing-democrat-white-house/story?id=74178625.

16. Mike Allen, "Democrats Are Destroying Republicans in a Historic 'Green Tsunami' of Fund-raising," *Axios*, October 18, 2020, www.axios.com/democrat-fund-raising-green-tsunami-01f3b59f-90c0-4d4a-9656-85cc63c73eeb.html.

17. Unless otherwise noted, all figures are in 2020 constant dollars to allow for accurate comparisons over time.

18. Federal Election Commission, "Joint Fund-Raising with Other Candidates and Political Committees," FEC.gov, https://www.fec.gov/help-candidates-and-committees/joint-fund-raising-candidates-political-committees/ (accessed January 1, 2022). Note that the FEC data sometimes contain individual contributions reported twice when the contribution is collected via a JFC. So, interpret these data carefully. Contributions to a JFC beyond the statutory limits may be reallocated to other JFC participants with the approval of the donor.

19. Center for Responsive Politics, "Joint Fund-Raising Committees 2020," *OpenSecrets*, 2022, https://www.opensecrets.org/jfc/top.php?type=C&cycle=2020. This is the number of JFCs reported on OpenSecrets.org on March 1, 2022.

20. Center for Responsive Politics, www.opensecrets.org/jfc/top.php?type=C&cycle=2020.

21. Compiled by authors from Federal Election Commission data.

22. Karl Evers-Hillstrom, "Trump Raised Record Money for State Parties, Then His RNC Took It Back," *OpenSecrets News*, February 24, 2021, www.opensecrets.org/news/2021/02/trump-raised-record-sums-for-state-parties-rnc/.

23. Hillary Clinton's JFC in 2016 and Mitt Romney's JFC in 2012 also engaged in similar money shuffles to and then from state parties. The 2016 Clinton JFC operated like Trump Victory, with state parties transferring their JFC proceeds to the DNC, though the 2012 Romney Victory Committee featured four state party committees that then transferred money to *other* state party committees in battleground states rather than to the RNC. See Diana Dwyre and Robin Kolodny, "Party Money in the 2016 Election," in *Financing the 2016 Election*, ed. David Magleby (Washington, DC: Brookings Institution Press, 2019), 274–75, www.brookings.edu/book/financing-the-2016-election/; Diana Dwyre and Robin Kolodny, "Party Money in the 2012 Elections," in *Financing the 2012 Election*, ed. David B. Magleby (Washington, DC: Brookings Institution Press, 2014), 196.

24. Bob Biersack, "How Wealthy Donors Fund the National Party by Giving to the States," *OpenSecrets News*, July 24, 2017, www.opensecrets.org/news/2017/07/wealthy-donors-fund-national-party-giving-to-states/; Michael Malbin, "McCutcheon Could Lead to No Limits for Political Parties—With What Implications for Parties and Interest Groups?" *New York University Law Review* 89, no. Online Symposium (2014): 92–104.

25. Georgia Trump Victory with Senator David Perdue and the RNC (raised $774,450); New Jersey Trump Victory with Representative Jeff Van Drew (raised $172,918); Colorado Trump Victory with Senator Cory Gardner (raised $1,113,347); and South Carolina Trump Victory with Senator Lindsey Graham (raised $259,340).

26. Center for Responsive Politics, "Joint Fund-Raising Committees 2020."

27. Center for Responsive Politics. "Joint Fund-Raising Committees 2020."

28. David Primo and Jeffrey Milyo, *Campaign Finance and American Democracy: What the Public Really Thinks and Why It Matters* (Chicago: University of Chicago Press, 2020), 106–8.

29. "National Party Conventions," Campaign Finance Institute, 2008, http://www.cfinst.org/federal/conventions.aspx; see "Sources of Funding for National Party Conventions, 1980–2004" and "2008 Conventions Reports"; R. Sam Garrett and Shawn Reese, "Funding of Presidential Nominating Conventions: An Overview" (Washington, DC: Congressional Research Service, May 4, 2016).

30. The 2014 Gabriella Miller Kids First Research Act, H.R. 2019; P.L. 113–94.

31. The Consolidated and Further Continuing Appropriations Act of 2015, H.R. 83; P.L. 113–235.

32. In 2012, an individual's contributions to all PACs and parties was capped at $70,800 (see Federal Election Commission, "Archive of Contribution Limits," FEC.gov, https://www.fec.gov/help-candidates-and-committees/candidate-taking-receipts/archived-contribution-limits/ [accessed February 27, 2022]).

33. These maximum contributions for individuals and PACs to the national party committees are calculated in the following manner: the maximum possible contribution to a party committee x 3 (the party's 3 national party committees) x 2 (limit is per *year*, so a contributor may give twice in a two-year election cycle) + the maximum possible contribution to each of the party's special committee (convention, recount and HQ) x 7 (1 convention committee, 3 recount committees and 3 HQ committees) x 2 (limit is per *year*) = maximum possible contribution.

34. Federal Election Commission, "Political Party Data Summary Tables, 2019–2020," FEC.gov, 2021, https://www.fec.gov/campaign-finance-data/political-party-data-summary-tables/.

35. For the latest research, see Michael Barber, "Donation Motivations: Testing Theories of Access and Ideology," *Political Research Quarterly* 69, no. 1 (2016): 148–59, https://doi.org/10.1177/1065912915624164; Jesse Crosson, Alexander Furnas, and Geoffrey Lorenz, "Polarized Pluralism: Organizational Preferences and Biases in the American Pressure System," *American Political Science Review* 114, no. 4 (2020): 1117–37, https://doi.org/10.1017/S0003055420000350.

36. Eric S. Heberlig and Bruce Larson, *Congressional Parties, Institutional Ambition, and the Financing of Majority Control* (Ann Arbor: University of Michigan Press, 2012); Robin Kolodny, *Pursuing Majorities: Congressional Campaign Committees in American Politics*, Congressional Studies Series, vol. 1 (Norman: University of Oklahoma Press, 1998).

37. Federal Election Commission, "Political Party Data Summary Tables, 2019–2020," tables 5, 6, 7, and 8.

38. Compiled by authors from Federal Election Commission, "Political Party Data Summary Tables, 2019–2020," tables 5 and 6.

39. We show spending from 2002, after BCRA banned party soft money, because soft money spending is incredibly difficult to track accurately.

40. Soo Rin Kim, "How Trump's Team Spent Most of the $1.6 Billion It Raised over 2 Years," *ABC News*, October 24, 2020, https://abcnews.go.com/Politics/trumps-team-spent-16-billion-raised-years/story?id=73795897.

41. Elizabeth McKenna and Hahrie Han, *Groundbreakers: How Obama's 2.2 Million Volunteers Transformed Campaigning in America* (New York: Oxford University Press, 2015).

42. A. B. Stoddard, "Dems Beware—the RNC Is Crushing It," *RealClearPolitics*, October 25, 2019, https://www.realclearpolitics.com/articles/2019/10/25/dems_beware_--_the_rnc_is_crushing_it_141582.html.

43. Shane Goldmacher and Maggie Haberman, "How Trump's Billion-Dollar Campaign Lost Its Cash Advantage," *New York Times*, September 7, 2020, sec. U.S., www.nytimes.com/2020/09/07/us/politics/trump-election-campaign-fund-raising.html.

44. Brian Slodysko and Zeke Miller, "How Trump Plowed through $1 Billion, Losing Cash Advantage," AP News, April 20, 2021, https://apnews.com/article/election-2020-virus-outbreak-joe-biden-donald-trump-impeachments-8ac355b6ebd62b19d8a44fedcbf5b128.

45. Lachlan Markay and Sam Stein, "Trump Campaign Spent Nearly Half a Million on Fireworks," *Daily Beast*, September 22, 2020, sec. politics, https://www.thedailybeast.com/the-trump-campaign-spent-nearly-half-a-million-on-convention-fireworks.

46. Slodysko and Miller, "How Trump Plowed through $1 Billion."

47. Olivia Nuzzi, "Donald Trump Is Paying Himself to Run for President: The GOP Frontrunner Likes to Brag That He Self-Funds His Presidential Campaign. What He Doesn't Mention Is That He's Profiting off It as Well," *Daily Beast*, March 1, 2016, http://www.proquest.com/docview/1782287143/abstract/D7B2AF62E6114202PQ/1; Dean Baker, "Trump Family and Friends: In Your Pockets," *HuffPost*, May 16, 2017, https://www.huffpost.com/entry/trump-family-and-friends-in-your-pockets_b_591a4c05e4b0f31b03fb9e7c.

48. S. V. Date, "Trump's Doral Resort Spikes Its Room Rates Ahead of His RNC Visit: The Doubling of Rates May Have Increased Taxpayer Costs for Housing Secret Service and Other Staff Who Traveled There Ahead of the President's Trip,"

HuffPost, January 23, 2020, www.huffpost.com/entry/trump-doral-room-rates_n_5e285b24c5b6779e9c2b6521.

49. Date, "Trump's Doral Resort Spikes Its Room Rates Ahead of His RNC Visit."

50. Fredreka Schouten and Christopher Schnaars, "More Than $1 Million in Campaign Donors' Money Went to Trump Properties in 2017," *USA Today*, www.usatoday.com/story/news/politics/onpolitics/2018/02/07/more-than-1-million-campaign-donors-money-went-trump-properties-2017/315453002/.

51. Slodysko and Miller, "How Trump Plowed through $1 Billion, Losing Cash Advantage."

52. Matt Holt, "State Parties Are Building the Groundwork for Trump's Comeback," *National Journal Daily A.M.*, February 2, 2021.

53. Holt, "State Parties Are Building the Groundwork for Trump's Comeback."

54. Shane Goldmacher, "Democratic Party Enters 2021 in Power—and Flush with Cash, for a Change," *New York Times*, January 31, 2021, sec. U.S., https://www.nytimes.com/2021/01/31/us/politics/democratic-party-finances.html.

55. Goldmacher, "Democratic Party Enters 2021 in Power."

56. Goldmacher, "Democratic Party Enters 2021 in Power."

57. Elena Schneider, "How ActBlue Has Transformed Democratic Politics," *Politico*, U.S. edition, October 30, 2020, https://www.proquest.com/politicalscience/docview/2455932478/citation/15DBF7D59BA74D42PQ/2.

58. Darlene Superville, "The RNC Has Spent Almost $200,000 on Donald Trump Jr.'s Legal Fees for the Russia Investigation," *Time.com*, September 19, 2017, 80.

59. Ann E. Marimow, Beth Reinhard, and Josh Dawsey, "Trump's Impeachment Defense: Who Is Paying the President's Lawyers? As Trump Faces Mounting Legal Bills, He Is Drawing on National Party Coffers Flush from Energized Donors," *Washington Post*, January 28, 2020, www.washingtonpost.com/local/legal-issues/trumps-impeachment-defense-who-is-paying-the-presidents-lawyers/2020/01/27/5ac18268-3eec-11ea-8872-5df698785a4e_story.html.

60. Eric Lipton, "How Trump Draws on Campaign Funds to Pay Legal Bills," *New York Times*, September 6, 2020, https://www.nytimes.com/2020/09/05/us/politics/trump-campaign-funds-legal-bills.html.

61. Compiled by authors from FEC spending reports.

62. The NRSC spent the entire limit of $1.6 million on the Loeffler runoff and $163,123 on the Perdue runoff. Before November 3, 2020, the NRSC spent none of the allowed coordinated expenditures to help Loeffler but spent $1.4 million to help Perdue. Compiled by the authors from FEC sources.

63. Compiled by the authors from FEC sources.

64. Dwyre and Kolodny, "Party Money in the 2016 Election."

65. All figures in this paragraph calculated by the authors from original FEC reports for the 2020 cycle. For generalized figures, see Federal Election Commission, "Political Party Data Summary Tables, 2019–2020."

66. Diana Dwyre and Evelyn Braz, "Super PAC Spending Strategies and Goals," *The Forum* 13, no. 2 (January 1, 2015): 245–67, https://doi.org/10.1515/for-2015 -0020; Diana Dwyre, "The Origin and Evolution of Super PACs: A Darwinian Examination of a Campaign Finance Species," *Society* 57, no. 5 (October 1, 2020): 511–19, https://doi.org/10.1007/s12115-020-00523-1.

67. For an analysis of the partisan behavior of party-allied Super PAC and other groups, see Robin Kolodny and Diana Dwyre, "Convergence or Divergence? Do Parties and Outside Groups Spend on the Same Candidates, and Does It Matter?," *American Politics Research* 46, no. 3 (2018): 375–401, https://doi.org/10 .1177/1532673X17719896; Paul S. Herrnson, "The Roles of Party Organizations, Party-Connected Committees, and Party Allies in Elections," *Journal of Politics* 71, no. 4 (2009): 1207–24, https://doi.org/DOI; http://dx.doi.org/10.1017 /S0022381609990065.

6

Interest Group Money in the 2020 Election

Jay Goodliffe

When Herbert E. Alexander published *Financing the 1960 Election*, interest groups were a modest but seminal factor in federal campaign finance. In 1960, more than a dozen labor union committees had strong ties to the Democratic Party. The business and ideological committees, fewer than a dozen, largely operated in a bipartisan or nonpartisan fashion. Meanwhile, large donations from the wealthy were a staple of campaign finance and tilted toward the Republican Party. By the 2020 election, these seeds had sprouted, grown, spread, and mutated into an extensive set of interest group organizations, taking three principal forms in federal campaign finance: Traditional PACs, Super PACs, and tax-exempt groups. Large donations from the wealthy are still a staple of campaign finance but in support of both political parties.

In the 2020 election cycle, Traditional PACs disbursed $1.9 billion, including $447 million in contributions to congressional candidates and $87 million in independent expenditures to influence federal elections. Super PACs (including Hybrid PACs; see below) spent $2.6 billion in independent expenditures to influence federal elections. And tax-exempt groups spent $127 million in independent expenditures, which is only part of what they spent on elections generally. The major change in how interest groups influence elections over the past ten years (and past sixty years) is the rise of Super PACs, which are substantially funded by wealthy individuals.

TRADITIONAL PACS

Federal campaign finance law has traditionally allowed a variety of political action committees (PACs) to raise and spend money in elections. First, corporations; trade, membership, and other associations; and labor unions may sponsor a Connected PAC. In addition, political groups without a sponsoring organization may form Non-connected PACs. Such PACs typically pursue issues, ideologies, or other causes but can also be organized by individual politicians. The latter are called Leadership PACs because the organizer typically holds or aspires to a formal leadership position (see chapters 3 and 4). For ease of presentation, the combination of Connected, Non-connected, and Leadership PACs can be labeled Traditional PACs (see chapter 2).

Table 6.1 displays the number of Traditional PACs and their disbursements in the 2008–2020 presidential election cycles, broken down by category (in constant 2020 dollars).[1] In total, the 6,014 PACs in 2020 spent $1.9 billion.[2] Connected PACs included 1,669 corporate and 1,091 trade/membership/other association PACs (including cooperatives and

Table 6.1 Traditional PACs, Disbursements ($ in millions) and Number, 2008–2020 Presidential Elections

(Number)	2008	2012	2016	2020
CONNECTED:				
Corporate	$373	$387	$416	$409
	(1,841)	(1,851)	(1,803)	(1,669)
Trade/Membership/Other*	$381	$324	$347	$301
	(1,286)	(1,152)	(1,119)	(1,091)
Labor	$302	$315	$357	$386
	(299)	(300)	(289)	(275)
NON-CONNECTED:				
Issue, Ideology, Cause	$373	$209	$252	$596
	(1,841)	(2,160)	(1,981)	(2,252)
Leadership	†	$147	$135	$213
		(532)	(572)	(727)
TOTAL	**$1,415**	**$1,382**	**$1,508**	**$1,905**
	(5,220)	**(5,995)**	**(5,764)**	**(6,014)**

*Includes cooperatives and corporations without stock
†FEC did not separate Leadership PACs in 2008. They are included with Issue, Ideology, Cause.
Source: Analysis of FEC Data, "Political Action Committee Data Summary Tables," https://www.fec.gov/campaign-finance-data/political-action-committee-data-summary-tables/?year=2020&segment=24, https://www.fec.gov/campaign-finance-data/political-action-committee-data-summary-tables/?year=2016&segment=24, https://www.fec.gov/campaign-finance-data/political-action-committee-data-summary-tables/?year=2012&segment=24, https://www.fec.gov/campaign-finance-data/political-action-committee-data-summary-tables/?year=2008&segment=24)

corporations without stock) and 275 labor PACs. Thus, business-oriented PACs outnumbered labor PACs ten to one, but their spending was less unbalanced: the former spent $710 million and the latter $386 million in 2020. Over time, business-oriented PAC spending has fluctuated somewhat (between $710 and 763 million), whereas labor spending has been increasing from $302 million in 2008 to $386 million in 2020. Non-connected PACs included 2,252 issue, ideological, or cause PACs, spending $596 million; and 727 Leadership PACs, spending $213 million. Taken together, disbursements by Non-connected PACs—both issue/ideology-oriented and Leadership—more than doubled from 2016.

The rise in disbursements by Non-connected PACs parallels the rise in partisan and ideological Super PAC disbursements discussed below, both influenced by the uncertainty of which party would control the House and Senate. And the rise in Leadership PAC disbursements is driven by the increasing importance of fund-raising for leadership positions in Congress.[3] This increase in disbursements (and the required fund-raising to support it) has taken place even though the contribution limits to and from Traditional PACs have not changed over the past fifty years (see chapter 2).

Traditional PAC Contributions

Figure 6.1 shows Traditional PAC contributions to congressional candidates alongside the expenditures by such candidates from 1978 to 2020. Both figures increased steadily over time, but while candidate expenditures

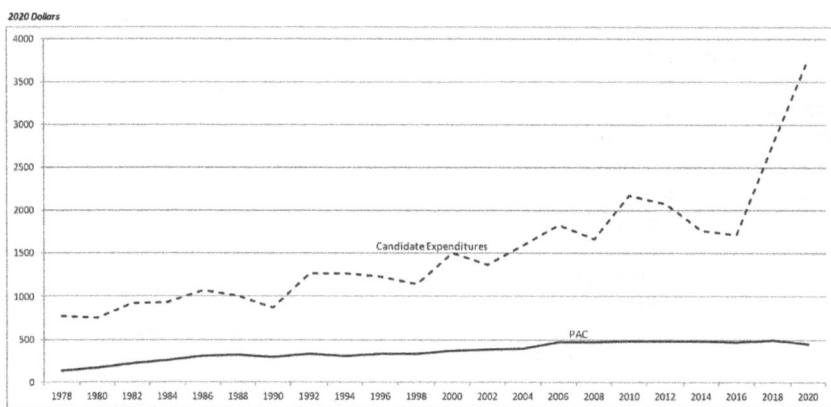

Figure 6.1   Congressional Candidate Expenditures and Traditional PAC Contributions to Congressional Candidates, 1978–2020. *Source*: https://www.fec.gov/campaign-finance -data/congressional-candidate-data-summary-tables/?year=2020&segment=24 and http:// cfinst.org/data.aspx

increased markedly from 2016 to 2018, and again from 2018 to 2020, PAC donations have remained steady since 2006. Until 2016, about one-quarter of candidate expenditures were funded by Traditional PAC contributions. But in 2020, only 12 percent of candidate expenditures were funded in this fashion because candidates relied more on contributions from individuals (see chapter 4). Part of this change might be attributed to changes in the law in 2004 (see chapter 2), which increased contribution limits for individuals while keeping Traditional PAC contribution limits the same. However, these figures both before and after 2004 show hardly any difference, so it could be that this shift is more reflective of new fund-raising technology that allows individuals to contribute more easily (such as ActBlue and WinRed fund-raising platforms).

Table 6.2 lists the top twenty Traditional PACs based on terms of congressional candidate contributions in 2020, along with the percentages contributed to Democratic and Republican candidates.[4] The top donor was the National Association of Realtors PAC (NARPAC), which contributed almost $4 million. Some of the business-oriented PACs gave more to

Table 6.2 Top Twenty Traditional PACs, Total Congressional Contributions and Recipient Party, 2020 Election

Name	Contributions	% Dem	% Rep
National Association of Realtors (NARPAC)	3,993,798	52%	48%
National Beer Wholesalers Assn.	3,174,500	52%	48%
Credit Union National Assn.	2,854,000	53%	47%
AT&T	2,776,500	46%	54%
Comcast Corporation & NBC Universal	2,712,500	46%	54%
American Crystal Sugar Co.	2,697,500	54%	46%
American Bankers Assn.	2,656,500	32%	68%
Majority Committee	2,545,000	0%	100%
National Automobile Dealers Assn.	2,431,000	28%	72%
National Air Traffic Controllers Assn.	2,375,300	67%	33%
American Federation of State County & Municipal Employees	2,364,500	99%	0%
American Federation of Teachers	2,323,500	100%	0%
International Brotherhood of Electrical Workers	2,294,400	97%	3%
American Association for Justice	2,242,500	98%	2%
Honeywell International	2,211,500	55%	45%
Lockheed Martin	2,145,000	45%	55%
United Brotherhood of Carpenters and Joiners	2,143,300	80%	20%
Home Depot	2,122,000	45%	55%
Northrop Grumman	2,058,500	52%	48%
Machinists/Aerospace Workers Union	2,028,000	98%	2%
Council of Insurance Agents & Brokers	2,009,000	34%	66%

Source: OpenSecrets, "Top 20 PACs to Candidates, 2019–2020," https://www.opensecrets.org/political-action-committees-pacs/top-pacs/2020, updated by author

Republicans in 2020 (e.g., AT&T, National Automobile Dealers Association), and some gave more to Democrats (e.g., Credit Unions, American Crystal Sugar Company). This pattern was a change from 2016, when all the top business-oriented PACs gave more money to Republicans. Meanwhile, the labor union PACs gave between 67 and 100 percent of their contributions to Democrats, continuing a longtime trend. The remaining entry, Majority PAC, was a Leadership PAC associated with then House Minority Leader Kevin McCarthy, which contributed 100 percent to fellow Republican candidates.

The top Traditional PAC contributors to congressional candidates have not changed much over time.[5] From 2000 to 2020, the top contributor to congressional candidates was NARPAC, contributing more than $41 million about equally to Democrats and Republicans. Six of the top ten corporations and trade associations in 2020 were also in the combined top ten from 2000 to 2020. Most of these organizations contributed more over time to Republicans than to Democrats. Two unions (Electrical Workers and AFSCME) as well as the American Association for Justice (trial lawyers) are in the top twenty in the 2020 election cycle as well as in the top ten combined from 2000 to 2020. These organizations contributed substantially more over time to Democrats than to Republicans.

Continuing the trend of previous election cycles, Traditional PACs gave most of their donations to incumbents. Figure 6.2 displays how much was contributed to incumbents, challengers, and open-seat candidates in U.S. House general elections from 1996 to 2020. In 2020, Traditional PACs contributed $346 million to U.S. House candidates—$306 million to House incumbents (89 percent), $20 million to challengers (6 percent), and $19 million to open-seat candidates. These percentages were approximately the same as 2016. Traditional

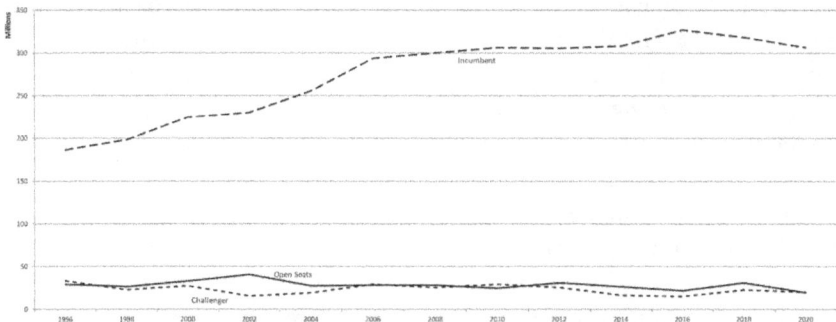

Figure 6.2   Traditional PAC Contributions to U.S. House General Election Candidates by Candidate Type, 1996–2020. *Source*: OpenSecrets, www.fec.gov/data/browse-data/?tab=bulk-data

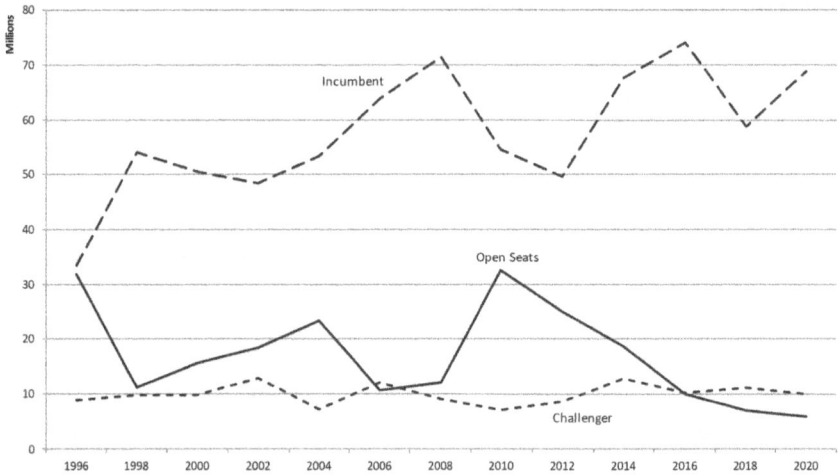

Figure 6.3   Traditional PAC Contributions to U.S. Senate General Election Candidates by Candidate Type, 1996–2020 (2020 dollars). *Source*: OpenSecrets, www.fec.gov/data /browse-data/?tab=bulk-data

PACs help maintain good relationships with House incumbents who, given their high reelection rate, will likely remain in office.

A similar, but less extreme, pattern is found for Senate candidates. Figure 6.3 displays how much was contributed to incumbents, challengers, and open-seat candidates in U.S. Senate general elections from 1996 to 2020. In the 2020 election cycle, Traditional PACs contributed $85 million to Senate candidates. The aggregate difference with the House is explained by the number of candidates: the House has many more candidates each election cycle than the Senate, and the contribution limits are the same for House and Senate candidates (see chapter 2). Traditional PACs contributed $69 million to incumbents (81 percent), $10 million to challengers (12 percent), and $6 million to open-seat candidates (7 percent). The lower percentage to incumbents can be explained in part by the lower reelection rates of incumbents in the Senate. The amounts given to different kinds of Senate candidates (relatively and absolutely) has changed more over time than the amounts given to House candidates. This result is partly due to the prospect of the chamber changing the majority party as well as the specific states with Senate seats up in a particular election cycle (as well as the differential costs of campaigns).

The total amounts given to different parties have also varied over time. In figure 6.4, Traditional PAC contributions to U.S. House general election candidates are separated into Republicans and Democrats. From 1996 to

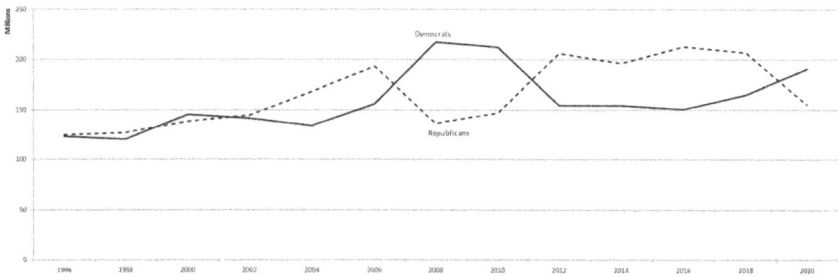

Figure 6.4 Traditional PAC Contributions to U.S. House General Election Candidates by Party, 1996–2020. *Source*: OpenSecrets, https://www.fec.gov/data/browse-data/?tab =bulk-data

2002, the amount spent supporting Republicans and Democrats was roughly equal. From 2004 to 2006, and from 2012 to 2018, Republicans received more contributions; from 2008 to 2010, and in 2020, Democrats received more contributions. This aligns perfectly with the majority party in the House going into the election cycle. In 2020, 55 percent of the $346 million contributed by Traditional PACs went to Democrats, who then controlled the House, but in 2016, these groups contributed 59 percent of their $363 million to Republicans, then in control of the House.

In contrast, the pattern in the Senate is not as strong. In figure 6.5, Traditional PAC contributions to U.S. Senate general election candidates are also separated into Republicans and Democrats. In most of the years, Republican candidates received more contributions; only in 2012 and 2018 did Democrats receive more PAC contributions. However, Republicans controlled the Senate going into the 2004 and 2006 elections, as well as the 2016 through 2020 elections; Democrats controlled the Senate going into

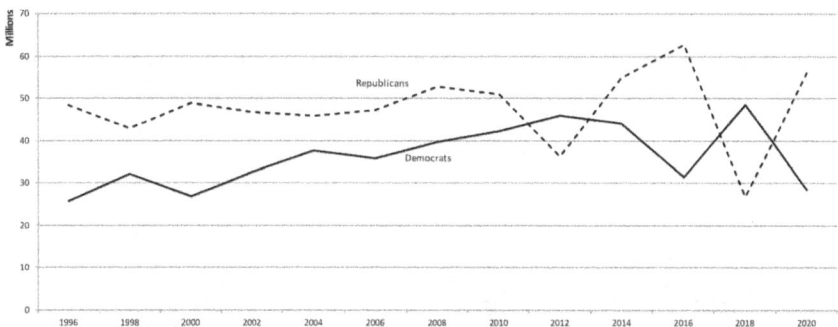

Figure 6.5 Traditional PAC Contributions to U.S. Senate General Election Candidates by Party, 1996–2020. *Source*: OpenSecrets, https://www.fec.gov/data/browse-data/?tab =bulk-data

the 2008 through 2014 elections. Thus, there is little correlation between Senate partisan control and the partisan distribution of PAC contributions. This aligns with the conventional wisdom that party control of the House is worth more than party control of the Senate.

Internal Communications

Traditional Connected PACs that businesses, trade/membership/other associations, and labor unions sponsor can expend funds to encourage their employees and members to vote for specific parties and candidates (see chapter 2). These internal communications may be seen as more credible to employees or members than messages from less well-known candidates or groups. These funds historically have come substantially from unions and favored Democrats over Republicans, but funds spent on internal communications have declined substantially over time. This trend continued as groups spent $31 million in 2016 and $22.7 million in 2020.[6] Relative to other kinds of interest group spending, these numbers are small. Even so, it is likely that some groups have moved funds from internal communications to independent expenditures.

Table 6.3 shows how much the top five Traditional PACs spent on internal communications in 2020. Two of the top spenders were unions: the AFL-CIO, which spent $4.1 million; and the National Education Association, which spent $2.2 million. An interest group—the League of Conservation Voters—and two business groups—the National Association of Realtors and the Credit Union National Association—are the other groups in the top five. The National Association of Realtors spent $3.8 million, which is also approximately how much the group contributed directly to federal candidates in 2020 (see table 6.2). What these organizations have in common is a large membership with whom political communication could be productive.

Table 6.3 Top Five Traditional PACs with Internal Communications Spending, 2020 Election

PAC	Amount
AFL-CIO	4,419,042
National Association of Realtors (NARPAC)	3,819,167
National Education Assn.	2,152,033
League of Conservation Voters	1,086,077
Credit Union National Assn.	1,044,151

Source: FEC, "Communication Costs by Corporations and Membership Organizations," https://www.fec.gov/resources/campaign-finance-statistics/2020/tables/cc/CC1_2020_24m.pdf

THE RISE AND SOURCES OF
INDEPENDENT EXPENDITURES

Since the U.S. Supreme Court ruled in favor of contribution limits but against expenditure limits in federal campaigns (see chapter 2), Traditional PACs and party organizations have been able to make unlimited independent expenditures for or against candidates—if the funds are raised within the contribution limits and are not coordinated with the candidate. Similarly, individual activists have also been able to make unlimited independent expenditures from their own funds on candidates of their own choosing. Eventually, new kinds of organizations developed to make independent expenditures, including Super PACs, Hybrid PACs, and tax-exempt groups (which will be discussed below).

Table 6.4 displays the independent expenditures from 2010 to 2020 by Traditional PACs, major party committees, Super PACs, Hybrid PACs, individual activists, and tax-exempt groups. Overall, independent expenditures have been larger in presidential than midterm election years, but they increased within each kind of election over this period. From 2016 to 2020 the increase was dramatic, rising from $2 billion to $3.3 billion. New types of organizations—Super PACs and Hybrid PACs—provided most of the growth in independent expenditures over this period, rising to 79 percent of all such expenditures in 2020.

The independent expenditures of party committees increased in absolute terms by $167 million from 2010 to 2020, but at the same time, party spending fell in relative terms from 33 percent of all such expenditures in 2010 to 12 percent in 2020. Meanwhile, the independent expenditures of Traditional PACs increased from $65 million to $87 million and accounted for just 3 percent of total independent expenditures in 2020. Interestingly, the pattern for independent expenditures by individual activists showed a similar relative decline, also accounting for just 3 percent of total independent expenditures in 2020. In 2010, tax-exempt groups spent $220 million in independent expenditures (including electioneering communications; see below), accounting for 32 percent of all such expenditures. In comparison, in 2020, tax-exempt groups spent $128 million, just 4 percent of all such expenditures. Tax-exempt groups are sometimes used as a conduit for so-called dark money, avoiding disclosure of donors, so it is interesting that their independent expenditures have decreased (although their expenditures in other areas may have increased).

Table 6.4 Independent Expenditures, Totals and Percentages by Source, 2010–2020

(2020 dollars, % within year)

Source	2010		2012		2014		2016		2018		2020	
Traditional PACs	65,300,222	10%	87,975,664	5%	53,382,915	5%	82,145,205	4%	61,387,653	4%	86,515,604	3%
Party	226,876,150	33%	284,475,556	16%	250,346,311	24%	274,442,505	14%	239,801,179	16%	393,499,533	12%
Super PACs	74,239,913	11%	684,027,436	38%	371,050,998	35%	1,139,237,851	57%	845,638,109	57%	2,019,535,095	62%
Hybrid PACs	na		14,558,678	1%	2,813,438	0%	50,317,831	3%	75,108,566	5%	552,212,295	17%
Individual Activists	94,866,428	14%	338,620,258	19%	183,714,995	18%	212,643,961	11%	119,015,630	8%	91,981,441	3%
Tax-Exempt Groups	220,353,462	32%	382,284,080	21%	184,887,954	18%	238,092,895	12%	141,203,797	10%	126,725,316	4%
Total	681,636,175		1,791,941,672		1,046,196,611		1,996,880,248		1,482,154,934		3,270,469,284	

Source: OpenSecrets, FEC report, "Communication Filings Data Summary Tables," https://www.fec.gov/campaign-finance-data/communication-filings-data-summary-tables/?year=2020&segment=24; and OpenSecrets, "Top 50 Federally Focused Organizations," www.opensecrets.org/527s/527cmtes.php?level=C&cycle=2020

Traditional PAC Independent Expenditures

Table 6.5 reports the most active Traditional PACs in terms of independent expenditures in presidential years from 2008 to 2020. In 2020, the Service Employees International Union (SEIU) spent the most in this regard, $16.7 million. SEIU was also the top spender in this regard in 2008, second-highest spender in 2012, and fourth-highest spender in 2016. In 2020, the second-biggest spender in independent expenditures in 2020 was End Citizens United, which started in the 2016 election cycle. It spent the third-largest amount in 2016 (about $15 million). The third-biggest spender in 2020 was another union, AFSCME, which was also the second- or third-biggest spender in 2008, 2012, and 2016. The NRA was the largest spender in 2012 and 2016, but then reduced its independent expenditures to $8.9 million in 2020—leaving it as the fourth-largest spender.

Table 6.5 also shows how some groups have changed their spending strategy, including new groups that came into existence (End Citizens United) or disbanded. For example, Life & Liberty PAC, a conservative group associated with Alan Keyes, spent $1.8 million in independent expenditures in 2008 but reduced its activity over the years until it had no activity in 2020. Moveon.org made independent expenditures as a Traditional PAC in 2008 and 2012 but in 2016 and 2020 made its expenditures as a Hybrid PAC.

SUPER PACS AND INDEPENDENT EXPENDITURES

Super PACs are the most significant recent development in federal campaign finance. Officially known as "independent-expenditure-only committees" (and technically considered Non-connected PACs), Super PACs can raise unlimited amounts from individuals, corporations, and unions, including directly from their general treasury funds (see chapter 2). This fund-raising fact is the primary difference between Super PACs and Traditional PACs, although both entities must disclose their donors to the FEC. A related innovation is Hybrid PACs, which are a Traditional PAC and Super PAC administered together with two separate segregated funds (see chapter 2). Many Hybrid PACs came into existence initially as Traditional PACs and then added Super PAC capabilities, but other Hybrid PACs started as Super PACs and then added Traditional PAC capabilities. These patterns show that both the "Traditional" and "Super" PAC approaches to campaign finance are useful pathways for seeking political influence.

As shown in table 6.4, Super PACs made the largest share of independent expenditures in 2020: $2 billion (62 percent); the next largest share came

Table 6.5 Top Traditional PAC Independent Expenditures, 2008–2020 Presidential Elections

Organization	2008	2012	2016	2020	Total
Service Employees International Union	51,848,292	18,458,734	11,457,637	16,667,098	98,431,761
National Rifle Association of America	21,603,923	18,661,053	20,809,198	8,888,865	69,963,038
American Federation of State County & Municipal Employees	12,724,014	14,033,628	16,455,556	10,238,910	53,452,107
End Citizens United	0	0	14,515,031	14,785,438	29,300,469
National Association of Realtors	8,109,499	4,274,374	0	2,992,300	15,376,174
Senate Conservatives Fund	0	3,998,078	1,022,820	5,372,954	10,393,853
Moveon.org	7,993,019	1,318,372	0	0	9,311,391
National Right to Life	4,444,671	2,986,896	512,176	116,905	8,060,648
American Hospital Association	769,265	2,233,300	1,378,204	1,646,676	6,027,445
Republican Majority Campaign	3,713,619	2,660,764	3,235	0	6,377,618
United Association of Journeymen and Apprentice Plumbers & Pipefitters	1,003,157	255,642	418,519	3,747,312	5,424,630
Credit Union National Assn.	637,903	920,363	1,955,337	1,850,176	5,363,779
United Auto Workers	5,864,854	0	0	0	5,864,854
Conservative Majority Fund	0	3,409,773	1,670,555	100,000	5,180,328
Club for Growth	4,276,914	807,464	221,714	171,688	5,477,780
International Association of Firefighters	2,618,000	2,073,919	54,554	302,754	5,049,227
American Federation of Teachers	4,649,411	61,314	443,719	0	5,154,443
Tea Party Majority Fund	0	0	3,869,856	174,068	4,043,924
United for Massachusetts	0	0	0	3,620,118	3,620,118
House Freedom Fund	0	0	107,835	3,518,222	3,626,057
National Federation of Independent Business	1,623,037	1,591,605	717,856	180,000	4,112,499
National Education Association	639,386	3,018,147	5,392	0	3,662,925
EMILYs List	3,849,999	0	0	0	3,849,999
American Medical Association	1,869,105	1,281,590	152,707	344,800	3,648,202
Freedoms Defense Fund	60,859	434,689	2,236,109	31,000	2,762,657
Government Integrity Fund Action Network	0	2,741,200	0	0	2,741,200
Life and Liberty PAC Inc.	1,774,213	901,804	3,235	0	2,679,252
Committee for Hispanic Causes—BOLD	0	0	107,043	1,954,433	2,061,476

Source: OpenSecrets coding of Federal Election Commission data on traditional PAC independent expenditures

from Hybrid PACs at $552 million (17 percent). By comparison, party committees spent $394 million (12 percent) in independent expenditures in 2020. The independent expenditures of party committees stayed roughly the same from 2010 to 2018, averaging $255 million, then increased by more than 50 percent in 2020. But this increase by parties is overshadowed by the increase in Super PAC spending. In 2010, the first year that Super PACs were allowed, parties spent more, but since then, Super PACs have spent more than parties, with larger differences in presidential election years. And the spending of Hybrid PACs jumped from $50 million in 2016 to $75 million in 2018 to $552 million in 2020. Thus, even as parties and Traditional PACs maintained their level of independent expenditures, they became a smaller percentage of total independent expenditures.

Super PAC Funding

When Super PACs first came into existence, a common concern was that businesses would spend substantial amounts from their treasury funds, "open[ing] the floodgates to special interests."[7] Figure 6.6 shows the amount that individuals, unions, and businesses contributed to Super PACs from 2010 to 2020. Clearly, the primary funders of Super PACs are not business treasuries per se (a primary concern of critics of *Citizens United*) but individuals. In the 2020 election cycle, Super PACs received $2.7 billion, almost doubling the $1.5 billion received in 2016. Of that $2.7 billion, individuals contributed $2.4 billion (89 percent), while corporation and union treasuries contributed about $160 million each (6 percent each).

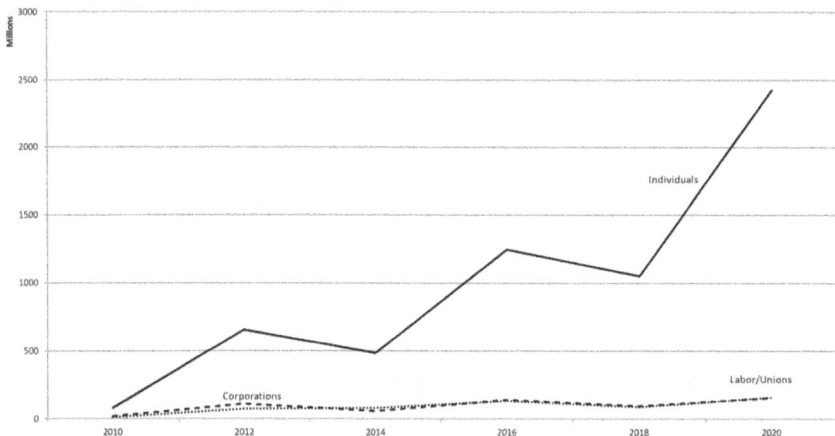

Figure 6.6   Super PAC Receipts from Individuals, Corporations, and Unions, 2010–2020. *Source*: OpenSecrets, www.fec.gov/data/browse-data/?tab=bulk-data

Table 6.6 Top Individual Contributors to Super PACs, 2020 Election

Donor	Total Given to Super PACs	# of Super PACs Donor Gave To	Total Given to Other Committees/ Candidates	Top Other Recipient
Adelson, Sheldon G. & Miriam O.	215,100,000	7	4,553,800	Trump Victory
Bloomberg, Michael R.	97,566,350	23	1,719,978	Democratic Grassroots Victory Fund
Uihlein, Richard	65,017,100	17	5,120,382	Republican National Committee
Steyer, Thomas	63,882,292	8	3,273,630	Biden Victory Fund
Mellon, Timothy	60,000,000	4	144,800	Scalise Leadership Fund
Griffin, Kenneth C.	58,250,000	9	2,086,917	Take Back the House 2020
Schwarzman, Stephen A.	33,500,000	5	2,846,300	Republican National Committee
Yass, Jeffrey S.	30,378,000	5	224,700	Rand Paul Victory
Perlmutter, Laura	22,400,000	5	2,551,100	Republican National Committee
Marcus, Bernard & Billi Wilma	20,511,390	12	6,780,588	Take Back the House 2020
Jurvetson, Karla	19,775,100	26	4,846,913	Democratic Grassroots Victory Fund
Ricketts, John J. & Marlene M.	19,110,000	7	4,654,050	Trump Victory
McMahon, Vincent K. & Linda E.	17,823,443	6	1,010,300	Trump Victory
Simons, James H. & Marilyn H.	15,510,000	8	2,262,591	DNC Services Corp
Schwab, Charles R. & Helen O.	15,250,000	10	4,934,700	National Republican Senatorial Committee
Ryan, Shirley	15,000,000	5	1,716,300	Senate Georgia Battleground Fund
Stephens, Warren A. & Harriet C.	13,150,000	13	2,872,100	Republican National Committee
Singer, Paul E.	12,693,227	13	2,606,600	McCarthy Victory Fund
Simon, Deborah J.	12,558,600	18	4,747,600	Democratic Grassroots Victory Fund
Wynn, Stephen A. & Andrea	12,500,000	4	3,636,100	Trump Victory
Cameron, Ronnie	11,825,000	13	3,062,500	Take Back the House 2020
Sprecher, Jeff, & Loeffler, Kelly	11,500,000	2	2,514,400	Republican National Committee
Beckenstein, Joshua & Anita	11,050,000	15	4,924,587	DNC Services Corp
Sussman, S. Donald	10,500,000	11	3,565,600	Democratic Grassroots Victory Fund
Warren, Kelcy L.	10,375,000	4	5,774,845	Republican National Committee

Source: OpenSecrets, https://www.opensecrets.org/outsidespending/summ.php?disp=D

Super PACs can fund all the logistics of independent expenditures: campaign consultants, pollsters, media creation and placement, reporting requirements, and so forth, something individual activists wishing to make independent expenditures on their own often find difficult to do. Such individuals can now send their contributions to Super PACs that align with their interests and work with other similar-minded individuals through a Super PAC.

Although businesses per se are not directly providing the bulk of funds for Super PACs, wealthy individuals associated with specific businesses are the largest contributors. Table 6.6 shows the top individual contributors to Super PACs in 2020. The largest individual contributors were Sheldon and Miriam Adelson, who gave $215 million to Super PACs, $137 million more than in 2016. The late Sheldon Adelson was the founder, chairman, and CEO of the Las Vegas Sands, which owns or operates several casinos; the Adelsons gave to seven Super PACs that supported Republican candidates. For example, the Adelsons contributed $90 million to the Preserve America PAC, a Super PAC that supported Donald Trump by making independent expenditures against Joe Biden. Beside Super PAC donations, the Adelsons also gave $4.6 million to other committees and candidates—of which the top recipient was Trump Victory, a joint fund-raising committee (JFC) between the Trump campaign and the Republican National Committee (see chapters 3 and 5).

Michael Bloomberg was the second-largest contributor in 2020, giving $98 million to twenty-three different Super PACs—about four times more than the $24 million he contributed to Super PACs in 2016. A former mayor of New York City and billionaire businessman, Bloomberg ran for the 2020 Democratic presidential nomination, spending $1 billion of his own money on his campaign (see chapter 3). Once he dropped out of the race, Bloomberg's largest contribution was $67 million to his own Super PAC, Independence USA PAC, which spent the entirety of its independent expenditures supporting Joe Biden. Bloomberg also gave $1.7 million to

Table 6.7   Characteristics of Donors and Size of Donations to Top Super PACs, 2020 Election

Sectors	Average Amount	Median Amount
Business	186,726	25,000
Labor	405,323	75,000
Individual	2,432	35
Issue/Ideology	3,743,568	38,700

Source: OpenSecrets coding of Federal Election Commission data on Super PAC contributions

other committees and candidates, of which the largest recipient was the JFC Democratic Grassroots Victory Fund.

The rest of the top Super PAC contributors follow a similar pattern. Most of an individual's contributions go to Super PACs that support one party's candidates (candidate-aligned), while the individual makes additional contributions to that same party committee or party's candidates (party-aligned). There is both change and continuity in these top donors: of the twenty-five donors who contributed more than $10 million to Super PACs in 2020, thirteen contributed more than $10 million in 2016 as well. In all, these top twenty-five individuals gave $875 million to Super PACs, a high proportion of the total raised.

Although large donors to Super PACs get the most attention, many donors to Super PACs give far less. Table 6.7 shows the average and median donation from different sectors to the top Super PACs (as listed in table 6.8). When a business contributes its treasury funds to these Super PACs, its average donation is $187,000, and the median donation is $25,000. When a labor organization contributes from its treasury to these Super PACs, its average donation is $405,000, and the median donation is $75,000, both larger than the business donations. When an issue-oriented or ideological donor gives to a top Super PAC, its average donation is $3.7 million, and its median is $38,000. This pattern means that some very large issue donors (i.e., outliers) are in these contributions. In contrast, the median donation by an individual to a Super PAC is $35, which means that more than half of individual donors are unitemized small donors.[8] However, more than two-thirds of the money from individual donations comes from the top one hundred donors.[9]

Super PAC Spending

The total independent expenditures by Super PACs and Hybrid PACs in 2020 was $2.6 billion (see table 6.4). As shown in table 6.8, the top twenty-five Super PACs accounted for almost $2 billion of these expenditures, a concentration even higher than donations. Considering Super PAC funding and spending together, this means that most Super PAC funding comes from the top one hundred donors, and this money flows mostly through the top twenty-five Super PACs. These figures indicate a system of financing that is highly concentrated. The division between the parties was roughly equal: $1.045 billion supporting Democrats, $939 million supporting Republicans.[10]

Table 6.8 Top Twenty-Five Super PACs, Independent Expenditures, 2020 Election

Super PAC	Type	Amount	For Dems/ Against Reps	For Reps/ Against Dems
Senate Leadership Fund	Party (R)	293,731,548	774,083	292,957,465
Senate Majority PAC	Party (D)	230,406,668	230,406,668	0
Congressional Leadership Fund	Party (R)	142,524,130	466,775	142,057,355
Future Forward USA	Biden	141,585,894	141,585,894	0
House Majority PAC	Party (D)	138,867,515	138,867,515	0
America First Action	Trump	133,819,980	0	133,819,980
Priorities USA Action	Biden	127,513,342	127,513,342	0
Preserve America PAC	Trump	102,983,479	0	102,983,479
American Crossroads	Party (R)	79,476,030	0	79,476,030
Club for Growth	Issue Group	65,439,435	11,110,208	54,312,367
American Bridge 21st Century	Party (D)	59,719,576	59,719,576	0
Independence USA PAC	Biden	56,530,420	56,530,420	0
Lincoln Project	Biden/Anti-Trump	49,186,930	49,186,930	0
Americans for Prosperity	Issue Group	47,732,979	93,107	47,639,872
League of Conservation Voters	Issue Group	42,266,596	42,266,597	0
Unite the Country	Biden	38,923,591	38,923,591	0
Peachtree PAC	Loeffler/Perdue (R-GA)	37,845,498	0	37,845,498
EMILY's List	Issue Group	36,769,678	34,332,837	2,436,841
Black PAC	Issue Group	31,989,594	31,989,594	0
VoteVets.org	Issue Group	25,949,540	25,949,540	0
Everytown for Gun Safety	Issue Group	21,202,222	21,202,231	0
Georgia United Victory	Loeffler/Perdue (R-GA)	20,787,073	14,710,781	6,076,292
Restoration PAC	Party (R)	19,777,016	0	19,777,016
National Rifle Assn.	Issue Group	19,452,528	0	19,452,528
Georgia Honor	Warnock	19,243,246	19,243,246	0
Totals		1,983,724,508	1,044,872,935	938,834,723

Source: OpenSecrets, "2020 Outside Spending, by Group," https://www.opensecrets.org/outsidespending/summ.php?cycle=2020&chrt=V&disp=O&type=A

Table 6.8 classifies Super PACs into three types: party-aligned, candidate-aligned, and issue-based.[11] Four of the top five spending Super PACs are the party-aligned congressional leadership Super PACs: one for each major party in the House and in the Senate (see chapters 4 and 5). These Super PACs spend in races that are expected to be close. Steven Law, president of the top-spending Senate Leadership Fund, said, "the top priority races for us [are] the ones that will be competitive."[12] Indeed, the congressional leadership Super PACs *drove* some of the overall increase in Super PAC spending from 2016 to 2020. In 2016, the Senate Leadership Fund (a Republican-supporting Super PAC) spent $86 million in independent expenditures; in 2020, it spent $294 million. In 2016, the Senate Majority PAC (a Democratic-supporting Super PAC) spent $75 million; in 2020, it spent $230 million. The independent expenditures of the House Super PACs similarly increased at least threefold from 2016 to 2020. These expenditures increased partly because it was uncertain which party would control each chamber of the Congress, and thus the outcome was more likely to be influenced by these expenditures.[13]

After the congressional leadership Super PACs, the next four top spenders were candidate-aligned Super PACs associated with Biden or Trump (see chapter 3). Future Forward USA was founded in 2018; in 2020, it spent $141 million in support of Biden, supported by $61 million in receipts from its affiliated tax-exempt group, Future Forward USA Action, and $46 million from Dustin Moskovitz (cofounder of Facebook). The next largest Biden-supporting Super PAC was Priorities USA Action, which spent $127 million. Priorities USA was founded in 2011 to support Barack Obama's presidential reelection campaign, and in supporting Hillary Clinton, was the highest-spending Super PAC in independent expenditures in 2016 ($133 million). Priorities USA also got involved in three U.S. Senate races. Guy Cecil, the chair of Priorities USA, said, "Our number one responsibility is to make sure we are holding Trump accountable."[14]

The top Super PAC supporting Donald Trump in 2020 was America First Action. America First Action was created as the Super PAC arm of America First Policies, a tax-exempt group founded after Trump's inauguration to support his America First agenda. (The two organizations have overlapping personnel.) When Linda McMahon took over as chair in March 2019, she stated, "The goal for the Super PAC is [to raise] $300 million, and so that is clearly targeting a lot of large-money donors . . . to come in to clearly help us get to that bottom-line number."[15] America First Action ultimately raised $150 million, of which it spent $134 million supporting Trump. Besides receiving more than $21 million from America First Policies and more than $15 million from McMahon, many of its top donors are found in table 6.7: Mellon, Schwarzman, Perlmutter, Ricketts, and Sprecher. The other top Super PAC supporting Trump was Preserve America USA, which was founded in August 2020 and spent $103 million supporting Trump. Funded mostly by the Adelsons ($90 million), it also received $10 million from Bernard Marcus (cofounder of Home Depot, #10 Super PAC donor in table 6.6). The other candidate-specific Super PACs in table 6.8 were also associated with the presidential campaigns or for the elections for U.S. Senate seats from Georgia, which were both runoff elections that determined party control of the Senate.

The party-aligned Super PAC American Crossroads was started in 2010 (the year when Super PACs were created) and has been associated with the Republican operatives Karl Rove and Steven Law (who is also president of the Senate Leadership Fund). American Crossroads was involved mainly in Senate races in Georgia and North Carolina. Its top donor was another party-aligned Super PAC, the Senate Leadership Fund (noted above). As both Super PACs were run by former aides of Senator Mitch McConnell, the Senate Leadership Fund concentrated its attacks on Jon Ossoff in one of the Georgia Senate races, while American Crossroads concentrated its attacks on Raphael Warnock in the other Georgia Senate race.

Founded as a candidate-aligned Super PAC for an unsuccessful 2014 U.S. Senate candidate in Illinois, Restoration PAC expanded and now states that it is a "nonpartisan" organization that supports candidates on conservative principles.[16] In practice, it supports only Republican candidates and is largely funded by Richard Uihlein (#3 in the top Super-PAC contributors in table 6.6). On the Democratic side, American Bridge 21st Century was founded when Super PACs were made legal in 2010, like American Crossroads, but has mostly been a hub for opposition research for other Democratic entities. In the 2020 election, it produced its own media using independent expenditures to influence the presidential race and the two Georgia Senate races. Some of its funding came from its tax-exempt affiliate as well as from individual donors such as Beckenstein and Simon (on table 6.6).

Candidate-aligned Super PACs only spend supporting one candidate. They are sometimes active in a primary election to support that candidate, which means that they sometimes spend to oppose a candidate of the same party. An example of such a Super PAC was Georgia United Victory, which supported Republican Kelly Loeffler for U.S. Senate. It spent $15 million of its $21 million of independent expenditures opposing Doug Collins, another Republican candidate in the primary. The remaining $6 million was spent supporting Georgia U.S. Senate Republican candidates Loeffler and Perdue and opposing Democratic candidates Ossoff and Warnock in the runoff elections (discussed in more detail below).

Party-aligned Super PACs usually spend in support of only one party. The Republican congressional Super PACs each made an exception. The Senate Leadership Fund spent $774 thousand opposing Doug Collins, as Loeffler was the incumbent (although she had been appointed to the Senate). And the Congressional Leadership Fund spent $458,000 opposing Chris Putnam, who ran (and lost) against the incumbent Kay Granger in the 12th U.S. House District in Texas.[17]

The party-aligned Super PACs and candidate-aligned Super PACs sometimes overlap because the party-aligned Super PACs will sometimes fund the candidate-specific Super PACs. The largest instance was the Peachtree PAC, which was formed on November 6, 2020, to influence the Georgia Senate runoff elections and was funded solely by the Senate Leadership Fund. Thirteen other Super PACs in the 2020 election cycle received most or all their funds from the party-aligned congressional leadership Super PACs. Because some of these Super PACs were formed late in the election cycle, they did not disclose their funding before the election. For example, Truth Still Matters PAC was formed on October 19, 2020, to attack the Democratic North Carolina Senate candidate Cal Cunningham.[18] It received all of its funds from Future45, a Super PAC formed in the 2016 election cycle to support Donald Trump that had expanded in 2018 and 2020 to attack Democratic congressional candidates as well.[19] These late-forming Super PACs, sometimes called "pop-up PACs," have increased over the past three election cycles.[20] Jon Jones, founder of Relation PAC, a pop-up PAC that supported the Democrats in the Georgia Senate runoff elections, explained:

> We'll be disclosing [donors] at the end of the month like we're required to do. But honestly, if we wanted to hide who our donors were, we could. Just put a corporation in between your donor and the FEC and you can do that. It's a shame that that's possible to do. It's very easy. It's a couple of hours of paperwork from your lawyer, and you're good to go.[21]

The third type of Super PAC is issue-based. Some issue-based Super PACs find that their issue aligns directly with the party division. For example, the two gun-oriented groups in table 6.8 both spent to support one party: Everytown for Gun Safety, a gun-control group, spent $21 million supporting Democrats; the National Rifle Association, a gun-rights group, spent $19 million supporting Republicans. But both organizations (through their Traditional PACs) made conventional PAC contributions to both Democratic and Republican candidates in 2020.

The top spending issue-based Super PAC in 2020 was Club for Growth, spending $65 million. It aligns with the Republican party, but it spent $11 million opposing Republicans in Republican primaries. For example, Club for Growth spent more than $1 million opposing Jerry Carl in the Republican primary (and runoff) for the Alabama 1st U.S. House district and supported Bill Hightower (who lost the primary runoff). In 2018 and 2020, Club for Growth spent more in the general elections, moving more to a party-aligned strategy. Its president, David McIntosh, stated, "It really shows a paradigm shift for the Club for Growth. To be effective conservatives, we need to be part of the majority. You can't just play in primaries."[22]

Americans for Prosperity (AFP), a libertarian Super PAC associated with Charles Koch, moved in the other direction. In previous election cycles, AFP had only supported Republicans. But in the 2020 election cycle, Emily Seidel, CEO of AFP, declared that AFP would "support the primary election of lawmakers, regardless of political party, who stick their necks out to lead diverse policy coalitions."[23] AFP then spent $84,000 supporting House Democrat Henry Cuellar of Texas in the primary election and $9,000 supporting House Democrat of Georgia Sanford Bishop in the general election, thus moving from a party-aligned Super PAC to an issue-based Super PAC.[24]

Not all Super PAC spending is on independent expenditures. Besides administrative costs such as salaries and fund-raising, Super PACs spend money on research, polling, and voter registration. For example, Alex Morgan, executive director of the Progressive Turnout Project, a Hybrid PAC, declared the organization's plans to spend $52 million on "door-to-door canvassing" in seventeen states, as well as send thirteen million postcards to ten states: "Research from the 2018 election shows that personalized, handwritten messages boost turnout, so this year we're investing big in reaching voters on the door and through their mailbox. That's how we'll beat Donald Trump and flip the Senate."[25] If this spending were classified as independent expenditures, Progressive Turnout Project would be included in the top twenty-five in table 6.8.

In addition to these three types of Super PACs, business and labor organizations have their own Super PACs. Table 6.9 displays the total spending by different types of Super PACs. In 2020, business Super PACs spent $15 million, and labor Super PACs spent $40 million. Issue-oriented Super PACs spent $805 million, party-aligned Super PACs spent $859 million, and candidate-specific Super PACs spent $971 million. In addition to the $859 million in independent expenditures that party-aligned Super PACs spent, the parties spent $393 million in independent expenditures directly, not through Super PACs. These figures total $1.25 billion, which far exceeds the soft money that party committees spent before 2004 (see chapter 2).

Table 6.9   Total Spending by Types of Super PACs, 2020 Election

Super PAC Category	Amount
Business	14,922,210
Labor	40,189,426
Single-Candidate	971,337,333
Party-Aligned	859,176,856
Ideology/Issue	805,540,743
Total	2,636,054,932

Source: OpenSecrets, compiled from https://www.opensecrets.org/outsidespending/summ.php?cycle=2020&chrt=V&disp=O&type=A

Table 6.10 aggregates the independent expenditures by parties and groups for the top ten Senate races and top ten House races in 2020.[26] In the North Carolina Senate race (the second most expensive Senate race), the candidates spent $76 million, and independent groups spent $182 million, more than

Table 6.10   Top Senate and House Races, Aggregate Independent Expenditures, 2020 Election

Senate Race	Total	For Democrats/ Against Republicans	For Republicans/ Against Democrats
Georgia Senate	244,513,751	82,406,510	160,427,315
North Carolina Senate	182,873,007	93,130,099	87,699,843
Georgia Senate Special	162,888,084	70,400,932	91,645,112
Iowa Senate	126,245,577	69,181,563	56,077,618
Maine Senate	91,484,190	56,109,866	33,394,907
Michigan Senate	88,400,693	49,667,130	38,733,563
Montana Senate	75,364,325	39,530,081	34,290,186
Arizona Senate	67,159,259	30,432,735	34,665,037
South Carolina Senate	49,662,641	16,649,667	32,790,582
Kansas Senate	47,905,590	20,521,964	26,882,532
House Race	**Total**	**For Democrats/ Against Republicans**	**For Republicans / Against Democrats**
New Mexico District 2	16,023,844	8,156,109	7,867,735
New York District 11	15,297,820	9,751,527	5,546,293
Georgia District 7	13,272,252	4,934,399	8,337,853
Virginia District 7	13,070,209	4,858,852	8,211,357
New York District 22	12,965,252	5,541,312	7,423,940
Texas District 22	12,425,426	5,237,285	7,188,141
Texas District 21	12,279,288	3,282,918	8,996,370
California District 48	12,069,427	8,987,171	3,082,256
California District 25	11,886,209	5,682,997	6,203,212
South Carolina District 1	11,686,944	5,196,258	6,490,686

Source: OpenSecrets, "2020 Outside Spending, by Race," https://www.opensecrets.org/outsidespending/summ.php?cycle=2020&disp=R&pty=N&type=H

double. Similarly, in the Iowa Senate, candidates spent $86 million, and independent groups spent $126 million. In such circumstances, candidates have less control of the campaign in issues emphasized. In most of the other Senate races, however, the candidates spent more than the independent groups. Overall, Republicans won six of these races, and Democrats won four. (Because of their unusual dynamics, the Georgia Senate races, the first and third races in table 6.10 are discussed in more detail below.)

Compared to the Senate, the independent expenditure totals are not as high in the House but are still substantial. In the first six races, independent groups spent more money than the two candidates put together. For example, in New Mexico's 2nd District, candidates spent $11.4 million, while outside groups spent $16 million (and party committees spent $8.7 million more). In these ten House races, Democrats won three of the races, and Republicans won seven. There does not appear to be any relationship between which candidate won and which candidate spent the most or had independent groups spending the most in support.

Georgia Senate Runoff Races

The first and third top Senate races in table 6.10 were the Georgia runoff elections, and table 6.11 goes into further detail, highlighting the financial dynamics of the campaigns and the "team sport" nature of the cooperation between candidates, parties, and independent groups.[27] Table 6.11 divides the spending into time up to the general election (November 3, 2021) and after the general election to the runoff election (January 5, 2021).[28] The runoff (and total) spending amounts include the first five days of 2021, during which more than $16 million was spent by the candidates in the two Senate races alone, in addition to independent group spending.[29] Finally, the aggregate figures include independent expenditures by parties and all the "independent" groups that report to the FEC (Traditional, Super, and Hybrid PACs, as well as tax-exempt groups).

The Georgia Senate race between Ossoff and Perdue was the most expensive congressional race of the year. The candidates spent $246 million, while parties and independent groups spent $278 million. The spending by Republican-aligned groups balanced the Democratic candidate's spending advantage: Ossoff (the Democratic candidate) spent $157 million and had $90 million in support from parties and independent group spending; Perdue (the Republican candidate) spent $89 million and had $188 million in support from independent group spending.

In the special Georgia Senate race between Loeffler and Warnock, the candidates spent $245 million, while parties and independent groups spent

Table 6.11 Georgia Senate Runoff Races: Independent Expenditures by Parties and Other Groups, 2020–2021

(millions of dollars)

	General 1/1/2019 to 11/2/2020	Runoff 11/3/2020 to 1/5/2021	Total		Top Outside Spending Groups		
Georgia Senate							
Perdue							
Candidate	19.3	69.7	89.0				
Groups and Parties	68.0	↑119.6	187.6	←	92.2	SLF (mostly indiv contrib)	18.9 Peachtree (from SLF)
Ossoff							
Candidate	43.4	113.8	157.2				
Groups and Parties	37.5	52.6	90.2	←	31.4	SMP (mostly indiv contrib)	14.2 Georgia Way (from SMP)
Special Georgia Senate							
Loeffler							
Candidate	27.5	71.8	99.3				
Groups and Parties	0.7	106.2	106.9	←	46.0	American Crossroads (mostly from SLF)	18.9 Peachtree (from SLF)
Warnock							
Candidate	27.2	118.0	145.2				
Groups and Parties	4.9	56.9	61.8	←	19.2	Georgia Honor (from SMP)	

Source: Coding of FEC records by author

Note: Spending includes disbursements that are not refunds. Groups and parties' spending includes support of candidate or opposition of opponent.

$169 million. Again, the Republican-aligned spending evened out the Democratic candidate's spending advantage: Warnock (the Democratic candidate) spent $145 million and received $62 million in support from parties and independent group spending; Loeffler (the Republican candidate) spent $99 million and had $107 million in support from parties and independent group support.[30]

There is a strong difference in the spending levels of independent groups both between the two Senate races as well as between the general and runoff elections. In the Perdue-Ossoff election, independent groups were already involved in the general election: even without the runoff election, the independent spending would be the third highest in congressional races ($106 million). However, in the Loeffler-Warnock election, independent groups did not spend much in the general election, just $6 million. This pattern is likely because the race between Loeffler and Warnock was administered as a special election in Georgia (Loeffler had been appointed), which meant that it followed different election rules: there was no primary election, and all qualified candidates ran in the general election. With another Republican candidate, Doug Collins, also running in the race, it was clear that no candidate would receive 50 percent of the vote, which meant that there would be a runoff election. In contrast, Perdue and Ossoff were the only candidates of their respective parties, so it was possible that one of the candidates would receive more than 50 percent of the vote. Ultimately, Perdue received 49.7 percent, and Ossoff received 47.9 percent of the vote in the general election, requiring a runoff election.

After the general election, the Georgia Senate runoff races would determine which party controlled the Senate. In addition, interest in politics remained high after the election with President Trump's disputation of the election results. Thus, candidates, parties, and independent groups were able to raise and spend more funds. Each of the candidates spent more money in the runoff election period than the previous part of the election cycle, and the independent expenditures in support of each candidate were higher in the runoff election than the rest of the election cycle as well—dramatically so in the Loeffler-Warnock election.

More than one hundred groups spent money in one or both Georgia Senate races. But the bulk of funds came from the top two party-aligned Super PACs: the Republican Senate Leadership Fund (SLF) and the Democratic Senate Majority PAC (SMP). On the Republican side, SLF spent $92 million directly in the Perdue-Ossoff race and $2.6 million in the Loeffler-Warnock race. Peachtree PAC spent $19 million in each race, but it received all of its funding from SLF.[31] American Crossroads spent $46 million in the

Loeffler-Warnock race and received $77 million of its $80 million in funds raised from SLF.[32] Thus, SLF provided well over one-half of the spending in the Georgia Senate races, directly or indirectly through other groups. The president of SLF, Steven Law, explained the investment: "The fate of our country hangs in the balance in Georgia. This new activity through Peachtree PAC will articulate the stakes couldn't be higher as the future of freedom is on the ballot."[33]

On the Democratic side, SMP spent $31 million directly in the Perdue-Ossoff race and $1.4 million in the Loeffler-Warnock race. SMP was also the sole funder of Georgia Way, which spent $14 million in the Perdue-Ossoff race; and was the sole funder of Georgia Honor, which spent $19 million in the Loeffler-Warnock race. It is curious that both SLF and SMP mostly worked through other groups in the Loeffler-Warnock runoff election.

TAX-EXEMPT GROUPS AND ELECTIONEERING COMMUNICATION COSTS

In addition to the various kinds of PACs that the Federal Election Commission regulates, tax-exempt groups that the IRS regulates also engage in political spending (see chapter 2). These groups are organized under Section 527 of the tax code, including 501(c)(4) social welfare organizations, 501(c)(5) labor organizations, and 501(c)(6) business organizations. Further, some political groups have been organized generally under Section 527. Like Super PACs, these tax-exempt groups have no contribution or spending limits, but unlike Super PACs, they do not have to disclose their donors to the FEC (following the IRS rules instead, which guarantee taxpayer confidentiality). However, if these groups spend any money on independent expenditures, typically in the form of electioneering communication costs, they must report it to the FEC. They are not, however, required to report other kinds of spending that may influence campaigns.

Figure 6.7 shows the reported independent expenditures of the different kinds of tax-exempt groups from 2004 to 2020. Starting in 2008, the most money was spent by social welfare organizations, with $86 million in 2020; the high point was in 2012 with $290 million spent. In 2020, the next highest spending was by labor organizations at $23 million; their high point was in 2008 with $67 million spent. In 2020, business organizations spent $10 million; their high point was in 2012, with $62 million spent. Finally, 527 groups spent $134 million in 2004, which declined to just $8 million in 2020. Once Super PACs became available, general 527 groups were formed less frequently and were less active.[34]

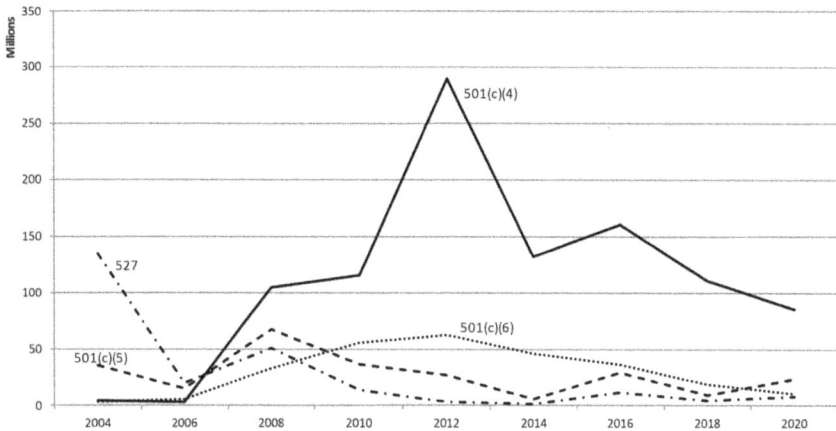

Figure 6.7 Tax-Exempt Groups, Aggregate Spending, 2004–2020 (includes spending reported to FEC—independent expenditures, electioneering communication costs, in 2020 dollars). *Source*: "Should This Be Higher in 2004?" https://www.opensecrets.org/527s/527cmtes.php?level=C&cycle=2004

Table 6.12 shows the top-spending tax-exempt groups from 2012 to 2020.[35] Very few such groups spent in all five elections. In 2020, the top spending tax-exempt group was Defending Democracy Together, an organization that spent $15 million attacking Donald Trump.[36] It also had an associated Super PAC, Republican Voters Against Trump, which spent $9 million. The second highest spending group was Americans for Constitutional Liberty, which was started in the 2020 election cycle to support Trump's reelection, spending $7.5 million. The third largest spending was by the U.S. Chamber of Commerce, which spent $5.7 million 2020; it was the overall top spender across the five election cycles. The top spender in 2016 was the NRA-Institute for Legislative Action, with $35 million. As shown in table 6.5, the NRA's Traditional PAC also spent $21 million in independent expenditures, for a total of $56 million. Such expenditures substantially declined from 2016 to 2020.[37]

Near the bottom of table 6.12 is the group Demand Justice, which is an affiliate of the Sixteen Thirty Fund. Sixteen Thirty Fund and Demand Justice illustrate some of the difficulties in tracking the finances of tax-exempt organizations. Demand Justice spent $3.7 million in electioneering communications in the 2020 election cycle. Sixteen Thirty Fund does not appear in table 6.12 because it did not spend any money directly on election campaigns. However, Amy Kurtz, president of the Sixteen Thirty Fund, wrote, "our organization invested hundreds of millions to shore up election

Table 6.12 Top-Spending Tax-Exempt Groups, 2012–2020

501(c) Organization	2011–2012	2013–2014	2015–2016	2017–2018	2019–2020	Total
U.S. Chamber of Commerce	35,657,029	35,464,243	29,099,947	10,908,413	5,747,676	116,877,308
Crossroads GPS	71,181,940	26,015,713	0	0	0	97,197,653
Americans for Prosperity	36,637,579	2,767,713	13,309,199	8,936,439	0	61,650,930
Majority Forward	0	0	10,116,977	45,871,118	3,972,402	59,960,497
NRA Institute for Legislative Action	8,607,876	12,675,153	35,157,585	1,347,056	895,451	58,683,121
American Future Fund	25,414,586	2,447,719	12,643,178	1,129,930	0	41,635,413
League of Conservation Voters	11,137,177	10,353,920	7,233,755	0	0	28,724,852
American Action Network	11,689,399	8,958,129	5,559,191	0	0	26,206,719
Patriot Majority USA	7,013,886	10,652,282	214,622	5,745,169	0	23,625,959
45 Committee	0	0	22,010,330	1,482,877	0	23,493,207
Americans for Tax Reform	15,794,552	122,500	0	0	0	15,917,052
Americans for Job Security	15,872,864	0	0	0	0	15,872,864
Defending Democracy Together	0	0	0	0	15,412,477	15,412,477
Environmental Defense Action Fund	0	2,905,996	4,285,793	4,779,773	349,952	12,321,514
Ending Spending	1,203,090	6,420,885	2,636,359	2,038,007	0	12,298,341
Planned Parenthood Action Fund	6,545,371	930,290	1,299,016	1,410,047	0	10,184,724
Americans for Responsible Leadership	9,793,014	0	0	0	0	9,793,014
VoteVets.org Action Fund	2,119,985	3,141,632	1,386,819	2,040,113	1,070,744	9,759,293
National Assn of Realtors	1,443,231	1,713,844	1,373,941	1,459,810	3,731,877	9,722,703
American Chemistry Council	648,600	2,382,566	3,455,206	2,488,814	0	8,975,186
Black Progressive Action Coalition	0	0	0	4,231,582	4,549,387	8,780,969
Kentucky Opportunity Coalition	0	7,573,748	0	0	0	7,573,748
Americans for Constitutional Liberty	0	0	0	0	7,548,879	7,548,879
Republican Jewish Coalition	4,595,666	0	486,320	1,379,394	0	6,461,380
NARAL Pro-Choice America	1,710,358	254,193	1,325,556	962,847	1,401,899	5,654,853
Club for Growth	660,220	481,773	4,061,719	391,710	0	5,595,422
60 Plus Assn.	4,615,892	814,100	121,897	0	0	5,551,889
Humane Society Legislative Fund	1,490,762	1,153,670	1,187,221	951,564	453,318	5,236,535

Big Tent Project Fund	0	0	0	0	4,819,710	4,819,710
Susan B. Anthony List	1,961,223	943,362	756,139	972,166	0	4,632,890
YG Network	2,874,481	1,597,680	0	0	0	4,472,161
Citizens for Responsible Energy Solutions	0	1,512,165	1,443,122	828,870	499,995	4,284,152
Demand Justice	0	0	0	317,696	3,732,553	4,050,249
iAmerica Action	0	0	3,870,474	0	0	3,870,474
One Nation	0	0	3,405,810	0	0	3,405,810
Carolina Rising	0	3,279,626	0	0	0	3,279,626

Source: OpenSecrets, "Political Nonprofits: Top Election Spenders," https://www.opensecrets.org/outsidespending/nonprof_elec.php

infrastructure, ensure access to the ballot, and educate communities around the country about what was at stake" in the 2020 election.[38]

From its Form 990, the Sixteen Thirty Fund disbursed $410 million to progressive groups and campaigns in 2020.[39] It also gave $164 million to other groups—including Super PACs—for expressly political purposes. Its biggest outlay was $128 million to America Votes, another progressive tax-exempt group that promotes voter registration and turnout. In addition, the Sixteen Thirty Fund donated $10 million to Defending Democracy Together, which was the top electioneering communication spender in 2020. And the Sixteen Thirty Fund contributed $61 million to other political groups,[40] including $33 million to Super PACs that supported Democratic candidates.[41] Although the names of the specific donors were not disclosed, the size of the donations was disclosed: $370 million came from thirty-five donations of $1 million or more; the largest donation was $86 million. Thus, all told, the Sixteen Thirty Fund raised and spent more than any Super PAC in 2020.

Although reported election spending by tax-exempt groups declined in 2020, this pattern may reflect strategies used by organizations. The top spender in 2018 was Majority Forward with $46 million. Majority Forward was associated with the Democratic leadership Super PAC, Senate Majority PAC. In 2020, Majority Forward spent $4 million directly but donated $51 million to the Senate Majority PAC, which made Majority Forward the top donor for the second-ranked Super PAC (in table 6.8). Similarly, One Nation (associated with Karl Rove) spent directly $3.4 million in 2016, nothing in 2020, but donated $85 million in 2020 to the Senate Leadership Fund, a Republican-aligned Super PAC, making it the top donor to the top spending Super PAC. One Nation was launched in 2015 and effectively replaced the once-dominant Crossroads GPS.[42]

CAMPAIGN ADVERTISING IN 2020

The most visible form of independent expenditure is campaign advertising. In 2000 and 2002, before party soft money was banned (see chapter 2), political parties aired almost 30 percent of such advertisements, more than double the percentage of advertisements aired by other groups. From 2004 to 2008, political parties still broadcast more ads than other groups, and in 2010, the first election in which Super PACs were allowed, parties and other groups aired about the same percentage of advertisements. Then in 2012, the first year that Super PACs were active throughout the election cycle, other groups aired about 30 percent of advertisements, more than double the percentage of political parties. Thus, parties and other groups had traded places. Through 2020, as funding of Super PACs increased, other groups continued to broadcast at least double the advertisements of political parties.[43]

Even before Super PACs developed, a division of labor existed between candidate campaigns, parties, and independent groups. Candidates aired advertisements introducing, explaining, and defining themselves to voters, whereas parties and independent groups aired advertisements attacking the candidate's opponent. The conventional wisdom was that parties and independent groups "can run ads attacking a candidate without as much worry about a backlash hurting their preferred candidate."[44]

The Wesleyan Media Project coded the tone of television ads in the 2020 election cycle as "promote," "contrast," and "attack." Following the long-standing pattern, about 40 percent of candidate ads "promoted" the candidate, and roughly another 40 percent were "contrast" ads between the candidates. Less than 20 percent were "attack" ads. Party and independent group ads had a different pattern: more than 70 percent were "attack" ads, while about 10 percent "promoted" a candidate. Thus, parties and independent groups and parties were the primary source of "attack" ads.[45] But interestingly, the 2020 presidential campaign ads had fewer attacks than in 2016, which had fewer attacks than in 2012.[46]

CONCLUSIONS

In 2020, interest groups continued their traditional campaign financial activities of contributing directly to candidates, engaging in internal communications, and making independent expenditures. They also continued to use tax-exempt groups (which do not need to disclose their donors) to encourage voting and influence elections. But the big story was the continued expansion of Super PACs, a vehicle that also grew among party committees and leadership groups. While most of the donations to Super PACs came from individuals, much of the money came from large donations from the wealthy supporters of both political parties.

As presidential elections will likely be closely contested,[47] and party control of both chambers of Congress could change in future elections, interest group activity in federal elections will likely continue or even increase. Although Super PACs can be used by like-minded individuals donating small amounts to work together to influence policy and elections, they can also be used by the wealthy to donate large amounts for the same purpose.

Thus, if they follow their current trajectory, Super PACs will likely continue to play a large—and expanding—role in federal campaigns.

NOTES

1. Unless otherwise noted, all figures in the text are in 2020 constant dollars to allow for comparisons over time.

2. Federal Election Commission, "Political Action Committee Data Summary Tables," https://www.fec.gov/campaign-finance-data/political-action-committee-data-summary-tables/?year=20XX&segment=24.

3. Damon Cann, *Sharing the Wealth: Member Contributions and the Exchange Theory of Party Influence in the U.S. House of Representatives* (Albany: SUNY Press, 2008); Eric S. Heberlig and Bruce A. Larson, *Congressional Parties, Institutional Ambition, and the Financing of Majority Control* (Ann Arbor: University of Michigan Press, 2012).

4. OpenSecrets, "Top 20 PACs to Candidates, 2019–2020," www.opensecrets.org/political-action-committees-pacs/top-pacs/2020.

5. David B. Magleby and Jay Goodliffe, "Interest Groups in the 2016 Election," in *Financing the 2016 Election*, ed. David B. Magleby (Washington, DC: Brookings Institution Press, 2019), 87–129.

6. These numbers have more uncertainty than usual because the FEC closed its offices during COVID and is still finishing some filings. Federal Election Commission, "Communication Costs by Corporations and Membership Organizations," https://www.fec.gov/resources/campaign-finance-statistics/2016/tables/cc/CC1_2016_24m.pdf, https://www.fec.gov/resources/campaign-finance-statistics/2020/tables/cc/CC1_2020_24m.pdf.

7. Barack Obama, 2010 State of the Union Address, https://obamawhitehouse.archives.gov/the-press-office/remarks-president-state-union-address.

8. OpenSecrets coding of Federal Election Commission data on super PAC contributions.

9. OpenSecrets, "Super PACs: How Many Donors Give," https://www.opensecrets.org/outside-spending/donor-stats/2020?type=I.

10. OpenSecrets, "2020 Outside Spending, by Group," www.opensecrets.org/outsidespending/summ.php?cycle=2020&chrt=V&disp=O&type=A.

11. David B. Magleby, "Classifying Super PACs," in *The State of the Parties*, 7th ed., ed. John Green, Daniel Coffey, and David Cohen (Lanham, MD.: Rowman & Littlefield, 2014), 231–50.

12. "Newsmakers: Steven Law," C-SPAN, January 24, 2020, www.c-span.org/video/?468377-1/newsmakers-steven-law.

13. Charles R. Hunt, "Campaign Finance: Trends and Developments," in *The Elections of 2020*, ed. Michael Nelson (Charlottesville: University of Virginia Press, 2021), 126–28.

14. "Newsmakers: Guy Cecil," C-SPAN, March 13, 2020, www.c-span.org/video/?470317-1/newsmakers-guy-cecil.

15. Quoted in Zack Stanton, "How to Raise $300 Million," *Politico*, June 19, 2019, www.politico.com/story/2019/06/19/linda-mcmahon-2020-america-first-trump-super-pac-1368075.

16. Restoration Action/PAC, "About Us," https://join.restorationofamerica.com/about_us.

17. OpenSecrets, "Congressional Leadership Fund," www.opensecrets.org/outsidespending/recips.php?cmte=C00504530&cycle=2020, updated by the author.

18. Campaign Legal Center, "Complaint to Federal Election Commission, July 2, 2021," https://campaignlegal.org/sites/default/files/2021-07/07-02-21%20super%20PAC%20affiliation%20complaint%20%28final%29.pdf.

19. OpenSecrets, "Future45," www.opensecrets.org/outsidespending/recips.php?cycle=2020&cmte=C00574533.

20. Michael E. Toner and Karen E. Trainer, "The $14 Billion Election," in *A Return to Normalcy? The 2020 Election that (Almost) Broke America*, ed. Larry J. Sabato, Kyle Kondik, and J. Miles Coleman (Lanham, MD: Rowman & Littlefield, 2021), 215–16.

21. Quoted in Kim Berryman and Kyung Lah, "Pop-Up Super Pacs Flood Georgia Runoff: 'It's about the Big Message,'" *CNN*, December 21, 2020, www.cnn.com/2020/12/21/politics/georgia-senate-runoff-pac-spending-cnntv/index.html.

22. Quoted in Simone Pathé, "It's No Longer All about Republican Primaries for the Club for Growth," *Roll Call*, March 7, 2019, www.rollcall.com/2019/03/07/its-no-longer-all-about-republican-primaries-for-the-club-for-growth/.

23. Emily Seidel, "A New Approach to Public Policy and Political Engagement," Memo to Americans for Prosperity Staff and Activists, June 6, 2019, https://fm.cnbc.com/applications/cnbc.com/resources/editorialfiles/2019/06/06/Kochnetworkpoliticalexpansion.pdf.

24. OpenSecrets, "Americans for Prosperity," www.opensecrets.org/outsidespending/recips.php?cmte=Americans+for+Prosperity&cycle=2020.

25. Quoted in John Bowden, "Democratic Group Plans to Send 13 Million Hand-Written Postcards to Voters in Swing States," *The Hill*, July 16, 2020, https://thehill.com/homenews/campaign/507521-dem-group-plans-to-send-13-million-hand-written-postcards-to-voters-in.

26. Open Secrets, "2020 Outside Spending, by Race," www.opensecrets.org/outsidespending/summ.php?cycle=2020&disp=R&pty=N&type=H.

27. David B. Magleby, "The 2012 Election as a Team Sport," in *Financing the 2012 Election*, ed. David B. Magleby (Washington, DC: Brookings Institution Press, 2014), 1–45.

28. In the regular Georgia Senate race between Perdue and Ossoff, there was a primary election on June 9, 2020. Perdue was unopposed in the Republican primary and spent $2.2 million to that point; Ossoff spent $4.7 million and won the Democratic primary with 53 percent of the vote where the next closest candidate received 16 percent. Outside entities spent $413,000 supporting Perdue and $32,000

opposing Perdue. As will be shown, these amounts are dwarfed by later spending. (Author coding of FEC records.) In the table, primary election spending is included in general election spending.

29. This 2021 spending is not included in most summaries. The figures were calculated using various queries to FEC databases by date. In addition, the campaign spending figures (i.e., disbursements) exclude campaign contribution refunds.

30. Author coding of FEC records.

31. Federal Election Commission, "Receipts," www.fec.gov/data/receipts/?committee_id=C00762377&two_year_transaction_period=2020&cycle=2020&line_number=F3X-11C&data_type=processed.

32. Federal Election Commission, "Financial Summary," www.fec.gov/data/committee/C00487363/?cycle=2020.

33. Quoted in Fredreka Schouten and David Wright, "A New McConnell-Aligned Super PAC Plans $43 Million Ad Blitz to Sway Georgia Runoffs," *CNN*, December 8, 2020, www.cnn.com/2020/12/08/politics/new-super-pac-to-spend-43-million-in-georgia-senate-runoffs/index.html.

34. Its high point was in 2004 with $135 million in spending. In 2004, one of the well-known 527 groups was Swift Boat Veterans and POWs for Truth, which attacked the Democratic presidential nominee, John Kerry, for his war record. At that time, 527 organizations were seen as a way around the BCRA prohibition on (unlimited) soft money donations. Open Secrets, "Top 50 Federally Focused Organizations," www.opensecrets.org/527s/527cmtes.php?level=C&cycle=2020.

35. This figure does not include spending on issues, which is not reported, or contributions to other organizations.

36. Karl Evers-Hillstrom, "Never-Trump Group Is 2020's Top 'Dark Money' Spender So Far," *Open Secrets*, October 7, 2020, www.opensecrets.org/news/2020/10/never-trump-groups-darkmoney-1020/.

37. As noted earlier, the high point in 501(c)(4) spending came in 2012, and the biggest spender with $71 million was Crossroads GPS, a group affiliated with American Crossroads super PAC discussed earlier. But Crossroads GPS stopped spending after 2014. Open Secrets, "Political Nonprofits: Top Election Spenders," www.opensecrets.org/outsidespending/nonprof_elec.php.

38. Amy Kurtz, "Our Democracy Needs a Reboot," *Medium*, April 8, 2021, https://amy-kurtz.medium.com/our-democracy-needs-a-reboot-92278c17647c.

39. "Form 990," Sixteen Thirty Fund, www.politico.com/f/?id=0000017d-2e2b-df97-a9ff-be7fdd190000.

40. Amy Kurtz, "Progressive Philanthropy Answered the Call in 2020," *Medium*, November 17, 2021, https://amy-kurtz.medium.com/progressive-philanthropy-answered-the-call-in-2020-57f038a6a5d2.

41. Scott Bland, "Liberal 'Dark-Money' Behemoth Funneled More Than $400M in 2020," *Politico*, November 17, 2021, www.politico.com/news/2021/11/17/dark-money-sixteen-thirty-fund-522781.

42. Karl Evers-Hillstrom and Yue Stella Yu, "Karl Rove-Linked 'Dark Money' Group Raised, Spent Big ahead of 2018 Midterms," *Open Secrets*, November 21, 2019, www.opensecrets.org/news/2019/11/dark-money-group-one-nation-2018/.

43. Wesleyan Media Project, "Political Ads in 2020: Fast and Furious," figure 6, https://mediaproject.wesleyan.edu/2020-summary-032321/.

44. John C. Tedesco and Scott Dunn, "Political Advertising in the 2020 Presidential Election," in *The 2020 Presidential Campaign: A Communications Perspective*, ed. Robert E. Denton Jr. (Lanham, MD: Rowman & Littlefield, 2021), 61.

45. Wesleyan Media Project provided the data for this analysis.

46. Wesleyan Media Project, "Political Ads in 2020: Fast and Furious," figure 5, https://mediaproject.wesleyan.edu/2020-summary-032321/.

47. Presidential elections will likely be closely contested in the Electoral College, if not in the popular vote.

7

Political and Policy Implications of the 2020 Election

Robert G. Boatright

In *Financing the 1960 Election*, Herbert Alexander reported on the political and policy implications of a close and historic campaign.[1] The main political issue Alexander raised was the inadequate funding of presidential and congressional campaigns, along with attendant pathologies: persistently high levels of campaign debt, inefficient and parochial fiscal management, and an overreliance on funds from wealthy "fat cats" and "special interests." The main policy issues Alexander raised were the potential remedies for these inadequacies: public subsidies for national campaigns, a greater reliance on small donations, and fuller disclosure of the sources and uses of money. Sixty years on, these concerns—and remedies—are still features of campaign finance politics and policy.

The question "does money matter in campaigns?" would not have made sense to Alexander and his contemporaries, but it has become an increasingly common query in an era of record-breaking expenditures in national campaigns. Most analyses conclude that it does, but campaign spending is not always correlated with outcomes. Most recently, David Magleby and Candace Nelson asked whether money mattered less than conventional wisdom expected in the 2016 presidential election, when Donald Trump and his team won despite being significantly outspent by Hillary Clinton and her team.[2] This pattern was nearly repeated in 2020: Team Trump almost prevailed despite being significantly outspent by Team Biden. Other analysts raised similar questions about the 2020 presidential primaries and congressional elections.[3] This question provides a useful context for reviewing the political and policy implications of the 2020 election.

In this regard, the most striking feature of the financing of the 2020 election may not be the record-breaking aggregates of political money but, rather, the symbolic value of campaign contributions in today's highly polarized political climate (see chapters 3 and 4). The post-2020 campaign finance reform agenda that congressional Democrats and their allies proposed reflects this development, with campaign finance regulation one of many highly partisan election reform issues. Although campaign finance reform remains a topic of conversation, however, those who harbor concerns about the health of American democracy have raised many other concerns in recent years, and campaign finance reform was not necessarily as high a priority in 2020 as it was in prior elections.

WHAT WAS DIFFERENT IN 2020?

As the preceding chapters note, the contrasts between the two parties' presidential candidates, polarization within the electorate, and prospects for a change in party control of Congress drew a record amount of money into the 2020 campaign. The disruption that the COVID-19 pandemic presented also altered fund-raising and expenditures. The best place to begin consideration of these matters is with the novel aspects of campaign finance in the 2020 election cycle.

Unusually Well-Known Candidates

One reason money may have mattered less than expected in 2016 and 2020 was Donald Trump's extraordinary ability to generate media attention. Indeed, it was estimated that Trump received the equivalent of $5.4 billion in coverage in 2016, slightly more than twice as much as Hillary Clinton received.[4] Although no such estimate is available for 2020, it is likely that Trump generated even more media attention from the White House. This pattern may have been intensified by Trump's announcement of his reelection bid on Inauguration Day in 2017 (far earlier than any previous president) and his assembly of an innovative fund-raising apparatus, with unprecedented integration with the Republican National Committee (RNC; see chapters 3 and 5). The Trump White House was unusually explicit about its focus on campaigning.

Trump's media attention had a downside, exacerbating divisions within the GOP and uniting the Democrats in seeking his defeat. Although he was already well known, former vice president Joe Biden became the "anti-Trump" candidate once he secured the Democratic nomination (see chapters 3 and 5), so his record-breaking general election war chest may not have mattered as much as expected. Thus, Magleby and Nelson's conclusions about 2016 may apply to 2020 as well: "Unless another presidential candidate can capture the news media's attention in the future the way Trump did . . . , we expect candidates' campaign financing in the future to more closely resemble the way Romney and Obama financed their races in 2012."[5]

New Emphasis on Small Contributions

It is customary for political scientists to draw distinctions between small and large campaign contributions. "Small" donors tend to be more driven by ideology and attraction to charismatic candidates than "large" donors, especially the very wealthy and well organized, who are more concerned with securing access to policy makers. Reform proponents have frequently advocated for increasing small contributions to dilute the influence of the large contributions. At the same time, some political scientists have warned that small donors also contribute to political polarization and refusal to compromise whereas larger donors tend to be more moderate and pragmatic in their politics.[6]

The increased reliance on small contributions was a significant part of the record-breaking fund-raising in 2020. Both parties took steps to encourage small contributions in the presidential campaign. The Democratic National Committee (DNC) established a threshold number of unique contributions (not the same thing as unique contributors) as one of the criteria for participation in primary debates. This approach soon became controversial because it appeared to advantage some candidates over others.[7] And this controversy became part of a broader debate about the role of money in politics (see chapters 3 and 4).[8] In the end, these arguments were not really about the money—Democratic primary candidates were treating contributions as symbols of grassroots support rather than as fuel for a campaign.

Although President Trump faced little opposition for renomination, he, too, emphasized small contributions. This decision resulted in part from Trump's successful fund-raising in 2016,[9] but it was also part of a strategy to tap the president's popular base. As with the 2020 Democratic candidates—as well as many candidates from previous elections—an initial, token donation could snowball over the course of the campaign. It is easier to coax previous donors into giving more money than it is to find new ones, and many donors are willing to enroll themselves in regular payment plans. Ironically, such efforts mean that many small donors eventually become large donors.

The Trump campaign's emphasis on small donors yielded a serious controversy with political and policy implications (see chapter 3). Beginning in April 2021, a series of *New York Times* articles investigated the "pre-checked box" strategy in the Trump campaign's fund-raising emails.[10] During the final two and a half months of 2021, Trump and the RNC refunded $64.3 million—more than ten times what Biden and the DNC refunded over the same period (over the entire campaign Trump refunded $122.7 million). These refunds were prompted by donors who unwittingly gave as much as six or seven times what they had initially intended to give.

Trump's fund-raising emails arrived accompanied with a set of pre-checked boxes at the bottom of the email or Web page, with small print accompanying the boxes reading "make this a weekly recurring donation," "make this a monthly recurring donation," or "donate an additional $100." Many donors failed to read through the entire page or failed to diligently uncheck all the boxes. The *Times* report was accompanied by various stories about people of modest means who faced financial difficulties because of these payments. At a minimum, the article suggested, these contributions, even if refunded, amounted to an interest-free loan to the Trump campaign at a moment when Trump was running behind Biden financially (see chapter 3). The Trump campaign was not unique in employing this strategy, however, and subsequent *Times* articles noted instances where Democratic Party fund-raising appeals had used this approach as well.[11]

Although such usage of pre-checked boxes may be deceptive, it is not necessarily illegal, and it exists on a continuum of aggressive marketing practices that encourage contributing. In May 2021, the Federal Election Commission (FEC) voted unanimously to ask Congress to pass legislation prohibiting the use of pre-checked boxes, and Senators Amy Klobuchar and Richard Durbin introduced such legislation later in the month.[12] Some opponents of this effort have worried, however, that such prohibitions could be a step toward a broader regulation of political fund-raising appeals, which might infringe upon speech.[13]

The increased importance of small donors transcended presidential politics in 2020, including congressional races as well (see chapter 4). One reason for this pattern was changes in fund-raising technology that made it easier for individuals to contribute. Democrats benefited from the success of ActBlue, the online contribution portal,[14] while Republicans benefited from a similar but newer operation, WinRed.[15] In large part because of its longer experience, ActBlue channeled small contributions to Democratic candidates far more successfully in 2020 than WinRed did for the Republicans.

Although these portals made it easy for donors to learn about candidates across the country, they can lead donors to make choices that party leaders might not prefer (see chapters 5 and 6). Two prominent examples from 2020 were Kentucky Democratic Senate candidate Amy McGrath, who raised $55.6 million in small donations and $94.1 million overall in her unsuccessful bid to defeat Senate Republican Majority Leader Mitch McConnell; and South Carolina Democratic Senate candidate Jaime Harrison, who raised $70.9 million from small donors and $130.5 million overall in his unsuccessful campaign against Republican Senator Lindsey Graham.[16] To put Harrison's totals in perspective, before 2020 only one Senate candidate had ever raised as much money in total small contributions as Harrison.[17]

Harrison and McGrath were both charismatic candidates who drew national attention, but both were running in red states against well-established incumbents in a presidential year. Thus, the funds they raised might have been deployed more effectively in more competitive Senate races. Because most competitive Democratic Senate candidates were already well funded, it is hard to tell if such a reallocation of funds would have produced better results for Democrats. Yet, the flood of money into campaigns such as these did show the weakness of party leaders in directing the flow of money to their candidates.

Uneven Deployment of Super PACs

The maturation of Super PACs was another factor in the 2020 election. Overall, Super PAC independent expenditures totaled almost $2.6 billion and generated extensive controversy, especially in instances where they were linked to very large donations from very wealthy individuals or to tax-exempt groups (see chapters 5 and 6). However, Super PACs played a much less significant role in the presidential nomination process than in the recent past, and their activities bore little resemblance to the 2012 and 2016 elections, in which some candidates were propelled by Super PAC spending that rivaled their own campaign spending.[18] Few of the numerous Democratic presidential candidates benefited from aligned Super PACs during the primary season (see chapter 3).[19] In fact, only one of the unsuccessful Democratic aspirants (Elizabeth Warren) had Super PAC support in excess of $5 million. And Super PACs aligned with Warren and Biden emerged too late in the primary campaign to influence the outcome. Some of the lower-profile candidates did have Super PACs, and others had relied on Super PACs in prior bids for office. Washington Governor Jay Inslee, for instance, received $1.8 million in aligned Super PAC support.[20]

The absence of Super PACs was a consequence of leading Democrats' opposition to them: Warren had pledged not to have a Super PAC, as had Bernie Sanders. And Warren received considerable criticism when she welcomed Super PAC support at a critical point in the primaries. Sanders was not unscathed in this regard, either; he did receive campaign support from a tax-exempt group, Our Revolution, which he had helped form in 2016.[21] Ironically, the nomination race eventually drew in two wealthy self-financed candidates, who spent far more than all the Super PACs active in the Democratic primaries (see chapter 3). It is worth noting, however, that Super PACs played a major role in many 2020 congressional campaigns (see chapter 4).

The Role of Scam PACs

A larger concern in 2020 for many campaign finance watchdogs was the role of so-called scam PACs. Scam PACs, as informally defined in a memorandum by FEC Commissioners Ellen Weintraub and Ann Ravel, are "political committees that collect political contributions, frequently using the name of a candidate, but which spend little to none of the proceeds on political activity benefitting that candidate."[22] Scam PACs have existed since the *Citizens United* decision, but it has been difficult to reach consensus on what they are, how much of a problem they are, or what legal steps might be taken to limit their activities.

The Weintraub and Ravel memorandum cited research suggesting that thirty-three such groups raised a total of $48.5 million in 2014. Although precise estimates from 2020 are hard to come by, Ciara Torres-Spelliscy of the Brennan Center wrote two short pieces suggesting that the problem had become much worse by the 2020 election and providing anecdotes of groups that seem to be clear cases of group entrepreneurs seeking exclusively to enrich themselves.[23] Political scientist Zhao Li found news articles from 2011 through 2020 alleging that ninety-nine different organizations were scam PACs.[24] The FBI also conducted highly publicized prosecutions in 2020 of individuals who had used scam PACs to enrich themselves and issued a warning to the public about how to spot them.[25] And a 2020 CNN investigation discussed a network of seventeen different groups that purported to be conducting election-related advocacy on behalf of the "Blue Lives Matter" movement but, in fact, converted tens of millions of dollars for personal use.[26]

In a political climate where disputes over truth and allegations about "fake news" are a tool of political warfare, it is easy to see why defining a scam PAC is difficult. For example, no legal standards set how much of its receipts a Super PAC must spend on behalf of candidates. And in its *Pursuing America's Greatness v. Federal Election Commission* (463 F. Supp. 3d 11 (D.D.C. 2020)) decision, the U.S. District Court for the District of Columbia held that the FEC cannot regulate Super PACs based on their use of a candidate's name.[27] The requirement of nonconsultation with candidates regarding Super PAC spending complicates the matter. Weintraub and Ravel both suggested that standards modeled on Charity Navigator's ratings of suspicious 501(c)(3) groups were a possibility, but it is unclear whether regulation might go beyond this approach.

Both the anecdotal evidence that Torres-Spelliscy provided and the quantitative measures that Li offered suggest that scam PACs have disproportionately been a problem on the political right. Li estimates that 82 percent of alleged scam PACs are conservative, and that these groups raise a disproportionate share of their money from older, less technologically savvy donors. This pattern poses the possibility of bipartisan action to restrain them. Although the leaders of these organizations sometimes have had prior experience running legitimate conservative groups, scam PACs' activities can interfere with the ability of legitimate groups to support candidates and causes. In fact, some within the Trump campaign claimed in 2019 that they were finding it difficult to compete with groups that used Trump's name in their fund-raising.[28] This concern suggests that scam PACs are not embedded in "normal" campaign strategy but are a separate, potentially deceptive practice.

Ann Ravel has suggested that learning more about scam PACs would require additional disclosure about other Super PAC activities—something that may be anathema to many Republicans.[29] During the 116th Congress, Reps. Katie Porter (D-CA) and Dan Crenshaw (R-TX) introduced legislation to increase the ability of the FEC to provide the public with information about scam PACs; similar legislation was introduced in the 117th Congress but with no Republican cosponsors.[30]

News Roles for Television and Social Media Advertising

Two changes in political advertising may have influenced campaign spending in 2020. First, the COVID-19 pandemic increased the amount of time Americans spent in their homes, which led Americans, in turn, to watch more than twice as much television as they had before the pandemic.[31] Although not all this increase was for broadcast television, political advertising on broadcast television did become more valuable for candidates and more expensive to purchase. The Wesleyan Media Project (WMP) estimated that the volume of television advertising in 2020 was roughly twice what it had been in 2016.[32]

Second, Americans' use of social media also grew in 2020; this increase was due partially to the pandemic and partially to the ongoing growth in digital technology use. The increase in candidate expenditures on social media advertising was not as substantial as it had been in 2016, but it often was associated with fund-raising and/or targeted content, both of which tend to consist of partisan and politically extreme rhetorical appeals. As in 2016, the Trump campaign outspent the Democratic nominee on social media advertising despite being heavily outspent in other types of advertising.[33] Tax-exempt groups spent a significantly smaller percentage of the overall advertising money in 2020 than in prior years.[34]

The WMP study emphasizes that the pandemic made it difficult to forecast whether this surge in advertising will continue, or whether the surge was a temporary response to changes in Americans' viewing habits.[35] Some of the changes in Americans' media use during the pandemic will be difficult for political advertisers to respond to. For instance, the largest category increase was in streaming video sites such as Netflix and Hulu, which are not all dependent on advertisements. It is noteworthy that the traditional relationship between campaign activity and voter turnout was upended in 2020: conventional wisdom has held that get-out-the-vote efforts, which are often conducted in person, are the best way to increase turnout, and that advertising has little effect. The 2020 election featured more advertising than ever before, while mobilizing volunteers for in-person campaign events was limited by the pandemic—and yet turnout skyrocketed.

Postelection Fund-Raising

The most unprecedented feature of the 2020 election was the degree of postelection fund-raising by the defeated presidential candidate. Donald Trump was the fourth incumbent president to be defeated since the advent of the modern campaign finance system in the early 1970s, and his 2024 presidential bid will be the first campaign waged by a defeated incumbent since the nineteenth century. This fact has many implications for campaign finance scholars, some of which became immediately visible in the weeks following the election.

First, the weeks between Election Day and the inauguration of President Biden were a time of frenzied campaign activity for the Trump campaign. A CNN report from December 4 estimated that Trump and his allies raised $207 million in the month following the election.[36] In fact, Trump raised more money in the month following Election Day than in the month preceding it. Much of this money went to the Trump campaign fund, but some contributions also were directed toward his recently formed Leadership PAC, Save America, and the RNC. Trump and the RNC spent some of this money on the Georgia Senate runoff elections, some on unspecified "election integrity" efforts—and some of it was transferred to Trump's super PAC, to other candidate-specific Super PACs, or to Trump-endorsed 2022 candidates. Yet, much of the Trump money remained unspent as of early 2023. The rhetoric employed in fund-raising for these efforts reinforced Trump's claims that the 2020 election had been stolen.

One analysis of postelection fund-raising concluded that approximately $10 million was spent on legal costs—a category that included the salaries of the lawyers who were challenging the election results—while more than $50 million was spent on online advertising and other fund-raising expenses.[37] Although it is not unusual for campaigns to allocate money for litigation surrounding close outcomes, it is unprecedented for so much money to be spent on advertising *after* Election Day.

Trump's fund-raising did not stop once the 2020 presidential election had been certified, however. As of January 31, 2022, the three major fund-raising vehicles connected with Trump—the Save America Leadership PAC, the Save America Joint Fundraising Committee, and the Make America Great Again Super PAC—had more than $120 million on hand, the majority of which was raised during the first four months of 2021. This total was more than the combined cash on hand for the NRCC or the NRSC at that time—and more than Trump had on hand at a similar point following his 2016 campaign.[38]

The fact that Trump had not, as of January 2022, formally declared his 2024 candidacy meant that donors to the various Trump Super PACs had given without a clear understanding of what they were giving money for: Trump variously promised to continue contesting the 2020 election, support other candidates, fight against the Biden agenda, and "save America." Similarly, the Trump-aligned Super PACs spent far less in 2021 than they raised, as in 2020.[39] This pattern meant that even before the dust had settled on the 2020 election, Trump had the financial resources to play the role of President Biden's chief antagonist. Trump's absence from social media has also meant that in terms of campaign money he entered the postelection period both "diminished and dominating."[40]

Trump continued to raise money throughout 2021 and 2022, although his pace slowed as the 2022 midterm election drew near. The RNC, NRSC, and NRCC continued to use Trump's name in their fund-raising appeals and to sell Trump-themed merchandise. Some Republican leaders worried, in fact, that Trump's fund-raising in 2022 was interfering with fund-raising efforts for the party's candidates in the midterm election.[41] This situation stands in stark contrast to other recent presidents. Other defeated one-term presidents have generally played little or no role in raising money for themselves or others in the years following their defeats, whereas former two-term incumbents such as Bill Clinton, George W. Bush, and Barack Obama raised little money for themselves because they could not run again but were still available to help raise money for other candidates. Trump effectively froze the 2024 Republican presidential primary field right after the 2020 election.

Second, the news media applied great scrutiny to post-2020 fund-raising by Republican members of Congress as well. In the weeks following the January 6 occupation of the Capitol, more than one hundred corporate PACs announced changes to their contribution strategies (see chapter 4). Some, such as Google, Archer-Daniels-Midland, and Goldman Sachs, announced that they were reviewing their contribution strategies; others, including Nike and Amazon, announced that they were suspending contributions to the 147 Republicans who had voted against accepting the electoral votes of some states.[42] Hallmark, which is based in Kansas City, went still further, demanding the return of its contributions to local Senators Josh Hawley (R-MO) and Roger Marshall (R-KS).[43]

These corporate decisions were clearly designed to send a message to consumers, shareholders, and the public that these companies condemned the events of January 6. However, a suspension of contributions during the first quarter of a two-year election cycle does not necessarily affect a candidate's overall fund-raising—the money can, of course, be donated later in the year. Although some watchdog groups have monitored these companies' subsequent contributions to these legislators, the good press the companies received from a temporary suspension could well outweigh the negative consequences of reestablishing their old contribution practices later in the year.[44] And it is also evident that many of the legislators who could be tied to the January 6 events had little need for corporate PAC support because other kinds of contributions made up most of their campaign funds. Indeed, Senator Hawley and Sen. Ted Cruz (R-TX) announced later in the year that they would decline all corporate PAC contributions, and the most outspoken Republican House members associated with January 6, such as Marjorie Taylor Greene (R-GA) and Madison Cawthorn (R-NC), raised substantial amounts of money in small contributions in the weeks following January 6.[45]

The attention given to corporate PAC donations was symptomatic, however, of a broader movement in analyses of campaign contribution practices. In April 2021, Public Citizen released a study of corporate PACs that have donated money to state and federal lawmakers who support restrictions on voting.[46] A

USA Today report explored the campaign contributions of individuals involved in the January 6 riot.[47] And a September *Houston Chronicle* report discussed the corporations that gave money to Texas legislators who supported the state's controversial abortion law.[48] These sorts of analyses are not entirely unprecedented. To give one high-profile example, in 2014 Mozilla CEO Brendan Eich resigned his position at the company following media disclosure of his $1,000 contribution to California's 2008 referendum to prohibit same-sex marriage.[49] Although it is not clear that anyone was forced out of a job in 2021 because of their campaign contributions, analyses of campaign contributions may become a more visible weapon of political conflict than had been the case in prior years.

Third, the weeks immediately following the 2020 election were atypical for Democrats as well. It has been the norm over the past several decades for first-term presidents to seek reelection (the last voluntary one-term president also held office in the late nineteenth century). Just as Trump's consideration of whether to run for president again effectively froze the Republican field, so uncertainty over whether Biden would seek reelection froze the Democratic field. As of early 2022, few of the unsuccessful 2020 Democratic candidates had significant cash on hand. Indeed, Bernie Sanders and Cory Booker were the only candidates with more than $2 million on hand as of January 31, 2022. Sanders will be eighty-three at the time of the 2024 election and has given no indication that he would run again. Fund-raising in 2022 by previous Democratic presidential aspirants such as Booker, Klobuchar, or John Hickenlooper does not indicate that they are planning another presidential run. It is rare for candidates to formally establish an exploratory committee until after the midterm elections. Yet the pattern since at least the 1980s has been that incumbent first-term presidents are assumed to be seeking reelection and rarely face significant primary challenges within their own party, and candidates begin jockeying for position early once an incumbent has been elected to a second term.

We may not know until 2024 or later whether these postelection changes are temporary aberrations or signs of a more enduring change in campaign finance. The answer to such questions depends in part on whether there is any legislative response to them.

THE POST-2020 REFORM AGENDA

Following the 2020 election, two major packages of federal campaign finance reforms were widely discussed. Collectively, the proposed reforms in these packages would reshape virtually every aspect of campaign finance law: they would increase disclosure of political donors, provide public financing for congressional and presidential elections, and curtail several types of independent spending. During the Democrat-led 117th Congress, there was little anticipation that these packages would pass both chambers and be signed into law in their original form, and there is even less chance that reforms such as these will pass in the Republican-led 118th Congress. These packages are far more partisan than past reform proposals, and they are not exclusively about campaign finance. Instead, the polarization and political disruptions of the past few years have prompted calls for changes to all aspects of American democracy, including voting laws, election systems, presidential power, fighting disinformation, election fraud, and foreign interference in elections. So, although ambitious reform plans exist, they serve more as a matter of political messaging for the Democratic Party than as a vehicle for change in the law.

The For the People Act and the Freedom to Vote Act

In the 117th Congress, as in the 116th Congress, the first piece of legislation introduced was the "For the People Act" (H.R. 1), a comprehensive set of election reforms designed, according to sponsor John Sarbanes (D-MD), to promote "clean and fair elections," "end the dominance of big money in our politics," and "ensure public servants work for the public interest."[50] Among other things, the bill would provide for automatic voter registration, restrict partisan gerrymandering, increase spending on election security, and enact new laws restricting the political activities of foreign governments and their agents.

The major campaign finance provisions of the For the People Act were introduced as stand-alone bills in the past and in the 117th Congress as well.[51] For instance, the bill included a revised version of the "Democracy Is Strengthened by Casting Light on Spending in Elections" (DISCLOSE) Act, first introduced in the House in 2010 in response to the U.S. Supreme Court's *Citizens United v. Federal Election Commission* (558 U.S. 310 (2010)) decision. The bill's disclosure provisions require disclosure of so-called dark money contributions of $10,000 or more to Super PACs or 501(c)(4) groups. Political groups that engage in print, video, or online advertising, or make prerecorded telephone calls, would be required to list the names of their largest donors in those communications. The bill also requires that corporations disclose more information to their shareholders about campaign-related contributions or expenditures.

H.R. 1 also included several provisions to reward candidates who raise small contributions. It proposed a voluntary small-donor matching system for House candidates. Candidates who opted into the program would receive a six-to-one match of public funds for contributions of up to $200; candidates would be required to raise a threshold number of small contributions to qualify. Participating candidates would be required to, among other things, limit their personal spending on the campaign and limit the size of the contributions they raise in both the primary and general election. The bill also establishes a presidential matching-fund system with similar guidelines but with a more complicated threshold for qualifying than the previous federal system. Essentially, these provisions of the law would revitalize the now-obsolete presidential public financing laws, applying the lessons of New York City's matching-fund program at the national level.[52]

Another major component of H.R. 1 was reform of the Federal Election Commission (FEC). The bill incorporated stand-alone legislation by Reps. Derek Kilmer (D-WA) and Brian Fitzpatrick (R-PA) that would reduce the size of the FEC from six commissioners to five, thus reducing the likelihood of partisan stalemate. It would empower a bipartisan panel to recommend potential commissioners to the president and give the president the ability to determine the FEC chair. The bill also would prohibit the practice of "holdover" commissioners—commissioners who remain on the FEC long after their term has been completed because the president has not nominated a replacement.[53] This component of the bill built upon long-standing arguments by legal scholars and by reform groups, such as Issue One and the Campaign Legal Center, about the FEC's inaction and flaws in comparison to election commissions in other nations.[54]

Finally, H.R. 1 included several narrower provisions that reform advocates had long championed, including ethics provisions related to candidate and interest-group fund-raising. For instance, the bill placed limits on the role foreign nationals can play in any decisions related to campaign spending, and it required the FEC to conduct periodic audits of foreign spending. It clarifies the definition of coordination between Super PACs and candidates or parties, limiting the practice of shifting campaign operatives back and forth between campaigns and ostensibly unconnected Super PACs, and giving the FEC greater power to penalize such coordination. One provision of the bill establishes a separate small contribution fund for parties, which can be used by the parties to make larger contributions to candidates than currently are permitted. Finally, H.R. 1 would expand the ability of candidates to use campaign funds for child care and other expenses that might discourage candidates of modest means from running for office.

H.R. 1 passed the House on March 3, 2021, with all Democrats but one voting in favor and all Republicans voting against it.[55] It failed to receive enough votes in the Senate to overcome a Republican filibuster, however, and Democratic Senator Joe Manchin also stated his opposition to the bill. In an effort to secure Manchin's support for a reform bill, and potentially for circumventing a filibuster to pass it, Democratic senators worked with Manchin to create a separate bill, the Freedom to Vote Act.[56] This bill removed much of the campaign finance section of H.R. 1 but retained provisions enhancing disclosure of large super PAC contributions, establishing a voluntary state-based small-donor matching program and limiting coordination between super PACs, candidate, or parties. However, most news coverage of the Freedom to Vote Act focused not on the remaining campaign finance provisions but on the new bill's voting provisions.[57] Campaign finance reform had gone from being a central piece of the legislation to being only one of several priorities.

This omnibus strategy may well have been a concession to political reality: the steadfast opposition of Republicans to most Democratic priorities has certainly encouraged the party to engage in symbolic legislating. In 2021, the sheer number of proposals packed into H.R. 1 gave Democratic senators, and perhaps some Republicans as well, many things to choose from. In an interview, Craig Holman of Public Citizen noted that he was optimistic that some of the ethics components of the bill, as well as the provisions requiring disclosure to shareholders of corporate political activities, might be moved separately and might acquire some bipartisan support.[58] Some of the components of H.R. 1 initially had cosponsors of both parties, so a piecemeal approach might attract Republicans, although the odds of overcoming a Senate filibuster remain slim. Indeed, on January 19, 2022, Democratic Senators Joe Manchin and Kyrsten Sinema joined with all Senate Republicans in rejecting an effort to change filibuster rules, thus dooming Democrats' hopes of enacting any campaign finance reform legislation during the 117th Congress.[59]

Republicans, meanwhile, have offered quite different reform proposals. The "Commitment to America," the party's 2022 platform document, includes among its government accountability proposals a pledge to pursue the "American Confidence in Elections (ACE) Act," which had been introduced in the 116th and 117th Congresses by Rep. Rodney Davis (R-IL).[60] Although most provisions of the ACE Act addressed Republican allegations about election security, it also included a set of provisions for raising contribution limits and disclosure thresholds; limiting the ability of the FEC, the SEC, and the IRS to investigate campaign finance violations;

and exempting several different types of campaign activity from being counted as contributions. There is little overlap between the ACE Act and the Democratic reforms, and the framing of the ACE Act as an effort to protect free speech and fight back against "woke" corporations marks it as a partisan statement. Although the ACE Act has been included among Republicans' agenda items for the 118th Congress, Davis was defeated in his primary, and it is unclear if the new chairman of the House Administration Committee will have any interest in working to pass legislation related to campaign finance.

The Protecting Our Democracy Act

In a fashion much like the H.R. 1 omnibus strategy, political scientists, government ethics watchdogs, and others who have raised ethics concerns about the Trump presidency have offered a slate of reforms that address many areas in which they believe Trump overstepped the bounds of presidential power—or, more broadly, where the presidency had acquired more power than it should have. Democrats in Congress rallied around the "Protecting Our Democracy Act," introduced by Rep. Adam Schiff (D-CA).[61] The reforms in this bill include limiting the use of emergency powers, strengthening whistle-blower protections, strengthening Hatch Act limitations on political activity by executive branch officials, placing limits on the presidential power to pardon, and changing the role of inspectors general. A slate of reforms that legal experts Bob Bauer and Jack Goldsmith proposed in their 2020 book *After Trump* goes even further, outlining ways to insulate the Justice Department and the media from political interference.[62]

This effort is not strictly about campaign finance, but the topic plays a part. Most consequentially, the bill would also require campaigns to report to the FEC and the FBI any foreign campaign assistance to a campaign—that is, it would classify foreign interference in an election as, in part, a violation of prohibitions on campaign donations by foreign nationals.[63]

The bill also includes a requirement that presidents release their tax information, which would make it more difficult for the president to receive illegal contributions to his personal businesses or his private financial accounts. To a similar end, it clarifies federal law to define and restrict the "emoluments" (personal gifts or other personal benefits) government officials may receive.

The Protecting Our Democracy Act also includes some of the ethics provisions first introduced in the For the People Act. Congressional Republicans and Democrats are likely to agree in principle that they would like to reassert congressional power in many of these areas; and at least prior to Trump, this principle would have produced bipartisan support for many, although certainly not all, of the provisions in this bill. Yet the packaging of the bill means that it is still likely to be seen as a partisan, anti-Trump exercise. As of early 2023, there is little indication that Republicans in Congress will pursue reforms of this nature.

Many of the corruption allegations or ethical questions raised during the Trump administration could also be addressed through executive orders. The president has the power to draft stricter conflict-of-interest rules for executive branch agencies and federal contractors, and to be more transparent about lobbyists' access to the president and the White House. Such efforts can help to clarify the relationship between the financiers of elections and the actions of the president. In a March 2021 editorial, Walter M. Shaub, former director of the U.S. Office of Government Ethics and a proponent of such reforms, criticized President Biden for promising to make these changes but not following through.[64] In Shaub's view, Biden has benefited from being less bad than Trump in the eyes of reform advocates and has not been pressured enough to remedy some of these problems. Other government watchdog groups were somewhat more positive about Biden's reestablishment or strengthening of Obama-era provisions about lobbying.[65]

Turning to the States

One avenue that reformers have pursued for a long time has been to champion reforms at the state or municipal level that might ultimately be suitable for implementation at the federal level. The matching-fund provisions included in H.R. 1, for instance, resembled the matching funds that have been used in New York City elections, and many states' public financing programs for gubernatorial elections have been studied by those interested in rejuvenating presidential public financing. One of the most consequential recent campaign finance innovations, however, has been Seattle's "democracy voucher" program, established in 2015.[66] Seattle residents are given $100 of vouchers, which they can contribute to the candidate or candidates of their choice in city elections. These candidates can, in turn, use these vouchers to fund a variety of campaign activities, with the names of voucher contributors publicly disclosed. A variety of recent studies have explored the effects of this program and the potential for vouchers to be applicable at the federal level.[67] Indeed, some aspects of state or municipal campaign finance laws such as these might be applicable to federal elections—in the same way that changes in voting systems such as the establishment of ranked choice voting have been adopted at the state level, yet used in federal elections in those states. However, such changes are unlikely to achieve serious consideration at the national level anytime soon.

A Deregulatory Supreme Court

The 2020 election occurred a decade after the *Citizens United v. Federal Election Commission* decision (see chapter 2). That decision, which ultimately led to the development of Super PACs, was initially met by a flurry of proposals for reversal. Liberal reform advocates had variously proposed constitutional amendments, state-level laws limiting nonparty groups, and expanded disclosure requirements. By 2020, however, it had become clear that the new members of the U.S. Supreme Court were even more skeptical of campaign finance regulation than were those on the court at the time of the *Citizens United* decision.

During his presidency Donald Trump nominated, and the Senate confirmed, three justices to the Supreme Court—Neil Gorsuch, Brett Kavanaugh, and Amy Coney Barrett. Gorsuch and Kavanaugh reinforced the original 5-4 majority in *Citizens United*; Barrett appears to have added a sixth vote to that majority. Indeed, the Supreme Court reaffirmed its stance on campaign finance through its unwillingness to consider a direct challenge to *Citizens United.*

On November 9, 2020, the court denied certiorari to the petitioners in *Lieu v. Federal Election Commission.*[68] Ted Lieu (D-CA), a sitting member of Congress, had spearheaded an effort supported by a number of liberal reform groups, political scientists, and law professors that contended that the record since 2010 showed that Super PACs had engaged in so many instances of de facto coordination with candidate campaign committees that it was wrong to consider their activities as independent political speech.[69] The court did not comment in its denial in this case, but few of the petitioners in the Lieu case had a great expectation of success.[70]

In its most consequential campaign finance case since 2016, *Americans for Prosperity Foundation v. Bonta* (594 U.S. ___ (2021)), the new court majority showed that it would be skeptical of state- or federal-level efforts to enhance disclosure laws regarding independent spending. The defendant in this case was the state of California, which had enacted laws requiring disclosure of the names of contributors of more than $5,000 to 501(c)(3) organizations operating in the state, on the grounds that disclosure would limit fraud or corruption. Americans for Prosperity, a 501(c) group that is part of the network of organizations supported by Charles Koch, challenged the law, arguing that disclosure might lead to reprisals against donors. Six of the justices sided with Americans for Prosperity, arguing in separate opinions that California's law placed a burden on donors' free speech rights and that the state had not demonstrated the need for the law.[71] Although the decision does not definitively close the door to enhanced disclosure laws for tax-exempt groups, it does signify that the court will apply strict scrutiny to any such efforts.

In 2022, the Court also heard *FEC v. Cruz* (596 U.S. ___ (2022)), a case filed by Sen. Ted Cruz challenging the federal restriction limiting candidates' ability to repay themselves after an election for loans of more than $250,000 of their own money to their campaigns.[72] In a 6-3 decision written by Chief Justice John Roberts, the court struck down this restriction, arguing that it served no anticorruption interest while inhibiting candidate speech. The *Cruz* decision is part of a trend in court decisions toward blurring the distinction between legal campaign contributions and illegal personal gifts to candidates, while at the same time tightening the definition of corruption. A good example of this tightening is *McDonnell v. United States* (579 U.S. ___ (2016)). The case concerned federal corruption charges made against former Virginia governor Robert "Bob" McDonnell. McDonnell and his wife were given or loaned the equivalent of $175,000 by a lobbyist seeking state support. In a 9-0 decision, the court concluded that the gifts offered to the McDonnells were not part of any measurable quid pro quo and that they may have been offered because of the donor's friendship with the McDonnells. In this decision, the court clarified that it would set a high bar for legal allegations of corruption.[73]

Meanwhile, authors of particularly ambitious campaign finance reform proposals have sought to broaden the definition of corruption. For instance, Lawrence Lessig has contended that expanded regulation is necessary to prevent what he calls "dependence corruption," the reliance of legislators on donors rather than on voters. Zephyr Teachout has explored the ways in which political discourse can be corrupted by the quest for campaign resources.[74] Both have presented arguments that might influence future Supreme Courts, if not the current one.

After an administration deemed by many to have engaged in overtly corrupt behavior, the public may well be primed to be more receptive to arguments about corruption than in the past. But as David Primo and Jeffrey Milyo argue, the public tends to consider a very wide range of completely legal aspects of politics to be corrupt, and the language of corruption is used extensively by politicians both on the left and the right to criticize their opponents.[75] The widespread rhetorical use of the term, coupled with the Supreme Court's narrow definition of the term, suggests that it may be tempting for reform advocates to use the sort of framing that Lessig and Teachout proposed, but this fact does not necessarily mean that they will be successful in doing so. Unless Trump (or another wealthy candidate with such complicated personal finances) runs in the future, it is likely that his transgressions will be treated as sui generis or as issues related to the power of the presidency, not to campaign finance.

Thus, the court's activities since Trump's election suggest that it will maintain its deregulatory approach to campaign finance and that efforts to revert to the pre-*Citizens United* status quo will not succeed until the composition of the court changes. For some liberals, arguments about the Supreme Court since the 2020 election have shifted from a strategy to persuade the court to the more ambitious notion of expanding the number of justices on the court. Although President Biden has at best given lukewarm support for this idea, any movement in this direction would certainly draw on concerns about *Citizens United* but would have implications that go well beyond campaign finance matters.[76]

During the 2020 campaign, however, President Biden did promise to work toward a constitutional amendment that would overturn elements of *Citizens United* (and perhaps even *Buckley v. Valeo*) to reestablish restrictions on independent expenditures and allow for full public financing of elections.[77] Although Biden's proposal is not the first to offer a constitutional route toward extensive changes in campaign finance law, like other reform proposals, it is unlikely to become law in the near future. Absent major changes to how the Supreme Court considers campaign finance law, however, a constitutional amendment may be necessary to achieve such ends.

THE POLITICS OF REFORM

Campaign finance reform has rarely been at the top of the list of Americans' concerns, and when it has been given priority, it has often been due to scandals where campaign funds played a major role. After the 2020 election, such reforms have a characteristically low priority.[78] One can also see evidence in the presentation of campaign finance issues in the two parties' platforms since 2012.

In 2012, Democrats began their platform with a list of economic priorities aimed at responding to the effects of the 2008 recession.[79] Immediately after listing these, they shifted to cutting waste in government and making sure that "everyone plays by the same rules." The platform devoted four para-graphs to matters related to campaign finance and lobbying reform, arguing that wealthy Americans (such as the Republican nominee Mitt Romney) held too much sway over policy makers. Campaign finance reform was iden-tified as a necessary response to these problems.

In 2016, Democrats discussed campaign finance in even more detail but with a different focus. In a section titled "Protect Voting Rights, Fix Our Campaign Finance System, and Restore Our Democracy," the party listed its campaign finance reform priorities second among five democratic reforms—behind enhanced voting rights and ahead of judicial appointments, D.C. statehood, and improving government management.

By 2020, however, campaign finance merited just two paragraphs in the Democratic platform, and the discussion of election reform began with a lengthy discussion of voter suppression and gerrymandering and concluded with a long discussion of support for U.S. territories, strengthening the postal service, and enhancing ethics laws governing the executive branch. The issues remained the same, but the priorities had shifted.

Campaign finance also disappeared from the Republican Party platform during this period. The party's 2012 platform includes a robust defense of *Citizens United* on free speech grounds, stating that Republicans "support repeal of the remaining sections of McCain-Feingold, support either raising or repealing contribution limits, and oppose passage of the DISCLOSE Act or any similar legislation designed to vitiate the Supreme Court's recent decisions protecting political speech."[80] The 2016 Republican platform contains only one brief reference to campaign finance—a condemnation of the use of union dues for political purposes. Republicans did not adopt a new platform in 2020.

As noted previously, it seems clear that the salience of campaign finance reform has declined among officeholders and activists relative to election reform. This pattern will likely lead to shifts in where politicians, policy advocates, lobbyists, and activists choose to direct their efforts and energy. Legislative compromises may drop campaign finance provisions, and phil-anthropic funds and think tank focus may move away from research on the topic. In addition, politicians who claim the reformist mantle will feel less pressure to practice what they preach when raising funds or responding to Super PAC spending.

The Symbolic Value of Campaign Finance

The declining salience of campaign finance reform and attendant shifts in effort may reduce the chances of enacting reforms. But such developments do not mean that campaign finance will disappear from political discourse. On the contrary, criticisms of campaign finance practices may become valuable symbols in political combat. They can help distinguish friend from foe (within and between political parties), demonstrate virtue, and show commitment to broader causes. Such symbols can work for reformers as well as for opponents of reform.

Although enhanced disclosure laws have been a major part of reformers' proposals over the past decade, the events surrounding the 2020 election show that disclosure laws are now far more easily weaponized than was the case in the past. Corporate decisions to suspend contributions to some Republican members of Congress after the January 6, 2021, riot and occupation of the Capitol (discussed above) are one such example. Later in 2021, major corporations were also pressed by activists to withhold contributions in response to new restrictive voting laws in Georgia and Texas.[81] In each of these cases, corporate donors were being asked to take a symbolic stand for or against particular policy ideas. Similarly, some media outlets' explorations of citizens' contribution decisions show that it is easy for disclosure to be weaponized.[82] Campaign contribution records can now easily be used by candidates to determine how best to target fund-raising appeals, by data aggregators such as Catalist, as well as by social scientists seeking to predict candidate or donor behavior.

Such uses of campaign contribution data have implications for disclosure laws. Disclosure historically has been an area of bipartisan agreement—conservative opponents of campaign finance regulation have argued that disclosure is sufficient to prevent corruption, and liberal groups have emphasized enhanced disclosure and the threat of corruption in their responses to *Citizens United*. One risk of the increased emphasis on using direct contributions to candidates as symbolic litmus tests for donors is that it can draw the focus away from less easily measurable forms of financial support, such as what is provided by Super PACs or tax-exempt groups.

Another risk is that the consensus around disclosure will erode. The $200 reporting threshold for itemized individual contributions has not been raised since the 1979 amendments to the Federal Election Campaign Act, nor is it indexed to inflation, and some candidates and states disclose contributions smaller than $200. Changes in fund-raising technology also incentivize repeat giving and make it more likely that small donors may ultimately exceed the $200 threshold without realizing that their contributions will be disclosed. What once may have seemed like a reasonable compromise between preventing corruption and protecting donor privacy may need to be revisited. Some libertarian organizations, such as the Cato Institute, have recently published calls for loosening disclosure rules in the name of encouraging anonymous speech.[83] Some left-leaning reformers have also argued for many years that donor anonymity would reduce the incentive for legislators to reward large donors.[84]

The Murky Policy Implications of the 2020 Election

Despite the unusual circumstances surrounding the 2020 election, the financing of the election does not represent a radical break from the trend that has been evident throughout the past decade. The cost of elections continued to climb, and the types of independent expenditures that had become prominent in the years following the *Citizens United v. FEC* decision continued to play a role at the presidential and congressional level. Although the incumbent president was outspent, he almost prevailed, and there was less disparity between the two major party presidential nominees than had been the case in 2016.

The absence of a clear story about how campaign finance laws shaped the 2020 election may make it hard to anticipate what the consequences of the election will be for campaign finance. America emerged from the 2020 election with a host of concerns about the health of its democracy. For many, these may be a matter of more immediate concern than are campaign finance laws and practices.

In part, this situation may exist because Donald Trump's presidency broke with many well-established norms about presidential behavior. This is not to say that no ethical concerns were raised in the 2020 presidential campaign in relation to campaign finance law. Many reform advocates raised questions about the favorable treatment of some campaign donors or the threat of corruption inherent in, for instance, use of President Trump's Washington, D.C., hotel or his other properties. Among the allegations that swirled around President Trump's first impeachment were questions about whether foreign money had made its way into the campaigns of either presidential candidate. Yet, these questions have little direct relationship to the questions that have preoccupied campaign finance scholars for the past two decades. Addressing these sorts of matters is quite different from reconsidering contribution limits, public subsidies for campaigns, or other types of systemic changes. These matters have little to do with how much money is involved in elections.

Although campaign finance reform has rarely been a major concern of voters, one could draw upon past volumes of this book to argue that political elites use changes in campaign finance to tell the stories of past elections.

For instance, 2000 was the year that the presidential public financing system broke down, 2004 was the first election following the passage of the Bipartisan Campaign Reform Act, 2008 was the race in which small donors became more important than ever before and public funding in the general election died, 2012 was the first election after the *Citizens United* decision, and 2016 was an election in which the presidential candidate who was substantially outspent still won. Many stories likely will be told about 2020, but few of them would place campaign finance in a starring role.

Progressive reform advocates may need to wait for a new story—or some sort of major scandal—to attract attention and increase the salience of campaign finance reform. They may well choose to focus their attention on state and local reforms, and these reforms may percolate for a very long time before accruing a track record that would lead to serious consideration at the federal level. At the same time, many scholars have had misgivings about the diminished role of the parties, about the chaotic presidential primaries of 2016 and 2020, and about the 2016 victory of a candidate who owed so little to his party's power brokers. These misgivings may mean that reform proposals that strengthen the role of parties in financing election campaigns could also receive more serious consideration. In short, the policy implications of the 2020 election for campaign finance reform are far murkier than has been the case in the aftermath of most other recent elections.

NOTES

1. Herbert E. Alexander, *Financing the 1960 Election* (Princeton, NJ: Citizens' Research Foundation, 1962), 89–90.

2. David B. Magleby and Candace Nelson, "Political and Policy Implications following the 2016 Election," in *Financing the 2016 Election*, ed. David B. Magleby (Washington, DC: Brookings Institution, 2019), 299–350.

3. See Charles R. Hunt, "Campaign Finance: Trends and Developments," in *The Elections of 2020*, ed. Michael Nelson (Charlottesville: University of Virginia Press, 2021), 134–35; and Calce Myers, "Campaign Finance and Its Impact on the 2020 Campaign," in *The 2020 Presidential Campaign: A Communications Perspective*, ed. Robert E. Denton Jr. (Lanham, MD: Rowman & Littlefield, 2021), 170–71.

4. Charles Hunt, "Campaign Finance."

5. Charles Hunt, "Campaign Finance," 301.

6. Raymond J. LaRaja and Brian F. Schaffner, *Campaign Finance and Political Polarization* (Ann Arbor: University of Michigan Press, 2015); Richard H. Pildes, "Small-Donor Based Campaign-Finance Reform and Political Polarization," *Yale*

Law Journal Forum, November 18, 2019, www.yalelawjournal.org/pdf/Pildes_Sma
llDonorBasedCampaignFinanceReformandPoliticalPolarization_1nbukg72.pdf.

7. Reid J. Epstein and Matt Stevens, "Democratic Debate Rules Will Make It
Harder to Get Onstage," *New York Times*, October 2, 2019.

8. Bill Scher, "The Democrats' Donor-Measuring Contest," *Politico*, March
20, 2020, www.politico.com/magazine/story/2019/03/20/democrats-donors-2020
-debates-225884/.

9. John C. Green, "Financing the 2016 Presidential Nomination Campaigns,"
in *Financing the 2016 Election*, ed. David B. Magleby (Washington, DC: Brookings
Institution, 2019), 131–86.

10. Shane Goldmacher, "How Trump Steered Supporters into Unwitting Donations," *New York Times*, April 3, 2021, www.nytimes.com/2021/04/03/us/politics/
trump-donations.html.

11. See, for example, Shane Goldmacher, "G.O.P. Group Warns of 'Defector'
List If Donors Uncheck Recurring Boxes," *New York Times*, April 7, 2021, www
.nytimes.com/2021/04/07/us/politics/republicans-donations-trump-defector.html.

12. Shane Goldmacher, "FEC Asks Congress to Ban Prechecked Recurring
Donation Boxes," *New York Times*, May 6, 2021, www.nytimes.com/2021/05/06
/us/politics/fec-trump-donations.html; Shane Goldmacher, "Klobuchar to Propose
Ban on Prechecked Donation Boxes in Political Donations," *New York Times*, May
24, 2021, www.nytimes.com/2021/05/24/us/politics/klobuchar-recurring-dona-
tions.html.

13. Goldmacher, "How Trump Steered Supporters into Unwitting Donations."

14. Elena Schneider, "How ActBlue Has Transformed Democratic Politics,"
Politico, October 30, 2020, www.politico.com/news/2020/10/30/democrats-actblue
-fundrasing-elections-433698.

15. Melissa Holzberg, "ActBlue Still Outraises WinRed, But the GOP Platform
Is Catching Up," *OpenSecrets*, August 4, 2021, www.opensecrets.org/news/2021/08
/actblue-outraises-winred-gop-catching-up/.

16. "Kentucky Senate 2020 Race," *OpenSecrets*, www.opensecrets.org/races/
candidates?cycle=2020&id=KYS1&spec=N; "South Carolina Senate 2020 Race,"
OpenSecrets, www.opensecrets.org/races/summary?cycle=2020&id=SCS2.

17. The lone prior candidate to raise in excess of Harrison's small-donor total
is Beto O'Rourke, a 2018 candidate for the Senate in Texas. See "Texas Senate 2018 Race," *OpenSecrets*, www.opensecrets.org/races/summary?cycle=2018
&id=TXS2. Despite increased spending overall in 2022, no candidate in
2022 matched Harrison's small-donor total either.

18. See Green, "Financing the 2016 Presidential Nomination Campaigns";
and John C. Green, Michael E. Kohler, and Ian P. Schwarber, "Financing the
2012 Presidential Nomination Campaigns," in *Financing the 2012 Election*, ed.
David B. Magleby (Washington, DC: Brookings Institution, 2014), 77–122.

19. This is calculated from the aggregate totals provide in Karl Evers-Hillstrom,
"Most Expensive Ever: 2020 Election Cost $14.4 Billion," *OpenSecrets*, February 11,

2021, www.opensecrets.org/news/2021/02/2020-cycle-cost-14p4-billion-doubling -16/.

20. "Act Now on Climate," *OpenSecrets*, www.opensecrets.org/outsidespending/ detail.php?cmte=C00697300&cycle=2020.

21. Karl Evers-Hillstrom, "Pro-Warren Super PAC Tops Outside Spenders— and Super Tuesday Voters Don't Know Its Donors," *OpenSecrets*, March 3, 2020, www.opensecrets.org/news/2020/03/warren-super-pac-st; Andrew Kerr, "Inside the Dark Money Boosting Bernie's Campaign," *National Interest*, January 10, 2020, https://nationalinterest.org/blog/buzz/inside-dark-money-boosting-bernies-cam- paign-112561.

22. Ellen L. Weintraub and Ann M. Ravel, "Proposal to Attack Scam PACs," Federal Election Commission, September 26, 2016, www.fec.gov/resources/about -fec/commissioners/weintraub/statements/2016-09_Memo--Scam-PACs.pdf.

23. Ciara Torres-Spelliscy, "Beware of Scam PACs in This Crowded Presidential Field," Brennan Center for Justice, March 19, 2019, www.brennancenter.org/our -work/analysis-opinion/beware-scam-pacs-crowded-presidential-field; Ciara Torres- Spelliscy, "Beware of 'Scam PACs' and PACs That Scam," Brennan Center for Justice, May 11, 2021, www.brennancenter.org/our-work/analysis-opinion/beware -scam-pacs-and-pacs-scam.

24. Zhao Li, "Lemons in the Political Marketplace: A Big-Data Approach to Detect 'Scam PACs,'" Princeton University, Department of Political Science, https://csdp.princeton.edu/sites/csdp/files/media/zhao_li_lemons_in_the_political _marketplace.pdf.

25. Federal Bureau of Investigation, "Scam PACs Are on the Rise," Federal Bureau of Investigation, April 25, 2021, www.fbi.gov/news/stories/scam-pacs-are-on -the-rise-041521.

26. Blake Ellis and Melanie Hicken, "Donations Have Surged to 'Scam' Political Group That Claims to Help Police Officers," *CNN*, October 16, 2020, www.cnn .com/2020/10/16/us/police-super-pac-political-group-invs/index.html.

27. Federal Election Commission, "Court Declares Regulation Unconstitutional in *Pursuing America's Greatness v. FEC* (D.D.C. 1:15-cv-01217-TSC)," Federal Election Commission, March 28, 2021, www.fec.gov/updates/court-declares-regula- tion-unconstitutional-in-pursuing-americas-greatness-v-fec/.

28. Maggie Severns, "Trump Campaign Plagued by Groups Raising Tens of Mil- lions in His Name," *Politico*, December 23, 2019, www.politico.com/news/2019/12 /23/trump-campaign-compete-against-groups-money-089454.

29. David A. Graham, "A First Step in the Fight against Scam PACs," *The Atlantic*, May 14, 2020, www.theatlantic.com/ideas/archive/2020/05/scam-pacs /611566/.

30. H.R. 6854 (116th), "Stop Scam PACs Act," www.govtrack.us/congress/bills /116/hr6854; H.R. 6494 (117th), "Scam PAC Act," www.govtrack.us/congress/bills /117/hr6494.

31. Nielsen Corporation, "COVID-19: Tracking the Impact on Media Consumption," *Nielsen Insights*, June 16, 2020, www.nielsen.com/us/en/insights/article/2020/covid-19-tracking-the-impact-on-media-consumption/.

32. Travis N. Ridout, Erika Franklin Fowler, and Michael M. Franz, "Spending Fast and Furious: Political Advertising in 2020," *The Forum* 18, no. 4 (2021): 465–92.

33. Ridout et al., "Spending Fast and Furious."

34. Ridout et al., "Spending Fast and Furious."

35. Ridout et al., "Spending Fast and Furious."

36. Fredreka Schouten, "Trump Raises More Than $207 Million since Election Day as He Pushes Baseless Election Fraud Claims," *CNN*, December 4, 2020, www.cnn.com/2020/12/03/politics/trump-fund-raising-election-day/index.html.

37. Shane Goldmacher and Rachel Shorey, "Trump Has Built War Chest of More Than $100 Million," *New York Times*, July 31, 2021, www.nytimes.com/2021/07/31/us/politics/trump-donations.html.

38. Michael Scherer and Josh Dawsey, "Trump Looks to 2024, Commanding a Fundraising Juggernaut, as He Skirts Social Media Bans," *Washington Post*, October 29, 2021, www.washingtonpost.com/politics/trump-fund-raising/2021/10/29/5b5a2e64-31b1-11ec-a1e5-07223c50280a_story.html.

39. Karl Evers-Hillstrom, "Trump Has 10 Times More Campaign Cash Than He Did Four Years Ago," *OpenSecrets*, April 9, 2021, www.opensecrets.org/news/2021/04/trump-has-10x-more-cash-2021/.

40. Anne Karni and Maggie Haberman, "At Once Diminished and Dominating, Trump Begins His Next Act," *New York Times*, June 5, 2021, www.nytimes.com/2021/06/05/us/politics/donald-trump-republican-convention-speech.html.

41. Jessica Piper, "GOP Donor Pool Unexpectedly Shrinks as Midterm Nears," *Politico*, September 8, 2022, www.politico.com/news/2022/09/08/gop-shrinking-donor-pool-midterms-00055317, discusses these concerns but presents data suggesting that there is little evidence to support them.

42. Alyce McFadden, "A Look at the Companies Freezing PAC Contributions after Capitol Riot," *OpenSecrets*, January 13, 2021, www.opensecrets.org/news/2021/01/corporate-pac-contibutions-paused-to-josh-hawley-and-others/.

43. Kevin Hardy and Allison Kite, "Hallmark Asks Hawley, Marshall to Return Political Donations," *Kansas City Star*, January 12, 2021, www.kansascity.com/news/politics-government/article248424220.html.

44. Citizens for Responsibility and Ethics in Washington, "Corporations Have Given $10 Million to the Sedition Caucus," September 24, 2021, www.citizensforethics.org/reports-investigations/crew-reports/corporations-have-given-10-million-to-the-sedition-caucus/.

45. Luke Broadwater, Catie Edmondson, and Rachel Shorey, "Fund-Raising Surged for Republicans Who South to Overturn the Election," *New York Times*, April 17, 2021, www.nytimes.com/2021/04/17/us/politics/republicans-fund-raising-capitol-riot.html.

46. Public Citizen, "The Corporate Sponsors of Voter Suppression," April 5, 2021, www.citizen.org/article/corporate-sponsors-of-voter-suppression-state-law-makers-50-million/.

47. Rachel Axon, "Many Accused in the Capitol Attack Placed Their Campaign Cash on Trump, Republicans," *USA Today*, March 25, 2021, www.usatoday.com/story/news/2021/03/25/accused-capitol-attackers-sent-trump-republicans-campaign-cash-riot-insurrection/6970294002/.

48. Monique Welch, "The Money behind the Politics: These Companies Are Top Donors to Sponsors of Texas' Abortion Law," *Houston Chronicle*, September 10, 2021, www.houstonchronicle.com/politics/article/The-money-behind-the-politics-These-companies-16444025.php.

49. Salvador Rodriguez, "Some Mozilla Employees Ask CEO to Resign for His Support of Prop 8," *Los Angeles Times*, March 28, 2014, www.latimes.com/business/technology/la-fi-tn-mozilla-ceo-brendan-eich-step-down-antigay-prop-8-20140328-story.html.

50. Congressman John Sarbanes, "HR 1, the For the People Act," press release, https://sarbanes.house.gov/issues/hr-1-the-for-the-people-act.

51. For a detailed discussion of the provisions of the bill and the individual pieces of legislation the bill draws from, see the Brennan Center for Justice, "An Annotated Guide to the For the People Act of 2021," March 18, 2021, www.brennancenter.org/our-work/policy-solutions/annotated-guide-people-act-2021.

52. Gregory Clark, Hazel Millard, and Mariana Paez, "Small Donor Public Financing Plays Role in Electing Most Diverse New York City Council," Brennan Center for Justice, November 5, 2021, www.brennancenter.org/our-work/research-reports/small-donor-public-financing-plays-role-electing-most-diverse-new-york.

53. "H.R. 1414 Restoring Integrity to America's Elections Act," www.govtrack.us/congress/bills/117/hr1414.

54. Cory Combs, "Issue One Applauds Introduction of Bipartisan Bill to Fix the Federal Election Commission," Issue One, February 25, 2021, /issueone.org/articles/issue-one-applauds-introduction-of-bipartisan-bill-to-fix-the-federal-election-commission/; Campaign Legal Center, "Three Big Ways the For the People Act Would Fix the FEC," February 23, 2021, campaignlegal.org/update/three-big-ways-people-act-would-fix-fec.

55. "H.R. 1 For the People Act of 2021," www.govtrack.us/congress/bills/117/hr1.

56. Mike DeBonis, "Revised Democratic Voting Bill Drops Controversial Provisions, Tweaks Others as Pressure for Action Mounts," *Washington Post*, September 14, 2021, www.washingtonpost.com/politics/revised-democratic-voting-bill-drops-controversial-provisions-tweaks-others-as-pressure-for-action-mounts/2021/09/14/6c59def8-150a-11ec-9589-31ac3173c2e5_story.html.

57. Nate Cohn, "A Bill Destined to Fail May Now Spawn More Plausible Options," *New York Times*, June 24, 2021, www.nytimes.com/2021/06/23/us/politics/voting-rights-bill.html.

58. Craig Holman, Government Affairs Lobbyist, Public Citizen, interview by Robert Boatright, October 26, 2021.

59. Mike DeBonis, "Manchin, Sinema Join with GOP in Rejecting Attempt to Change Filibuster Rules, Effectively Killing Democratic Voting Bill," *Washington Post*, January 19, 2022, www.washingtonpost.com/politics/democrats-brace -for-likely-defeat-of-voting-rights-push-due-to-gop-filibuster/2022/01/19/2f9a734c -792d-11ec-bf97-6eac6f77fba2_story.html.

60. Rodney Davis, "A Comprehensive Plan to Restore Confidence in American Elections," *The Hill*, July 27, 2022, thehill.com/opinion/congress-blog/3575843-a-c omprehensive-plan-to-restore-confidence-in-american-elections/.

61. "H.R. 5314 Protecting our Democracy Act," www.govtrack.us/congress/bills /117/hr5314.

62. Bob Bauer and Jack Goldsmith, *After Trump: Reconstructing the Presidency* (Washington, DC: Lawfare Press, 2020).

63. *The Fulcrum*, "Explaining the Protecting Our Democracy Act," April 1, 2021, protectdemocracy.org/update/explaining-the-protecting-our-democracy-act/; Stephen Spaulding, Lisa Gilbert, and Craig Holman, "Two Smart Ways to Deter Foreign Money and Dirt Digging from Our Elections," *The Fulcrum*, March 25, 2021, https://thefulcrum.us/campaign-finance/foreign-interference-8902348.

64. Walter M. Shaub, "Biden Promised Massive Ethics Reforms. Why Hasn't He Started Yet?," *Washington Post*, March 17, 2021, www.washingtonpost.com/outlook /2021/03/17/biden-ethics-reforms-lobbyists/.

65. Virginia Canter, "Biden, Trump and Obama Ethics Pledges, Compared," Citizens for Responsibility and Ethics in Washington, February 9, 2021, www.citi- zensforethics.org/reports-investigations/crew-reports/biden-ethics-pledge-compared -obama-trump/.

66. www.seattle.gov/democracyvoucher.

67. Geoffrey Henderson and Hahrie Han, "If We Build It, Only Some Will Come: An Experimental Study of Mobilization for Seattle's Democracy Voucher Program," *Journal of Experimental Political Science* (2020): 1–16, doi:10.1017/ XPS.2020.32.

68. www.fec.gov/resources/cms-content/documents/Lieu_sc_denial_certiorari .pdf, November 9, 2020.

69. Brief of Amici Curiae, *Lieu v. Federal Election Commission*, July 22, 2020, www.supremecourt.gov/DocketPDF/19/19-1398/148404/20200722140445391 _19-1398%20-%20AmicusMD.pdf.

70. This is my own observation as one of the authors of the political scientists' brief.

71. Adam Liptak, "Supreme Court Backs Donor Privacy for California Chari- ties," *New York Times*, July 1, 2021, www.nytimes.com/2021/07/01/us/supreme -court-donor-privacy.html.

72. Adam Liptak, "Supreme Court Rules for Ted Cruz in Campaign Finance Case," *New York Times*, May 16, 2022, www.nytimes.com/2022/05/16/us/politics/ ted-cruz-supreme-court-campaign-finance.html.

73. Adam Liptak, "Supreme Court Vacates Ex-Virginia Governor's Graft Conviction," *New York Times*, June 27, 2016, www.nytimes.com/2016/06/28/us/politics/supreme-court-bob-mcdonnell-virginia.html.

74. Lawrence Lessig, *Republic, Lost* (New York: Twelve Books, 2012); Zephyr Teachout, *Corruption in America: From Benjamin Franklin's Snuff Box to Citizens United* (Cambridge, MA: Harvard University Press, 2014).

75. David M. Primo and Jeffrey D. Milyo, *Campaign Finance and American Democracy: What the Public Really Think and Why It Matters* (Chicago: University of Chicago Press, 2020), 128–32; see also Daron R. Shaw, Brian E. Roberts, and Mijeong Baek, *The Appearance of Corruption* (New York: Oxford University Press, 2021).

76. Robert Barnes and Ann E. Marrimow, "Adding Justices or Term Limits Sparks Sharp Debate of Supreme Court Commission," *Washington Post*, October 15, 2021, www.washingtonpost.com/politics/courts_law/commission-on-supreme -court-warns-of-political-dangers-in-reform-proposals/2021/10/14/7a4c1d2a-2d45 -11ec-baf4-d7a4e075eb90_story.html.

77. https://joebiden.com/governmentreform/.

78. DeBonis, "Revised Democratic Voting Bill Drops Controversial Provisions, Tweaks Others as Pressure for Action Mounts."

79. Transcripts of all Democratic Party platforms are available at www.presidency .ucsb.edu/people/other/democratic-party-platforms.

80. Republican Party 2012 platform, www.presidency.ucsb.edu/documents/2012 -republican-party-platform. Other years' Republican Party platforms are available at www.presidency.ucsb.edu/people/other/republican-party-platforms.

81. Brian Schwartz, "Companies Quiet on Whether They Will Keep Donating to GOP Supporters of Georgia Voting Bill," *CNBC*, April 1, 2021, www.cnbc.com /2021/04/01/georgia-voting-law-corporate-donations-to-gop-under-scrutiny.html; Ashley Lopez, "Voting Rights Groups in Texas Are Asking Corporations to Do More to Fight GOP Election Bills," *Houston Public Media*, April 6, 2021, www .houstonpublicmedia.org/articles/news/politics/2021/04/06/395217/voting-rights -groups-in-texas-are-asking-corporations-to-do-more-to-fight-gop-election-bills/.

82. Axon, "Many Accused in the Capitol Attack Placed Their Campaign Cash on Trump, Republicans."

83. Eric Wang, "Staring at the Sun: An Inquiry into Compulsory Campaign Finance Donor Disclosure Laws," Cato Institute Policy Analysis no. 829, 2017, www.cato.org/policy-analysis/staring-sun-inquiry-compulsory-campaign-finance -donor-disclosure-laws.

84. Bruce Ackerman and Ian Ayres, *Voting with Dollars: A New Paradigm for Campaign Finance* (New Haven, CT: Yale University Press, 2004).

Index

ACE Act. *See* American Confidence in Elections Act

ActBlue, 11, 109, 160; small donations from, 196

activities, campaign finance policy regulating, 23–29

ad campaigns: in COVID-19 pandemic, 200; social media, 199–200; Super PACs and, 186–87; Team Biden, 86; Team Trump, 86; WMP on, 187, 200

Adelson, Miriam, 171, 175

Adelson, Sheldon, 171, 175

AFL-CIO, 164

AFP. *See* Americans for Prosperity

After Trump (Bauer & Goldsmith), 207

Alaska Republican Party, 133

Alexander, Herbert B., 2, 14, 16, 21, 99, 125, 193

Allen, Mike, 129

America First Action, 71; Trump and, 174–75

America First Policies, 71, 174–75

American Association for Justice, 161

American Bridge 21st Century, 69, 175

American Confidence in Elections (ACE) Act, 206–7

American Crossroads, 175, 181–82

American Possibilities, 69

Americans for Constitutional Liberty, 183

Americans for Prosperity (AFP), 177, 209–10

Americans for Prosperity Foundation v. Bonta, 209

America Votes, 186

appropriations bills, 28

approval ratings, 2–3

Archer-Daniels-Midland, 202

authorized committees, 24

Axios, 129

Barrett, Amy Coney, 209

Bauer, Bob, 207

BCRA. *See* Bipartisan Campaign Reform Act

Bernstein, Carl, 45n3

Biden, Joe, 3, 38, 55, 57, 101, 171; basement strategy of, 4; campaign expenditures of, 59; cash on hand of, 73–74; on *Citizens United*, 211; in debates, 77–78; DNC and, 129; fund-raising of, 59, 64; Future Forward USA and, 174; JFCs of, 60, 83, 133; Leadership PAC of, 69; PCC of, 8; receipts of, 72–73; victory of, 87. *See also* Team Biden

Biden Action Fund, 60, 133

Biden Fight Fund, 60

Biden Victory Fund, 60, 133

Bipartisan Campaign Reform Act (BCRA), 33–35, 37, 131, 150; policy implications of, 215

Bishop, Sanford, 177

Bloomberg, Michael, 1, 3, 56, 59, 62, 80, 143; Super PAC donations of, 171
Blue Lives Matter movement, 198
Boatright, Robert, 14
Bollier, Barbara, 117
Booker, Cory, 203
bridge period, 82–84
Buckley v. Valeo, 31–33, 88n4, 211
Bullock, Steve, 102
bundlers, 55; of Trump, 72
Bush, George W., 56, 100, 127, 202
business PACs, 177–78
Bustos, Cheri, 113
Buttigieg, Pete, 56, 57, 60; campaign expenditures of, 77, 78; Leadership PACs of, 70–71

campaign dynamics, 72–87
campaign expenditures: of Biden, 59; of Buttigieg, 77, 78; of Clinton, H., 61; of DSCC, 147; of Sanders, 59, 67, 77–78; from Super PACs, 172–79; Team Biden, 68, 80–81; Team Trump, 68, 80–81; of Trump, 60–62; of Warren, 65, 77. *See also specific topics*
campaign finance: Democrats on, 212; growth of, 1–2; post-2020 reforms, 203–11; Republicans on, 212; symbolic value of, 212–14. *See also specific topics*
campaign finance law, 22; resources, 54–55; rivals, 53–57; rules, 52–53
campaign finance policy: activities regulated by, 23–29; congress in, 28–29; Constitution affecting, 29–30; COVID-19 and, 39–42; early foundations of, 30–36; entities regulated by, 23–29, 25; foreign interference and, 39–42; implications of changes to, 36–40; importance of, 22–23; statutes affecting, 29–30; 2020 regulatory environment and, 36–43
Campaign Legal Center, 205
candidate-aligned Super PACs, 174, 175–76
candidate committees, 8
Capitol Hill riots, January 6, 5, 203; corporate response to, 213; Trump and, 117–18
Carey committees. *See* Hybrid PACs

Carl, Jerry, 177
cash on hand, *73*; of Biden, 73–74; of Sanders, 73–74
Cato Institute, 213–14
Cawthorn, Madison, 202
Cecil, Guy, 174
Census Bureau, 4
Center for Responsive Politics, 16
challenger spending, 115–17
Chamber of Commerce, U.S., 183
Cheney, Liz, 122n50
Citizens' Research Foundation, 14, 16
Citizens United case, 35–36, 169, 198, 204, 209; Biden on, 211; policy implications of, 214–15
CLF. *See* Congressional Leadership Fund
Clinton, Bill, 128
Clinton, Hillary, 56, 59, 69, 100, 147, 174, 193; campaign expenditures of, 61; JFCs, 152n23
Club for Growth, 177
Clyburn, Jim, 80
CNN, 200
Coats, Dan, 41
Collins, Doug, 102, 175–76, 180
Collins, Susan, 111
Commitment to America, 206–7
Committee on House Administration, 28
Committee to Defend the President, 71–72
congressional campaign committees, 18n25; limits on, 103; noncandidate expenditures in, *107*
congressional campaign finance: Hybrid PACs in, 107; JFCs in, 105–6; party-connected contributions, *104*; structure of, 102–9; Super PACs, 107; Traditional PACs in, 103–4
congressional elections, 100–102; receipts, *103*; Traditional PAC contributions in, *159*. *See also* House races; Senate races
Congressional Leadership Fund (CLF), 108
Connected PACs, 45n12; defining, 26
Consolidated and Further Continuing Appropriations Act, 136
Constitution, U.S.: campaign finance policy and, 29–30; First Amendment, 30
contribution limits, 27, 29, 31, *33*, 34, 44, 136–37; federal, *38*; Supreme Court

ruling on, 165; Traditional PAC, 160, 162

Cook Political Report, 101

Cooper, Roy, 143

coordinated expenditures: of DCCC, 146–47; of NRCC, 146–47; party contributions, *106*

Corporate PACs, 118

Corrado, Anthony, 37

corruption, 208; defining, 210–11

The Costs of Democracy (Heard), 14–15

COVID-19, 3–4, 17n15, 102, 109–10, 143–44, 194; ad campaigns and, 200; campaign finance policy and, 39–42

Credit Union National Association, 164

Crenshaw, Dan, 110, 199

Crossroads GPS, 186; spending of, 190n37

Cruz, Ted, 202

Cuellar, Henry, 177

Cunningham, Cal, 176

dark money, 12, 42, 85

Date, S. V., 144

Davis, Rodney, 206–7

Davis, Wendy, 110

DCCC. *See* Democratic Congressional Campaign Committee

Dean, Howard, 56

debates: Biden in, 77–78; DNC, 76–77; Warren in, 77

Defending Democracy Together, 183, 186

Demand Justice, 183

democracy voucher program, 208

Democratic Congressional Campaign Committee (DCCC), 18n25, 103, 112, 131; coordinated expenditures of, 146–47

Democratic Grassroots Victory Fund, 133, 172

Democratic National Committee (DNC), 18n25, 24, 53–54, 68, 127, 195; Biden and, 129; convention accounts, 136–37; debates sponsored by, 76–77; in 2020, 73–82

Democratic National Convention, 84

Democratic Senatorial Campaign Committee (DSCC), 18n25, 130; campaign expenditures of, 147

Democrats, 2–3, 211–12; on campaign finance, 212; candidate donations, 90n23; in House of Representatives, 100–101; PCCs of, 58–60; Super PACs opposed by, 198; 2024 candidates, 203

Department of Justice (DOJ), 29, 43

direct campaign expenditures, 5–7, *6*; historic context of, 12–13; in presidential elections 1976-2020, *12*

disbursements: Leadership PACs, 159; net, of PCCs, 57–62; Non-connected PACs, 159; party committees, *143*; of Traditional PACs, 157, *158*

DISCLOSE Act, 204, 212

DNC. *See* Democratic National Committee

DOJ. *See* Department of Justice

DSCC. *See* Democratic Senatorial Campaign Committee

Ducey, Doug, 101

Durbin, Richard, 196

Dwyre, Diana, 14

Eich, Brendan, 203

Election Day, 54, 82

Election Defense Fund, 88

electioneering communication costs, 182–86

election integrity efforts, 201

Electoral College, 4–5, 100

electoral college votes, 88

Ellison, Keith, 129

End Citizens United, 167

entities, campaign finance policy regulating, 23–29, *25*

ethics, 206–8

Everytown for Gun Safety, 108, 176

exploratory committees, 55

express advocacy, 23

Facebook, 174

fake news, 198–99

FCC. *See* Federal Communications Commission

FEC. *See* Federal Election Commission

FECA. *See* Federal Election Campaign Act

FEC v. Cruz, 210

Federal Communications Commission (FCC), 29

Federal Corrupt Practices Act, 31
Federal Election Campaign Act (FECA), 15, 22, 24, 31–33, 40, 132
Federal Election Commission (FEC), 16, 22, 28–29, 116; on JFCs, 132; reform of, 205; on transparency, 42–43
filibusters, 206
Financing the 1960 Election (Alexander), 2, 14–16, 21, 99, 193
First Amendment, Constitution, 30
Fitzpatrick, Brian, 205
Floyd, George, 4
follow the money, 45n3
Follow the North Star Fund, 71
Forbes, Steve, 56
Ford, Gerald, 2
foreign interference, campaign finance policy and, 39–42
For the People Act, 41, 207–8; on matching funds, 208; passage of, 204–6; provisions in, 205
Freedom Caucus, 114
Freedom to Vote Act, 206
funding sources, 8
fund-raising, 55–56; of Biden, 59, 64; impeachment and, 145–46; party, 130–42; postelection, 88, 200–203; of Sanders, 59, 78–80; of Team Biden, 81; of Team Trump, 81; technology, 213; of Trump, 60–61, 65, 195–96, 200–201
Future45, 176
Future Forward USA, 69; Biden and, 174

Gallup polls, 2
Garrett, R. Samuel, 13
general election campaigns, 78; Team Biden in, 84–87; Team Trump in, 84–87
Georgia, 5; JFC receipts in, *135*; runoff elections in, 129–30, 148, 151, 176, 179–82, 189n28
Georgia Honor, 109
The Georgia Way, 108
Gideon, Sara, 111
Gingrich, Newt, 57
Ginsburg, Ruth Bader, 4, 111
Glavin, Brendan, 16
Goldman Sachs, 202

Goldsmith, Jack, 207
Goodliffe, Jay, 14
Google, 202
Gorsuch, Neil, 209
GOTV, 142
Graham, Lindsey, 111, 197
Granger, Kay, 176
Great American Committee, 71
Great America PAC, 71
Green, John C., 13, 15
Greene, Marjorie Taylor, 202

Harris, Kamala, 5, 56, 57, 60, 83, 130; Leadership PAC of, 71
Harrison, Jaime, 111, 145, 197
Hatch Act, 207
Hawley, Josh, 202
Heard, Alexander, 14
Heersink, Boris, 127
Hersh, Eitan, 111
Hickenlooper, John, 203
high-dollar strategies, 55–56; JFCs in, 57; super PACs in, 57
Hightower, Bill, 177
Hitting Home PAC, 70
Hold the House Victory Fund, 133
Holman, Craig, 206
House Administration, 28
House Energy and Commerce Committee, 28
House Government Reform and Oversight Committee, 28
House Judiciary Committee, 28
House Majority PAC, 108
House of Representatives, 4–5; Democrats in, 100–101
House races: independent expenditures in, *178*; party expenditures on, *146*; Traditional PAC contributions to, *161*, 162–63, *163*
House Senate Victory Fund, 133
H.R. 1. *See* For the People Act
Huffington Post, 144
Hulu, 200
Hybrid PACs, 11, 51, 172; in congressional campaign finance, 107; defining, 167; development of, 36

ICAs. *See* intelligence community assessments

IEOCs. *See* independent-expenditure only committees

IEs. *See* independent expenditures

impeachment: fund-raising and, 145–46; of Trump, 128–29, 145–46, 214

incumbent spending, 115–17

Independence USA PAC, 69, 171

independent-expenditure only committees (IEOCs), 27

independent expenditures (IEs), 45n4, 82, *180*; in House races, *178*; party contributions, *106*; in presidential elections, *168*; rise of, 165–67; in Senate races, *178*; sources of, 165–67; of Super PACs, 167–82; of tax-exempt groups, *183*; of Traditional PACs, 165–67

independent spenders, 11–12

indirect campaign expenditures, 5–7, *6*

individual contributors: disclosure of, 213; party receipts from, 137–38; to Super PACs, *170*

influence operations, 42

Inslee, Jay, 197

Instagram, 75

intelligence community assessments (ICAs), 41

interest group money, Traditional PACs and, 158–64

internal communications, 164

Internal Revenue Code (IRC), 23; Section 501(c), 27; Section 501(c)(4), 27, 182, 190n37; Section 501(c)(5), 27, 182; Section 501(c)(6), 27, 182; Section 527, 182

Internal Revenue Service (IRS), 19, 29, 43

invisible primary, 52

Iowa caucuses, 78

Iowa Senate, 179

Iranian government, 42

IRC. *See* Internal Revenue Code

IRS. *See* Internal Revenue Service

Isakson, Johnny, 102

issue ads, 57

issue-based Super PACs, 174, 176–77

Issue One, 205

January 6. *See* Capitol Hill riots, January 6

Jayapal, Pramila, 113

JFCs. *See* joint fund-raising committees

Johnson, Lacy, 111

joint fund-raising committees (JFCs), 9, 37–39, 126, 171; of Biden, 60, 83, 133; of Clinton, H., 152n23; in congressional campaign finance, 105–6; FEC on, 132; Georgia runoff receipts, *135*; in high-dollar and small-dollar strategies, 57; national party share of, *133*; party fund-raising and, 131–35; of Romney, 152n23; of Trump, 61, 133

Jones, Doug, 101, 114

Jones, Jon, 176

Jordan, Jim, 110

Kavanaugh, Brett, 209

Kerry, John, 190n34

Keyes, Alan, 167

Kilmer, Derek, 205

Kitchen Table Conversations, 71, 78

Klacik, Kimberly, 110

Klobuchar, Amy, 56, 57, 78, 196, 203; Leadership PAC of, 71

Koch, Charles, 177, 210

Kolodny, Robin, 14

Kurtz, Amy, 183–84

Kyl, Jon, 101

labor PACs, 159, 161, 177–78

labor unions, 27

Las Vegas Sands, 171

Law, Steven, 174, 175, 182

LCV. *See* League of Conservative Voters

Leadership PACs, 27, 45n13, 55, 114; of Biden, 69; of Buttigieg, 70–71; disbursements from, 159; of Harris, 71; of Klobuchar, 71; of Sanders, 70; of Warren, 70

League of Conservative Voters (LCV), 86

Li, Zhao, 198

libertarians, 213–14

Lieu, Ted, 209

Lieu v. Federal Election Commission, 209

Life & Liberty PAC, 167

Lincoln Project, 86

Loeffler, Kelly, 102, 114, 175–76, 179–81
LyinComey.com, 127

Magleby, David B., 15, 193, 195
Majority Forward, 186
Majority PAC, 161
major party finances, 126–30
Make America Great Again Super PAC, 201
Manchin, Joe, 206
Marcus, Bernard, 175
Marshall, Roger, 117, 202
matching-fund provisions, 208
McCain, John, 56, 57, 101, 127
McCarthy, Kevin, 110, 133, 161
McCarthy Victory Fund, 133
McConnell, Mitch, 34–35, 111, 133, 175, 197
McConnell v. FEC, 33–35
McConnell Victory Committee, 133
McCutcheon v. FEC, 29, 37, 105, 132
McDaniel, Ronna Romney, 127
McDonnell v. United States, 210
McGrath, Amy, 111, 197
McIntosh, David, 177
McMahon, Linda, 174–75
McSally, Martha, 101, 111
Mfume, Kweisi, 110
midterm elections, voter turnout in, 100
Milwaukee Host Committee, 84
Milyo, Jeffrey, 210–11
momentum, from primaries, 54
Moran, Alex, 177
Moskovitz, Dustin, 174
Mueller, Robert F., 41
multi-candidate primaries, 54–55

Nancy Pelosi Victory Fund, 133
National Association of Realtors PAC (NARPAC), 160, 164
National Institute on Money in Politics, 16
National Intelligence Council, 41
National Republican Congressional Committee (NRCC), 18n25, 26, 103, 112, 118, 122n50, 131; coordinated expenditures of, 146–47
National Republican Senatorial Committee (NRSC), 18n25, 26, 130–31

National Rifle Association, 108, 176; Traditional PACs associated with, 183
Nelson, Candace, 193, 195
Netflix, 200
New Hampshire caucuses, 78
New Mexico, 179
New York City, 208
Nixon, Richard, 32
nomination campaigns, 53–57
noncandidate expenditures, 13, 65–68; in congressional campaign committees, *107*; independent, *86*; sources of, *150*; from super PACs, 67
Non-connected PACs, 10–11, 45n12; defining, 26; disbursements, 159
nonparty spending, *117*
NRA-Institute for Legislative Action, 183
NRCC. *See* National Republican Congressional Committee
NRSC. *See* National Republican Senatorial Committee
NRSC Targeted State Victory, 133
Nunes, Devin, 110
Nurses Super PAC, 78

Obama, Barack, 56, 57, 127, 174, 195, 202
Ocasio-Cortez, Alexandria, 110
officeholders, party receipts from, 138–42
Olympic Media, 111
Omar, Ilhan, 111
omnibus bills, 28
One Nation, 186
open-seat races, 116
OpenSecrets, 16, 86, 112, 190n34
organizational networks, 68–72
Ossoff, Jon, 102, 110, 175, 176, 179–81, 189n28
Our Revolution, 70, 198

PAC for a Level Playing Field, 70
PACs. *See* political action committees
partisan polarization, 2–3
party accounts, special, 136–37
party-aligned Super PACs, 148–50, 174
party candidates, party receipts from, 138–42

party committees, 9–10; disbursements, *143*; receipts of, *131*; sources of money, *132*; Super PACs and, 148; 2020 election as historic for, 150–51

party contributions: congressional campaign finance, *104*; coordinated expenditures, *106*; independent expenditures, *106*

party dues, 113

party expenditures, 142–50; on House races, *146*; RNC, 142–43; on Senate races, *147*

party fund-raising, 130–42; JFCs and, 131–35; special party accounts, 136–37

party independent expenditures, 147–48

party money, 14

party networks, Super PACs and, 149–50

party receipts: hard and soft money, *131*; from individual contributors, 137–38; from officeholders, 138–42; from party candidates, 138–42; small donations, 138; by source, *139–41* ; from Traditional PACs, 138; from transfers, 135

party recount, 145–47

Paul, Ron, 56

PCCs. *See* principal campaign committees

Peachtree PAC, 108, 176, 181

Pelosi, Nancy, 110, 113, 128, 133, 142

Pence, Mike, 71

People Standing Strong, 71

Perdue, David, 102, 114, 129–30, 155n62, 175, 179–81, 189n28

Perez, Tom, 129, 145

permanent campaign, 72, 88

Perot, Ross, 59

Persist PAC, 78, 80

Pew Research Center, 3

Pocan, Mark, 113

political action committees (PACs), 7–8; defining, 26. *See also specific types*

pop-up PACs, 176

Porter, Katie, 110, 199

postelection fund-raising, 88; of Trump, 200–203

postprimary campaign, 80–82

POWs for Truth, 190n34

Preserve America PAC, 171; Trump and, 175

The Presidential Election and Transition, 14

presidential public funds, 36–39

President's Commission on Campaign Costs, 14–15

Priebus, Reince, 127

primaries: California, 53–54; of Democrats in 2020, 54–56; momentum from, 54; multi-candidate, 54–55. *See also specific topics*

Primo, David, 210–11

principal campaign committees (PCCs), 24, 27, 51, 53, 56, 89n11, 114; of Biden, 8; calculation of expenditures, 94n88; Democratic, 58–60; net disbursements, 57–62; net receipts, 57–62; receipts for Democratic candidates, 62–65; receipts for Republican candidates, 65; receipt sources, 62–65, 103; Republican, 60–62; total funds raised by, 57–58; of Trump, 8

Priorities USA Action, 69, 83, 174

Progressive Turnout Project, 177

Progressive Voters of America, 70

Protecting Our Democracy Act, 207–8

Public Citizen, 202, 206

public funding, 136–37

Publicity Act, 31

Pursuing America's Greatness v. Federal Election Commission, 199

Ravel, Ann, 198

receipts: of Biden, 72–73; congressional elections, *103*; cumulative, of DNC, *73*; net, of PCCs, 57–62; party, from transfers, 135; of party committees, *131*; sources of PCC, 62–65, 103; from Super PACs, *169*. *See also* fund-raising

Reed, Mike, 142

reform agenda, 203–11

Relation PAC, 176

Republican National Committee (RNC), 1, 18n25, 24, 51, 68, 126, 194; party expenditures, 142–43; Trump and, 127; voter outreach of, 85

Republican National Convention, 84

Republicans, 2–3; on campaign finance, 212; PCCs of, 60–62

Republican Voters Against Trump, 183

Restoration PAC, 175

Reynolds, Molly E., 13–14
RNC. *See* Republican National Committee
Romney, Mitt, 56, 57, 127, 195, 212;
    JFCs, 152n23
Romney Victory Committee, 152n23
Roosevelt, Theodore, 30
Rove, Karl, 175, 186
runoff elections, in Georgia, 129–30, 148,
    151, 176, 179–82, 189n28; group
    expenditures in, 181–82; Trump on, 181
Russian government, 41

same-sex marriage, 203
Sanders, Bernie, 3, 56, 57, 129, 203;
    campaign expenditures of, 59, 67, 77–
    78; cash on hand of, 73–74; fund-raising
    of, 59, 78–80; Leadership PAC of, 70;
    small donations for, 62–64, 75–76; on
    Super PACs, 198
Santorum, Rick, 57
Save America, 88, 201
Save America Joint Fundraising Committee,
    201
Save America Leadership PAC, 201
Scalise, Steve, 105, 110, 113–14, 142
Scam PACs, 198–99
scare-off effects, 116
Schiff, Adam, 110, 207
Seattle democracy voucher program, 208
Seidel, Emily, 177
self-financed candidates, 59
Senate Judiciary Committee, 28
Senate Leadership Fund (SLF), 108, 174,
    175, 176, 181
Senate Majority PAC, 186
Senate races: independent expenditures
    in, *178*; party expenditures on, *147*;
    Traditional PAC contributions to, *162*;
    Traditional PACs in, *163*
Senate Rules and Administration
    Committee, 28
Senate Rules Committee, 28
separate segregate fund (SSF), 10;
    emergence of, 26; types of, 26–27
Shaub, Walter M., 208
Sinema, Kyrsten, 101, 206
Sixteen Thirty Fund, 183–84; Form 990, 186
SLF. *See* Senate Leadership Fund

small-dollar strategies, 56; JFCs in, 57
small donations: from ActBlue, 196;
    emphasis on, in 2020, 195–97; party
    receipts, 138; for Sanders, 62–63,
    75–76; for Trump, 195–96; for Warren,
    62–64; from WinRed, 196
social media, 75; advertising, 199–200;
    American use of, 200; Trump on, 200
soft money, 34
South Carolina primary, 80
special party accounts, 136–37
Speech Now v. FEC, 35–36
SSF. *See* separate segregate fund
Steyer, Tom, 56, 59, 62, 76–77, 80
Stop Hillary PAC, 71–72
streaming video, 200
Superbowl ads, 143
Super PACs, 1, 11, 51, 53, 75, 99, 125;
    ad campaigns and, 186–87; Bloomberg
    donations to, 171; campaign expenditures
    from, 172–79; candidate-aligned,
    174, 175–76; congressional campaign
    finance, 107; Democrat opposition to,
    198; funding, 169–72; in high-dollar
    strategies, 57; independent expenditures
    of, 167–82; individual contributors to,
    170; issue-based, 174, 176–77; major
    party aligned, *108*; maturation of, 197;
    noncandidate expenditures from, 67;
    partisan goals of, 138; party-aligned,
    148–50, 174; party committees and, 148;
    party networks and, 149–50; receipts
    from, *169*, Sanders on, 198; tax-exempt
    groups and, 182–86; Team Biden and,
    85–86; top donors to, *171*; top party-
    aligned, *142*; top twenty-five, *173*; of
    Trump, 71–72, 174–75, 201; types of,
    174, 178; uneven deployment of, 197–
    98; Warren support by, 197
Super Tuesday, 53–54, 80
Supreme Court, US, 29, 44; on
    contribution limits, 165; deregulatory,
    209–11; Trump-appointed justices, 209
Swift Boat Veterans, 190n34

Take Back the House 2020, 133
tax-exempt groups, 27, 157, 165;
    electioneering communication costs and,

182–86; independent expenditures of, *183*; Super PACs and, 182–86; top-spending, *184, 185*

Teachout, Zephyr, 210

Team Biden, 53, 193; ad campaigns, 86; in bridge period, 82–84; campaign expenditures, 68, 80–81; fund-raising of, 81; in general election campaign, 84–87; Super PACs and, 85–86

Team Trump, 53, 193; ad campaigns, 86; campaign expenditures, 68, 80–81; fund-raising of, 81; in general election campaign, 84–87

Ted Cruz for Senate v. FEC, 44

Tillis, Thom, 102

Tillman Act, 30

Torres-Speliscy, Ciara, 198

trade associations, 27

Traditional PACs, 10–11, 37, 51, 75, 132; in congressional campaign finance, 103–4; in congressional elections, *159*; contribution limits, 160, 162; contributions from, 106–7; defining, 27; disbursements of, 157, *158*; in House races, *161*, 162–63, *163*; independent expenditures of, 165–67; interest group money and, 158–64; internal communications in, 164; National Rifle Association and, 183; party receipts from, 138; in Senate races, *162, 163*; top twenty, *160*

transparency, FEC on, 42–43

Trump, Donald, 1, 2–3, 38, 56, 83, 126, 171; America First Action and, 174–75; approval ratings of, 2–3; bundlers of, 72; campaign expenditures of, 60–62; in Capitol Hill riots, 117–18; concession refusal of, 88; fund-raising of, 60–61, 65, 195–96, 200–201; on Georgia runoff elections, 181; impeachment, 128–29, 145–46, 214; JFCs of, 61, 133; legal costs of, 201; media attention on, 194–95; norms broken by, 214–15; opposition to, 195; PCC of, 8; postelection fund-raising of, 200–203; Preserve America PAC and, 175; re-election campaign of, 72, 194; RNC and, 127; small donations for,

195–96; on social media, 200; Super PACs of, 71–72, 174–75, 201; Supreme Court justices of, 209; 2016 campaign of, 72–73; unemployment under, 3. *See also* Team Trump

Trump Make American Great Again Committee, 133

Trump National Doral Miami, 144

Trump Tower, 144

Trump Victory Fund, 61, 87, 152n23

Truth Still Matters PAC, 176

2020 election, 1; context of, 2–5

Twitter, 75

2016 campaigns, of Trump, 72–73

Uihlein, Richard, 175

unemployment, during Trump presidency, 3

United States Code, 32

United the Country, 80

Unite the Country, 69

voter outreach, 82; of RNC, 85

voter turnout, 4–5; in midterm elections, 100

VoteVets.org, 78

Walker, Mark, 113

Walmart, 118

Warnock, Raphael, 102, 109, 129–30, 175, 176, 179–81

Warren, Elizabeth, 56, 57, 60; campaign expenditures of, 65, 77; in debates, 77; Leadership PACs of, 70; small donations for, 62–63; Super PAC support for, 197

Wasserman-Schultz, Debbie, 129

Watergate, 21, 32

Weintraub, Ellen, 198

well-known candidates, 194–95

Wesleyan Media Project (WMP), 199; on ad campaigns, 187.200

WinRed, 11, 109, 160; small donations from, 196

WMP. *See* Wesleyan Media Project

Woodward, Bob, 45n3

Zelenskyy, Volodymyr, 128

www.ingramcontent.com/pod-product-compliance
Lightning Source LLC
Chambersburg PA
CBHW022308280326
41932CB00010B/1024